We the People

Karl W. Bogott

Acknowledgments

I cannot possibly remember the names of all those who had an effect on this story because it is a story of a nation and of an adult life spent forming my personal views of that nation and its future. As a work of fiction however, I can make the simple disclaimer to the effect that fiction means 'never happened'. However, I would be remiss if I did not thank the following, with significant grammatical license: First and always foremost, my wife, Linda, for understanding and allowing me the time from grand-parenting and husbanding to write, National Novel Writing Month (NaNoWriMo) for the impetus to put flesh on the skeleton of a story, the Internet for the endless hours it took to accumulate and publish the historical facts that it took me only minutes to find, names from my Navy career that taught me 'attention to detail', independent thought and 'observation behind the obvious'; Dale Feltes, Phil Hannaford, Dr. R. Michael Maixner and Joe Reagan, to those who stepped in and provided personal insight to specific cultural or historical elements, Phil Miller and Claire Smith. And, finally, to my 'conceptual readers' Phil Miller, Kathy Robbins and Jack Markusfeld. I suppose I should note that, following every name in this paragraph should be letters that proclaim their service as retired members of the United States Armed Forces. I thank them for their services to me, for their help, and, more importantly, for their service to our nation.

A special acknowledgment goes to my wife, Linda, who, painstakingly, edited this revision.

Dedication

This story could not be written, much less published without the sacrifice of more than 1,320,000 American men and women who gave their lives to defend our freedom to speak out without fear of a midnight knock at the door.

Thank you.

Disclaimer

All characters and events in this story are fictional and, random names from my life notwithstanding, are unrelated to any actual person , living or dead or any actual event. Certain historical facts are matters of record and I have attempted to allude to them with historical accuracy.

"I am not an advocate for frequent changes in laws and constitutions, but laws and institutions must go hand in hand with the progress of the human mind. As that becomes more developed, more enlightened, as new discoveries are made, new truths discovered and manners and opinions change, with the change of circumstances, institutions must advance also to keep pace with the times. We might as well require a man to wear still the coat which fitted him when a boy as civilized society to remain ever under the regimen of their barbarous ancestors."

Thomas Jefferson

[Engraved on Panel 4 – Jefferson Memorial]

In Order to Form a More Perfect Union

Clarion Call

May 16, 2017 – Mentor, Ohio

The '(1)' appeared next to 'Inbox' on her Gmail® tab, but Kathy thought nothing of it. She had been corresponding all day with friends about studying for finals, advice on a term paper or the after-graduation party. She smiled reminding herself that graduation was less than a month away; 18 days to be exact. She completed the paragraph and thought on the summary of her term paper for AP English, then hit the 'Save' icon. "Done!" She sat back and rubbed her eyes and downed the last swallow of the soda sitting well away from her keyboard.

She touched the Gmail® tab and opened her Inbox on the screen. It was probably from Dana. She was putting together the graduation party and had been nagging about minutia. Kathy sniffed. Dana would rather party than study anyway, but she was generally a good friend; loyal, if lazy.

The message in bold font at the top of her list caught her attention. It was from '**The Jefferson-Hamilton Institute**' and the subject line was even more intriguing '**A Paid Summer Internship Offer – Not Spam**'.

Normally, a very conservative user of email, Kathy reached for the delete key and then paused. She hadn't thought much about the summer, except that it was three months in the way of her starting at State in the fall.

"Hey, it's online." She put her mouse on the message and clicked to open the message.

Ms. Greer. Thank you for reading our correspondence. My name is George Hanover, a staff member of the Jefferson-Hamilton

Institute. Please look at the paragraph below. I hope it will allay suspicions about this being a spam message or, worse yet, some scam. I assure you that what you will read is, not only genuine, but important.

The next two paragraphs were a synopsis of the Institute as well as several hyperlinks to references from and about it.

Ms. Greer. I do not expect you to believe everything you read from links I've sent you. Please do your own research on the Institute. I'm certain that you will find us, and our offer, credible. Now, please read on.

You, and 154 other young Americans have been selected to participate in an experiment in government. To protect the validity of the experiment, no details will be revealed until you have accepted the offer and terms of, shall we say, employment. The Internship lasts from Friday, June 16 to Friday, August 18. You will be away from home and at a protected location in Kentucky. Room and board are provided, along with a monthly stipend of $1,000, all state and federal taxes prepaid.

A separate email is in the inbox of your parent or guardian explaining this offer to them. Please discuss the offer with them and respond to me within two days, if you wish to entertain our invitation. Kathy, this is as important an opportunity as you may ever receive. It is important to you, as a learning opportunity, to the Institute and, in a very special way, to our Nation. I hope to hear soon. Your new friends are waiting.

George Hanover

Kathy turned in her chair and yelled, "Mom?"

May 21, 2017 – Camp Donelson, Kentucky

"Well, George, what are the numbers?"

George pushed back from his desk and tossed his reading glasses down. He rotated his chair and saw that it was Dean Elliot, one of the four founders of the Institute. Dean was 50 and looked like he was going on 35. He always dressed in khakis and a golf shirt and now pushed a pile of folders aside and leaned on the corner of a work table. George picked up a notebook. "Of 155 emails, letters and FedEx packages sent out, 18 have either refused or, we suspect, were deleted. I've already sent out offers to the first 18 alternates, based on the states, as required. Any push-back?"

Dean chuckled. "Well, if calls from two Senators, one Congressman, the FBI, two local sheriffs and one Archbishop can be considered push back, there's been some, yes. Oh, and 17 mothers and 6 fathers. Somehow, I don't think these kids trust us."

"That's a good start, then. Did you put them all at ease?"

"Well, the parents will never really trust us. And, of course, Senator Dewy, who, already knows about the experiment. The two sheriffs knew the kids and were just checking up for them. I'm not sure how the FBI got into it, but I gave the Deputy Director a call and he's going to put out a general memo to keep the waves down. Was there any pattern in who we lost from the first list?"

"We lost two more black kids, one boy and one girl, then we had hoped. But, I had enough in the alternates to avoid a skew. We also lost a few more from the Midwest than we wanted to, but we'll manage. May I send out the releases and information packages as soon as I have the required number?"

"Yeah. The Institutes Open Relations group is ready to deflect the press and media if one of the Interns lets something out. But, I hope that doesn't happen."

"What about the Devil's Advocates?"

A smile grew on Dean's face. "All five are ready to go. They were harder to convince than we thought, but Dr. Gilbert is very convincing. You know, George, since he came up with this weird idea, it's only been an academic experiment. Now that it's ready to start, it's both exciting and scary. What about you? Are you ready to be 'The Stage Manager'?"

"You make it sound like we're doing a production of 'Our Town'."

"In some strange way, aren't we?"

George snorted, "Hitchhiker's Guide to the Galaxy, more likely. You ever going to tell me who sponsored this experiment in futility?"

"Why futility, George? I think it's an excellent academic exercise in creative thought."

"Creative fiction, you mean."

"Let's hope not. I can't tell you who the sponsors are, George. That's in the contract. I can give you some loose idea, but that's all. The solicitation came from the Executive Branch and is being handled by the office of the Vice President. The Minority Whip is handling congressional liaison, along with Senator Dewy. I also know of one retired bank CEO, a well-known country music star and two Fortune 500 CEOs. We've got two Universities, an Associate Justice and at least one representative of an ultraconservative political action group. That's all you get. And, I need you to be a team player, George."

"Jeez, talk about herding cats."

"I would use the 'inmates running the asylum' analogy. But, it's a contract and, therefore, our job."

#

June 2, 2017 – Agana, Guam, Territory of the Mariana Islands

The FedEx truck stopped, and the driver glanced at the address on the delivery label. 'Oy Palomuto, 704 Patnetos Drive, Agana, Guam'. He glanced at the house number, hopped from the truck and jogged to the front door. He saw no doorbell on the typical Guamanian home and knocked on the door frame.

"Hafaday." The traditional Guamanian greeting came from inside the house, in a feminine voice.

"I have a signature required package for Oy Palomuto."

"I'm his mother. May I sign?"

The driver looked uncomfortable. "The delivery instructions are pretty specific. Is he not here, ma'am?"

The woman sighed. "He is here. Wait." She closed the door and he heard "Oy! The door."

After a moment, the door opened. "Hafaday." A young man displaying all the physical characteristics of a Chamorro, stood there wearing only shorts.

"Are you Oy Palomuto?"

"Yes."

"I have a package you need to sign for." He held out a large FedEx envelope, his tablet and stylus.

The young man looked at the packing label and a smile broke out. He quickly signed for the envelope. "Thank you." He turned toward the inside of the room. "Mama, it's from the Institute." As the door closed, the delivery driver heard the familiar sound of the opening string being pulled on the large envelope.

#

Internship Information:

1. Itinerary – Air: Agana, Guam (GUM) to Nashville, TN (BNA), Motor coach: Fort Campbell, KY - Camp Donelson (FMR).

1.1. Your confirmation code is GDRZ8 – Hawaiian Airlines.

1.2. Your passport or other valid U.S. issued identification will be required to both board the motor coach and gain entry to Ft. Campbell.

1.3. You may check in electronically to obtain seating and boarding passes.

1.4. An Institute staff member will meet you at baggage carousel #3 at the Nashville airport and will scan your Institute identification (enclosed).

2. Identification - Enclosed is a temporary ID card. The QR code is encrypted with identifying information that will positively identify you. Please have this card available when you arrive in Nashville. Without it, you will not be permitted to board the bus to the facility.

3. Recommended Clothing (See attached listing.)

4. Proscribed items – Please read the documentation provided.

5. Privacy and security statement and Release – to be signed prior to admittance to the compound.

6. Further information related to your travel or stay may be found at this site. Your user id is Opalo122 and your temporary password: 3ghX5#hvB2. You will be prompted to change your password the first time you sign on. Please do so before departure. You will also be prompted to create a userID and password for a family member who will serve as your personal outside contact. All correspondence outside the facility **will be** monitored. Further explanation will be provided upon arrival.

7. I look forward to meeting you in Kentucky. We appreciate your participation. Its importance cannot be underestimated. Thank you and travel safely.

George Hanover

June 16, 2017 – Nashville, Tennessee

Jay stepped off the USAirways flight from Phoenix and looked around. He saw no sign or anyone else waiting, so he tucked his Bible under his arm, clapped his Stetson on his head and began the trek to baggage claim, trailing his roll-on behind him. He patted the back-right pocket of his well-worn blue jeans to ensure that the laminated ID card was there.

#

George glanced down at his tablet. A green numeral '113' stood next to a red '42' displayed over the icon of a bus with the numeral '41' displayed. "Two more, Ellen, then you can head out. I show 42 not yet reported and I know at least 4 of those are driving from nearby states. I think the last flight arrives at 5:30 from JFK and I'll load them up and be on the road."

"Okay. Who's on this flight, anyway?" She looked absent-mindedly over her shoulder to see that the banner "Jefferson-Hamilton Institute Interns" was still hanging.

George swept a different app on his tablet. "Hmm. Two, it looks like, Jay Brigham, Phoenix, and Emelita Garcia from Nogales." He glanced up at the board. "Flight's on the ground. Look for a cowboy hat."

Ellen shook her head. "George, the flight is landing from Phoenix." She pointed down the concourse at a sea of Stetsons. "Ya think?"

A young woman in shorts, sandals and a simple white blouse with a colorful woven bag over her shoulder was walking up the concourse. Her eye caught the banner and she began to walk their way. As she converged on their location, as did Jay, about ten paces behind. When she reached them, she withdrew a laminated card from her shoulder bag and handed it to George.

"I am Emelita Garcia"

George took her card and scanned the QR code with his tablet. He smiled and looked up at her. "Emelita, welcome. Would you please tell me the name of your Civics teacher and the name of your boss at work?"

She looked somewhat surprised. "I'm sorry? Oh, Civics was taught by Mrs. Gordon and my boss is, surprisingly, her husband, Tom. How do you know this?"

Ellen took her by the arm. "We told you that we would make positive identification, Miss. Come on. The bus is this way. Oh, do you have luggage?"

"Yes, one bag." She and Ellen walked toward the carousel.

"Tom Harrison and I don't have a job, unless you count summers on Grandpa's ranch in Utah."

George turned back and saw Jay. He chuckled. "I doubt that the questions are the same, son. May I have your card, please?"

Jay reached into his pocket and handed over the card which George scanned. "Jay Brigham, Phoenix. Okay, what's the license plate on your dad's truck and", he glanced down at his tablet and shook his head, "without looking, the design on your boots. Man, research can sure pick 'em."

Jay cocked his head. "Wild. Well, my dad's license plate is 'AZSAINT' and I have a U.S. Flag on the right boot and a cross on the other; God and Country."

George handed back his card. "Welcome to the Institute, Jay. Do you have luggage?"

He swung his roll-on in front of him. "Nope, travel light."

The Convention

George, Ellen and Dean walked through the doors of the former 'mess hall', just as the rolling doors closed on the serving line. Ellen wore slacks and a collared pullover shirt, mostly white, but with a red and white strip running diagonally down the front and back. George and Dean both wore suits. George and Dean walked down the center aisle, as Ellen held the doors open for a train of six staff members pushing carts piled with tote bags on top and below; each with a picture ID attached to the handles. As the doors swung closed, another man, also in a suit but looking rumpled and harried, stopped one door in its swing and stepped into the room, dodging the log jam of carts as he caught up with George and Dean.

"Sorry. I'm behind a bit. Had a call from Senator Hines about one of our Interns. He didn't call home when he got to Nashville and they were worried."

George shook his head and sighed. "That's the third such call today, Doctor 'G'. I hope this 'helicopter parenting by proxy' isn't the start of a trend."

Dr. Gilbert straightened his hopelessly wrinkled suit jacket. "Alright, let's get our grand experiment underway." He started down the main aisle, followed by Dean and George, who, without thinking, fell into step behind him.

The universal clatter and chatter of young people enjoying a meal and each other, reduced to background levels. The three men approached the front of the room and mounted a platform set with chairs and a lectern to one side. A large screen hung down over the other. George approached the lectern and turned on the microphone.

"Take your seats, please. If your chair faces away, please turn it toward the platform." There was a general scraping and clatter which, after a moment or two, died down. The room grew quiet. "Thank you."

He scanned the room for a moment, looking at faces, all of which he had seen the day before at the airport or at the induction desk later in the evening. He turned and nodded at a staff member sitting at a laptop in the corner. The room darkened slightly, and the Institute logo appeared on the screen.

"Good morning and welcome to the Jefferson-Hamilton Institute's 'We the People' initiative. My name is George Hanover. Each of you received communication from me offering you an internship in this project. Each of you accepted. There are 155 of you; three from each state, one from Washington DC, one from Puerto Rico, one from the U.S. Marianas and one each from the other Atlantic and Pacific protectorates and territories. I hope the significance of this breakdown will become evident sooner, rather than later. However, that is the responsibility of Dr. Gilbert and Mr. Elliott.

"My position is, for lack of a better term, 'Stage Manager'. My job is to keep things going forward with some degree of organization and to manage the day to day interactions, that will allow you to do your job." He paused and scanned the side of the room for Ellen. "Ellen, please come up here and bring a tote with you." Ellen grabbed the last tote on the last cart and climbed the platform. "This young lady is Ellen Haley. She fills many rolls, some administrative and some related to your jobs. More on the latter, later. Please note her attire. Staff members wearing this shirt and, more importantly," he reached for the lanyard around her neck and removed it, "excuse me, Ellen, one of these badges, are the only Institute members with whom you may interact." He handed the lanyard back. "All other staff are support. They are not only unaware of why you are here but are instructed to have no interaction with you that is not specifically related to their jobs. They handle food service, laundry, retail, janitorial, security and other administrative tasks. There will be less confusion and disruption if you simply let them do their jobs while you do yours. Questions should always be directed to one of the marked staff, like Ellen.

"This is an important meeting. In just a moment, Dr. Gilbert and Mr. Elliott will explain the initiative to you and your tasks related to it. If, and I hope this is a wasted comment, you choose after that explanation not to participate, you are free to leave and return home. However, I must remind you that each of you signed a 'non-disclosure' agreement and that both civil and criminal action will be taken if, after you leave, you disclose any information about the initiative, before authorized public release." There was a murmur through the crowd. George held up his hand. "I know that sounds ominous. Bear with us. The importance of what you're doing will be evident right now." He turned and said "Please allow me to present Dr. Harold Gilbert, one of the founders of the Institute and the man from whom the initiative sprang, as a simple idea. Dr. Gilbert." George stepped away and took a seat, as Dr. Gilbert approached the lectern.

"Good morning. You have no idea how exciting the next two months will be. You may well be participating in history. For all our sake, I hope so. Let me begin.

"In 1786, it became apparent to the citizens and government of our very young country, that the structure they had given themselves was not working. I'm certain that you know I am referring to the Articles of Confederation. The central authority had, to put it lightly, no authority. I won't review its failings. They are 230 years unimportant. What is important, is that the leaders put together a group of men, sorry ladies, it was, then, a man's world, to 'fix' the articles and the structure they provided. They met in May 1787 and spent the next three months in secrecy. They quickly determined that the Articles were not capable of being 'fixed' and set out to write an entirely new, indeed they would be new to the whole world, document and structure to govern a new nation. That document and its initial amendments are, no surprise here, the Constitution and Bill of Rights.

The world has turned around more than 83,000 times in the intervening 230 years. In those revolutions have come other revolutions: steam, electricity, automobiles, flight, space travel, immigration from nearly every land on the earth, revolutions in medicine and communications and unimaginable changes in the human perception of itself and the responsibilities of government to it and, conversely, in the responsibilities of the citizenry to government.

Certainly, changes have been made, including amendments, laws and various interpretations to try and keep up. Valiant as the effort has been, it has also suffered from pressures of 'the times' with respect to population, infrastructure and perception. In short, the document can't keep up in any meaningful fashion any longer.

Regrettably, the legislators who might fix it are the very ones who have broken it for various reasons, some good, some not so good. You are all too young to remember a political cartoonist, the Doonesbury of his day, if you will, named Walt Kelly. His hero was a fuzzy character in a pork-pie hat named 'Pogo Possum'. During a particularly ugly period of post-World War II political upheaval, announced that 'We have met the enemy and they is us.' Well, ladies and gentlemen, we is them."

A low chuckle swept through the audience at the grammatical absurdity.

"Now, there is, within the halls of Congress, the Supreme Court and the White House, as well as at the state level, a growing sense of urgency to address the problem without causing, to put it bluntly, a violent response from everyone in defense of their own turf. It was for that reason that the Constitutional Convention met in absolute secrecy. It needed to keep the investigative reporters, lobbyists and busybodies of the day from disrupting the creative process. For that very same reason, secrecy is the watchword for this initiative."

A sense of expectation settled on the room. Many of the interns leaned forward. Any side conversation stopped.

"Let me cut to the chase. Ladies and gentlemen, you are going to write a new governing document for the political entity known to the world as the United States of America. And, you have only two months to do it."

"Holy shit!" was repeated a few times from various tables, along with "No Way!", "Yeah Right!", "We're going to do what?" and a few "You're kidding, right?"

Dr. Gilbert smiled for the first time since he had approached the lectern. He held up his hands to settle the uproar. "All of those statements, I believe, may apply, except the latter. I assure you, we are not kidding. Please settle down. Dr. Dean Elliott, also a participating founder of the Institute, will set the ground work. Thank you." He stepped away as Dr. Elliott stood and walked forward.

"That's a hard act to follow, but I wonder if the framers didn't make much the same comments, in somewhat more gentile manner, I would imagine, 230 years ago when they received their tasking." A ripple of polite laughter swept through the mess hall. "Alright. Moving on. My name is Dean Elliott. I'm going to spend a few minutes outlining the next few days. After that, we'll entertain a few questions. It's likely that there will be lots of questions. We hope that most of the answers will become apparent, as you move forward.

"Now, we are all on Camp Donelson, a former U.S. Army camp, dating from the Korean War. It is now part of Fort Campbell, Kentucky. You, I, the staff, in fact everyone but those folks you've been told not to talk to, will be here from now until the day we report out. Mostly, you have freedom to move about anywhere in the camp."

As he spoke, the large screen displayed a photo array of buildings in the compound.

"There is this facility, at which all meals are provided. There are laundry facilities, both self-service and a laundry/dry cleaning plant. There is a store, bowling alley, pool, gym, recreation area, library and a few other amenities. What there is not, is unmonitored contact with 'the outside world'. This is, roughly, the same secrecy that the Framers suffered, given the vast differences in communications between their time in Philadelphia and today."

"What about email and social media with our friends? You can't just cut us off." Dean turned his head and saw a petite young woman with a pony-tail standing, hands on hips.

Dean held up his hand. "Please, hold the questions until the end. I hope there will be fewer and," he smiled benignly, and looked at the young lady who had interrupted him, "somewhat less confrontational." He turned back to look over the audience.

"When you are assigned your permanent quarters," there was a rumble of conversation, "Oh, you stayed in enlisted barracks last night for convenience. In a few minutes, you'll be given your permanent ID card, please wear it at all times when you are outside of your room. You'll also be given a room assignment in what was the Bachelor Officers Quarters. Each of you has a private room, with bath. Your rooms have an electronic lock on the door to which only you and our security people have access. While we're diverted to that subject, we will make cleaning supplies and equipment available. This is not the Hilton. Your room is yours to organize and to keep clean. You have cable TV and a laptop computer. However, external access is severely restricted and, I'll say this slowly and loudly, so LISTEN!" he paused until the room was quiet, "all communications outside the camp are monitored, all of them. They are recorded, as well. No photographs or other files can be uploaded without specific permission; which we may grant, but on a case-by-case basis. I know it's hard to accept, but we are protecting the future of this country by being this harsh. For you, it's a question of two months of electronic, shall we say, deprivation versus the future of America.

"That sucks!"

"You don't trust us?"

"To be honest, no, we don't; not yet. But, we think that, within a week or two, you will be so excited about what you are doing that you will be too busy to 'tweet' and 'Facebook' much more than, we hope, 'having a wonderful time, wish you were here.' By the way, the same proscriptions and monitoring apply to everyone else in the Initiative, from Dr. Gilbert and me, to Ellen and her staff of helpers.

The mood seemed to relax.

"Okay, folks, I'll try and make this shorter. You can only eat so much of the elephant at a time. You have only a few things to do before Monday, but one of them is important. In a moment, you will receive a tote bag from Ellen's folks. Trade your temporary ID for your permanent badge and room key card. There is also a list of all Interns listed by state of residence. Please meet and get to know your state partners. In the bag is a map to the base, operating hours for the facilities and the mess, or dining room, if you wish. There is a 'snack bar' that will open tomorrow at the theater. There is also an office by the front door of this building, in which a staffer will be available 24x7.

"What we want you to do is, quite obviously, meet each other and get comfortable with your 'home away from home'. Send an email home. When you log on to the email package, you may set your own password. As I said, all correspondence is monitored. It is monitored electronically, looking for keywords and trends. We will not 'read' a message, unless the system alerts us to a word, phrase or idea.

"Also, as you meet and get acquainted, look for natural leaders or those you have an idea might contribute more to this effort than normal. We don't have the luxury of having George Washington, Alexander Hamilton or James Madison identified," he paused for effect, "yet! On Monday, you will debate and appoint a five-member Executive Committee to guide your efforts. That Executive Committee will include George over there, as Institute adviser. Each Executive serves at the pleasure of a two thirds majority, so, as new leaders appear that can contribute more, you may meet as a committee of the whole, to remove and replace, as you see necessary. We will advise, but not direct. We hope you will see those who can contribute most, before we do. Monday, we will outline the first week's efforts.

"One final note. Also, in the tote bag are four pieces of literature:

- <u>Founding Fathers</u> by M. E. Bradford, biographies of the men who wrote the Constitution

- <u>James Madison's Notes on the Constitutional Convention of 1787. One of the sets of notes taken during the convention.</u>

"There are also two reference documents:

- The Constitution of the United States of America and Amendments Thereto, and

- Organization Chart of the United States Government

"This is all the guidance we will give you. These items will give every one of you the same foundation for thought. Additionally, there is a great deal of additional background and research material in the library.

"Any questions about what I've said? Please, no questions about our job."

A well-tanned boy, on the right, stood and raised his hand, along with a few others scattered throughout the room.

"Okay, you first."

"Can we have guests in our rooms?"

"Absolutely, we expect that conversations, bull sessions, caucuses and other meetings need to be held somewhere. Your rooms are among those places."

"I meant social guests, sir."

"Young man, I'll say this loudly. We are not your parents. You are here to do the most adult and responsible task your nation can ask of you, except for going into life-threatening combat. That said, we expect you will conduct yourselves in an adult and responsible fashion. Much of what happens on this base is camera monitored and recorded. I promise you that your rooms and bathrooms are not. Next question."

A girl on the side waved her hand. Dean pointed to her. "Do we have input to the games, books, movies and menus?" A general titter ran through the room.

Dean smiled. "May I ask your name, miss?"

"Sally Jamison, sir, from Colorado."

Dean turned toward Ellen, who had a broad smile on her face. "Ellen, I believe we've found a volunteer for the 'Initiative Management Committee'." He turned back to her. "Yes, you do, Miss Jamison, in a manner of speaking. The committee I just alluded to, and which is a part of Monday's business, will manage the admin details of your stay here. I suggest that you volunteer for it, if that is something that interests you."

"Are there hours. That means things like reveille and lights out?"

Dean's head swiveled toward the question, settling on a young man standing erect. He had a familiar short haircut. "Let me guess, service brat?"

"Yes, sir. Mom is career Army."

"Thought so. I will repeat this. We are not your parents. Just keep to the published schedule, much of which you will create." He glanced at his watch. "Okay, we need to get out of here, so the staff can set up for dinner; which, I believe, is Pizza, Burgers and Ribs. In a moment, please head toward the cart with the sign that displays the first letter of your last name for your rooms, ID and reference materials."

A general scraping of chairs and an increase in noise level greeted his statement. Dean flicked the microphone. "A final note." He flicked it again. "A final note, if you please?" He paused and then continued. "On behalf of the organizations that have chartered this important effort and on behalf of the Institute and staff, our most grateful appreciation for the efforts you are going to undertake. Enjoy your weekend." He turned the microphone off and stepped back to Dr. Gilbert and George.

#

"Next, please."

Millie stepped to the table and handed over her temporary ID card. The tall man in his twenties took it and held it beneath a scanner. He glanced at a photo on the screen and glanced at Millie. He touched the check box on the screen. A large green check appeared, and a name and number appeared beneath it. "Hello, Millie. Welcome to 'We the People'. Let's see." He ran a finger up and down the rows of totes on the table until he found a matching number. "Okay. 121". He reached into the tote and withdrew a lanyard with ID card and room key card attached. He crosschecked the number with the screen, jotted a number on a card, stuffed the temporary card into the slot of a shredder and handed tote, lanyard and key card to Millie.

"Here you go Mildred Dickinson. Please always display the ID card, Miss Dickinson. You may remove the key card and keep it wherever you are most comfortable keeping it. Your room number is on this card. At least at the start, only you know what room yours is. We don't recommend that you write your room number on the key card. That way, if it's lost, it's only a key card and not automatic access to you or your belongings. Okay?"

"Millie, please." She looked at her picture on the ID, superimposed over the silhouette of Ohio, scrunched her nose at it, and slipped the lanyard over her neck. As she reached for the tote, she glanced at his badge. "Thank you, uh, Ishmael. Really? Your name is Ishmael?" She colored slightly as she realized her gaffe.

He grinned. "Yes, Millie. Just call me Ishmael. Don't worry. I've been living with that old line from grade school all the way through law school. Ishmael Thommason. A pleasure to meet you."

"Wow! You're a lawyer? I thought you guys passing out bags were, like, clerks or something."

"I suppose it's a clever deception; at least for the weekend. All the folks in shirts like this, are senior staffers with the Initiative. I'm one of the legal staff. I have a JD from George Washington and a PhD in Constitutional Law. Ellen is a Clinical Psychologist working on her Doctorate. There are three others, too; a total of five DAs. You'll meet all of us on Monday and, hopefully, understand more. Now, I hate to rush you along, but I've got a line and" he glanced at his table, "16 more totes to deliver."

Millie picked up her tote and turned to walk away. She stopped, turned her head back and said, "Thanks, Ishmael."

#

The lanky young man in dark dress slacks, a collared shirt buttoned to the neck, shiny tied shoes and wearing a yarmulke stepped to the table. He withdrew the temporary badge from around his neck and handed it to Ishmael. "Leonard Bromberg."

Ishmael pointed at the two remaining totes on the table. "I guessed that. The only other bag belongs to a Jane Abrams. You don't look like a Jane." He took the badge and scanned it, as he had a table full already. He picked up one of the two remaining bags and glanced at the room key, checking a code against the screen. "Yup, Room 223. Please always wear the ID, Mr. Bromberg. You may remove the key card and keep it wherever you are most comfortable. "

"I heard the spiel four times already. Spare me. But, I do have two questions."

Ishmael saw that there were still interns standing at the other tables, so he was not rushed. He had but one remaining at his, a young black woman listening intently for any useful information. "Shoot."

"I'm Jewish." He paused for any response from the man on the other side of the table.

"That was already a reasonable assumption on my part, given the headgear." He smiled and sat on the edge of the, now empty, table. "What's your question?"

"This is Friday and I have to observe Shabbat, if I can. I don't expect that you have enough Jews in the population to constitute enough for us to observe it correctly, but I sent an email to Mr. Hanover, asking if I would be able to keep Kosher and observe Shabbat. I hadn't heard by the time I left. The other question has to do with the acceptability of my prayer shawls," his hands drifted to his waist where the ends of the shawls could be seen tucked into his pockets, "and yarmulke."

Ishmael's brow furled for a moment and he glanced down at the screen. He pulled up a messaging app and typed in a quick line. "I've asked George to drop in to answer your question about Shabbat. I can address the question of your attire. Even though the standing Constitution is the item of issue here, it still guarantees you freedom to practice your religion in any way you see fit, so long as you break no laws. That said, if any intern or staff gives you any reason to believe otherwise, you find any DA or senior staff and tell them. Our job is to make sure you can do yours. Does that make it clear?"

The young lady listening in interrupted. "Excuse me, but I keep hearing the term DA. Just what is a DA, since I presume you are not all District Attorneys?"

Ishmael looked at the ID hanging on the remaining tote. "You would be Miss Abrams?"

"Jane Manning Abrams from Utah, yes." She held out her hand to Leonard. "Pleasure to meet you Mr. Bromberg." They shook hands and then she extended hers, in turn, to Ishmael. "And you Ishmael. Now, DA?"

Ishmael chuckled. "It means, simply, Devil's Advocate. You'll learn about the five of us on Monday, so please allow me not to go into depth, right now." He turned his attention back to Leonard. "And, you Mr. Bromberg? I see George headed this way." He handed Leonard his tote. "Welcome to the Initiative. May I ask you to step aside a moment while I welcome Miss Abrams, thankfully my last intern, but certainly not least, at least not in the single-minded purpose category." He smiled at her and tilted his eyebrows.

"My father has much the same opinion, sir. Our family has never been reticent to speak our minds." She handed him her temporary badge. He scanned it and handed over her tote, badge and key card."

"May I presume, as well, that you have overheard my introductory remarks?"

She giggled, "Shall I recite them? I have a very good memory."

"Spare me. I've heard it 24 times today … from me. And, I believe your memory will stand you in good stead here." He tipped her key card to read the code. Then he glanced down. "Room 121." George stepped to the table with Ellen at his side. "I look forward to working with all of you, Miss Abrams. Have a pleasant weekend." He turned to Leonard. "Leonard Bromberg meet George Hanover and Ellen Haley."

"One more thing, Ishmael?"

"Yes, Jane?"

"How many Mormons are here?"

"There are three, Miss Abrams." Ellen had the answer for her.

Jane turned toward her. "That doesn't seem like very many. Why?"

Ellen continued, "Actually, it emulates, very well, the actual population diversity in the U.S."

She looked a bit upset at being corrected on a question about the LDS church. "Oh. Okay. I was hoping there would be more."

George added. "You will have adequate opportunities to worship, if that's your question, Miss. We can arrange for a local minister."

"No, sir. That's not necessary. Any male Mormon can lead the service. Thank you." She picked up her tote and walked away. Four sets of eyes following her as she did.

George turned back first. "Mr. Bromberg. Your questionnaire and email indicated a desire to keep Kosher. After dinner, I will take you to meet our Executive Chef. He will work with you to make sure we do our best to help you keep your dietary restrictions."

"Thank you. I know it seems picky, but I promised my mother and my rabbi that I would try. And, since she asked first, how many Jews are here?"

Ellen again had the answer. "There are four." She saw his face fall.

"We have one senior staff and one support staff that are Jewish, Leonard, not quite a 'Minyan', I'm sorry. But, on the bright side, the rabbi from a conservative temple in Knoxville has offered to bring three more members along every second Friday, for worship. I'm afraid it's the best we can do."

Leonard looked at him with an expression just short of wonder. "How do you know so much about our requirements and customs? Almost no one in America cares."

His face was open, and his eyes sparkled. "I'm the senior staffer, Leonard. Shalom." The sound of metal doors filled the room "And, I see that the staff is ready to serve dinner. "Leonard, I will find you after dinner. In case, I don't find you in here, I will come to your room and get you." He glanced at Ishmael, a question on his face.

"Room 223, sir."

George nodded his head in gratitude, and walked toward the back of the room, where a dozen people in suits or 'business casual clothing' were seating themselves.

Ishmael looked at Ellen. "We've got us one heck of a group here. What do you think?"

"We've got the tools, that's for sure. Now we need fortitude and patience."

"Don't forget luck, lots of luck."

The Game is Afoot

The Weekend

June 16, 2017

"Aloha, bruddah." Kona Opana stopped at the empty four-person table occupied, solely, by Oy Palomuto. "Got room for one more?"

Oy set his burger down, wiped his hands on a third paper napkin, Oy liked his burgers sloppy, and pointed at the empty chair across from him. "Hafaday".

"You not Hawaiian?"

"Nope, Guamanian. You think they're gonna pack the place with Polynesians? At least I don't feel like a token islander anymore. Sit down and take a load off."

Kona set his tray down. It had a full half pizza and a large salad on it. "Sorry 'bout that."

"No sweat, man. I had some chick from Idaho, I think, that thought I was an Eskimo for Pete's sake."

"Land of the free, man, long as you're white." The big Hawaiian boy folded a large slice of pizza in half and took a bite. While he chewed, Oy took another bite of his burger followed by four fries dredged in mayonnaise. "What do you think about this, darn, I don't even know what to call it?"

"I think some of these guys have been conducting agricultural experiments. That's what I think."

The big boy laughed, mouth full of pizza. He swallowed and took a drink of iced tea. "Maybe just too much time in DC. I'll take the North Shore, any day." Oy joined in, hoisting his soda in a toast.

A feminine voice intruded on the laughter. "Hey, guys, the place is filling up. Got room for a girl from 'The Northstar State'?"

Oy turned and looked at the petite redhead, in a Vikings Jersey. The outline of Minnesota was on her badge, behind the name Lena Nordstrom. "Well, uh, Lena, I expect that 'The Rock' and 'The Aloha State' can handle a Vikings fan. Neither one of us can field a decent team, so pull up a chair."

Lena set her large salad, dressing on the side, and bowl of fruit on the table and then pulled her tote from the crook of her arm and set it down. She pulled out a chair and sat down. As she picked up her fork, she said, "I heard the last sentence or two as I was looking for a place to sit, that wasn't occupied by some smart mouthed jock. I think it's an exciting exercise."

"What is?" Kona tossed a crust on his plate. "You really think that a hundred-odd kids right out of high school can rewrite the Constitution?"

A fork full of salad, already dredged in a vinaigrette, was set down on her plate. "Why not? We don't know what the goal of this exercise is. It may just be a fishing expedition by some 'think tank' from the beltway." The fork was retrieved and emptied into her mouth. Two chews and she continued, "The point is that we, your 'hundred-odd' have the opportunity to 'recreate' if you will," she swallowed, "without some politician telling us why we 'can't' do something."

The conversation became a 'he said-she said' fork, pizza and french fry pointing argument until a coffee mug slapped down on the table. The three young heads twisted around to see a staff shirt sitting in the fourth chair. "Hi, Mike Eaves. Personally, I like what," he paused to look at the card hanging on a lanyard around Lena's neck, "Miss Nordstrom has to say. It's exactly what we want. Think outside the box. You are better educated, in the long view, than the Framers. You live this nation every day. You've got TV. You chat with people around the world and you've all done well in history and government classes.

Forget what you think you can't do. Be the Wright Brothers. Be Jonas Salk. Be Neil Armstrong. It's your country. Make it work the way you think it should work. Worst case? You get paid for two months of 'brainstorming', right? Then you all go off to your colleges and universities and leave the mess we're in neither worse nor better for the effort." He sat back, picked up his mug and looked into three pairs of wide-open eyes.

Lena tossed her fork down, put her hands flat on the table and leaned forward; speaking directly to Mike. "You make this sound hopeless. So, why are we here?"

"Lena, you, these young men and 152 others just like you, optimist and pessimist alike, are here exactly because the conventional wisdom says it's hopeless. We can't let that be. If we do go down that path, in twenty years, they'll be speaking Russian or Chinese in the halls of government in Washington or every non-Muslim citizen may well be in a concentration camp or on the path to extermination. I, for one, don't like those alternatives. We're taking a flyer that American youth aren't infected with despair ... yet." He stood, picked up his mug and looked at Oy and Kona. "Think about it."

#

Jay Brigham closed the door to his room and carefully placed his Stetson on the rack in the closet. He tossed his duffel on the bed and unzipped the closure. He removed two bound books; each with many ribbon markers scattered throughout and set them on the desk. He added the Bible he had carried all day and his cell phone.

He set them side by side and silently recited the titles: The Holy Bible, the Book of Mormon and Pearl of Great Price. Absentmindedly, he shuffled them a few times, ending with the Book of Mormon first in line on the left. He sat on the bed and pried his boots off. He placed them in the wardrobe and sat down at the desk.

He reached into the tote and withdrew the thin booklet that was the <u>Constitution of the United States and Amendments thereto with Annotations.</u> He placed that in the line and reshuffled the volumes. He pushed the <u>Pearl of Great Price</u> to the side and then made various geometric figures on the desk with the remaining three books as his mind processed what he had heard. Finally, after five minutes of rumination, he picked up the bible and slipped from the chair to his knees. Clutching the Bible to his chest, he began to pray.

#

Jane Abrams, tote on top of her rolling suitcase walked down the hall, silently counting off room numbers as she did. She extrapolated from 115 and noted that another girl was standing at the door to what should be 121, her room.

She stopped in her tracks as the girl's key card appeared to work and she pulled her bag into the room. Jane moved forward to the door. "Hi. Excuse me, but Ishmael said I was in room 121."

The other girl turned. "He told me that this is my room. I'm Millie Dickinson."

"Jane Manning Abrams. Hi. Let me try my key." She pulled the door closed and inserted her key card. She was rewarded with a red light. She withdrew the key and tried again; another red light. She knocked on the door and Millie answered it. "I guess not, but now I don't know what to do."

"Hang on." She walked to the phone and picked up the booklet of numbers next to it. She leafed through it until she found the number she sought. "They said there was always a staff member at this number. Here." She handed Jane the phone as she pressed three numbers.

Jane put the handset to her ear just as the phone was answered. "Bill Walters."

"Hi. I'm Jane Manning Abrams. When I checked in, Ishmael told me I was assigned to room 121." She pulled Millie's ID close to read the name. "Millie Dickinson was also told 121. Her key card works and mine doesn't."

"Hang on a second, Miss Abrams." The phone went silent for a moment. "I'll be right there. I'm not going to make a judgment over the phone. It has personal security implications. See you in two." The phone went dead.

"He says he'll be right here."

"Yeah, weird, right? Anyway, you want to sit down while we wait? Where are you from? I'm from Mentor, Ohio."

"I'm from Salt Lake City."

"Cool. You Mormon?"

"Yes."

"Wow, I didn't know there were any black Mormons."

Jane shook her head and smiled. "There are lots of us. My ancestor was the very first African American Mormon and my father is one of the Quorum of Seventy, the leaders of the church."

"Wow, equally cool. My dad's a state representative, but that's not nearly as cool." A knock sounded at the open door.

"Miss Abrams?" Jane stood. "May I see your ID, please?"

Jane handed it to him. "Right. Okay. I think Ishmael just messed up the numbers. Your room is 112, just down the hall. I'll be glad to show you."

Jane reached for her bag. "Thank you. Nice to meet you Millie."

"I'll see you around this weekend. We can talk about this and who we think should be leaders. Do you want to be one?"

"I don't know. I'm still trying to process what they told us we had to do. Whoever is on the Executive Committee has a big job. I'm not sure I'm up to that challenge."

"Well, I'll see you anyway. Sorry about the mix up."

"Not your fault, Millie. See you. Come visit. I'm in 112. Easy to remember, now." She pulled her bag through the door and turned down the hall.

"Miss Dickinson, good evening." Bill closed the door behind him.

#

Jay opened his eyes and stood. He sat on the desk chair as his thoughts raced. 'I can't do this myself. I can't protect the church from the way the country is denying the Son and leaning toward sin.' He picked up his cell phone and whispered to himself, "I've got to talk to the Bishop."

#

Bill walked into the office. All five DAs were there along with Dr. Elliot and George. "What was that all about?" George asked.

Bill walked to the coffee center and picked up his personal mug, a Victor style with 'I Know Why You Did That!'. He filled it with black coffee and took the last chair at the table. "It would appear that Ishmael", he tipped his mug toward the young black lawyer, "transposed a room assignment. I found two young ladies flipping a coin over who got the bed."

"Crap. Sorry. On the bright side, at least it was two girls."

Dr. Elliot shook his head.

George picked up his pen and poised it over a yellow legal pad. "Okay, folks, end of Day Zero. Observations?"

"I'll start." Heads turned toward Mike Eaves. "I was just walking around during dinner, observing how the peer groups were forming. Aside from calming two of our minorities from the Pacific, I found some formation around the natural leadership qualities of Eagle Scouts and folks headed to Ivy League and Military Academies. I expected that."

"Any young women stick out?", Dr. Elliot asked.

"None from my side. But, in defense, I guess I migrated toward the young men more than the women. Teen boys tend to form groups quicker than the girls, who take longer to 'scope each other out'."

Ellen jumped in. "I disagree with that, almost entirely. While that statement may not be sexist, it is certainly stereotyping the young ladies that we've invited; all of whom excelled in academics and outside pursuits."

"Ellen, studies show that male secondary peer groups form quicker, during these years ... "

George knocked his knuckles on the table. "Mike. Ellen. This discussion is as old as your specialties and will grow older, I'm sure, without resolution. Not tonight. We have only a few days to get this 'population sample' to coalesce and get to work. Please, keep your focus, people. Mike, continue."

"Sorry, Mike." Ellen did not appear to be ready to relinquish her stand. "We'll continue this later."

Mike chuckled. "The first round is on me."

A hardly subtle sotto voce comment, "Yeah, at the sound of the bell."

"Joyce!" George remonstrated.

Joyce held up her hands, palms out, but she was grinning at the success of her pointed jest.

Mike cleared his voice an insincere smile turned toward Joyce, "If I may be permitted to continue, I found three Eagle Scouts, but only one exuded true leadership in the few minutes of observation. His name is", Mike flipped open a small notebook, "Beau Williams, from Maryland."

"That's it? Just one Eagle Scout? That surprises me."

"George. Mike missed at least one." Joyce returned the false grin to Mike. "There's a young Hispanic from New York, Puerto Rican I guess, Juan Morales. He's an Eagle, as well as a National Merit Scholar, on a full boat to Princeton."

"What made him stand out, Joyce?"

"When I walked by, he was talking about, well lecturing, actually, the Atlantic territory intern on how being a territory is both good and bad. As near as I know, he knows more about the 'ins and outs' of being a citizen from a non-state than anyone at this table."

George wrote the young man's name on his pad. "That's one good candidate. Any other standouts?"

Bill lifted his hand slightly. "I've got one I haven't met, but I've heard about from a couple. Ishmael, you had a young black girl from Utah, right?"

Ishmael looked at his notes. "Oh yeah. Jane Abrams. She's a 4.0 from Salt Lake and headed to BYU, why? Nothing stuck out at check-in."

"One of the other Utah kids saw her and told me that she's sort of 'First Family of Utah". Her ancestor was the first black member of the Mormon church and her father is on the", he looked at his notes, "Council of Seventy. No, that's 'Quorum of Seventy'. Apparently, that's as close to the throne as you can get in the Mormon Church, without being around the big table in Salt Lake City. Anyway, she's apparently got it in her blood. She rises to the top of nearly anything she tries."

Dr. Elliot interrupted. "Let's keep her in standby. I'm unsure how the 'majority' membership will take a female African-American Mormon on the Executive Committee, regardless of how good she is. It might be a disruption."

George looked at him, eyebrows raised. "No guts, no Air Medal, Dr. E."

"I know. The coward dies a thousand deaths, etc. Let's keep her in our back pocket ... for now. She might be a better relief hitter than starting lineup. Any more?"

#

The phone rang three times. "Hello?"

"Bishop Benson?"

"Yes. May I help you?"

"Sir, it's Jay Brigham."

"Oh, Jay. I thought you were away in Kentucky on some hush-hush apprenticeship."

"I am sir. That's why I'm calling. I don't quite know how to explain it. In fact," His voice lowered. "I'm really not supposed to say anything about it, but what they want us to do ... I don't know."

"Jay, is it illegal or immoral?"

"No, sir. At least I don't think so. It's kind of a research project, I guess."

"Then what bothers you about it?"

"Well, I'm worried it might hurt the church."

"How so?"

"I don't know. It's just a feeling. Oh heck. I'm probably just tired from traveling. I shouldn't have called you."

"Jay, you're a good boy. I've known your dad for years and respected your granddad as much as I knew about him. You keep your ear to the ground and call me if you have any information, that I can use to find out if there is a threat to the church. Okay?"

"Yes, sir. Good night."

"Good night, Jay."

#

George put his pen down and pinched the bridge of his nose. He looked at the time on his cell phone. "Okay. I think that's all we can do for a first night." He picked up his pad. "Dr. Elliot, it appears that we may have identified four candidates for the Executive Committee; at least at this point. We have Beau Williams, Juan Morales and Millie Dickinson; and of course, our 'secret weapon', Miss Jane Manning Abrams. We've talked about how to 'schmooze, I believe, is the word' to either get these kids to run for a spot, or to find willing interns to 'nominate' them, without all the noise and steam of a railroad job. Okay? And keep your eyes and ears open for two or three more." He stood. "Get a good night's sleep, all. Tomorrow is Day One." Dr. Elliot walked from the room followed by George, who muttered over his shoulder, "Good night".

Six Degrees
June 17, 2017

"Hi, Millie. Got room for one more?"

Millie looked at the three empty chairs at her table and scrunched her face up. "Sit down, Jane." She picked up half a muffin and placed it on her plate. Then, she pushed the other half toward Jane, who sat across from her. "Have a muffin. These things are large enough to challenge a football team."

"Somebody mention football?" Two heads swiveled to see a freckled face beneath a bright shock of red hair. "Alvin Lee, ladies, state champion tight end and First Family from the sovereign Commonwealth of Virginia". He stretched out the pronunciation to resemble 'Vah-ginny-yah'.

Millie looked at Jane and made a face.

"Mind if I set myself down? This breakfast tray is a might heavy." He set his tray down with a thump and flopped down into a chair. The tray was so full that it might well have fed a football team. "So, where are you ladies from?"

"Utah" and "Ohio" came out almost simultaneous.

"Well, now, a darned Yankee and a Westerner. Ain't America great!"

Jane shook her head. "And, just what do you mean by 'first family', Mr. Lee? And, please dispense with the 'Southern Charm'. I expect that it's not really you behind that drawl."

Millie hid a grin and choked on a bit of toast. She reached for her hot tea.

Alvin flushed slightly at being chided by the smiling black woman on his right. "Well, I figured it was worth a shot to elicit a response." The theatrical drawl was replaced by an almost aristocratic southern lilt. "Do you mean you really don't know what First Family of Virginia means?"

"I'm not in the habit of displaying false ignorance, Alvin." Jane's voice had an edge to it.

Alvin held out his hands. "No offense, please. I'm a Lee, as in Robert E, Richard H and Lighthorse Harry. In Virginia, you can't BE any more Virginia than to be a Lee."

Millie giggled. "Somebody put in a call to Kevin Bacon. Mr. Lee, my name is Mildred Dickinson. You might say we share a heritage. My great times a bunch granddaddy was the Honorable

John Dickinson of Pennsylvania. Name ring a bell?" She saw Jane's head tilt in curiosity.

Alvin pushed his chair back, stood and bowed at the waist. "Well, it is truly an honor to meet another 'signer', Miss Dickinson. I do believe our forefathers were, to put a point on it, in opposition at one time. Let's hope that doesn't happen this time." He resumed his seat.

"Holy cow. Is this weird or what. Your granddaddies helped form this country and now your families are going to do it again. I thought I had a claim to heritage because my great grandfather was the first black man to become a Mormon."

Alvin looked at her, slightly differently than he had at the beginning of the conversation. He held out his hand. "In and of itself, I believe that also makes you a 'first family' if, perhaps, in a different way."

Jane took the hand, shook and held it. "I thank you for the inclusion, Mr. Lee. It will be interesting to see how we view 'the central government'." She let his hand drop. "Now, I expect you would like to pay attention to that plate of food before it causes a global warming episode."

Millie choked again, and Alvin laughed as he picked up his napkin. "I believe that is excellent advice, Miss Abrams."

#

Ellen was sitting with the three interns from Michigan. Somehow, they had found each other in just the few hours they had been together since check-in. The breakfast discussion revolved around the upcoming football season for Michigan and Michigan State; despite her best efforts to keep them on track. She sighed. No names would go on her list from Michigan. She picked up her mug, excused herself and walked away; looking for greener pastures on which to find leaders and innovators.

She had, however, overheard parts of the conversation between Millie and Alvin Lee. His name *would* go on her list as another natural. He exuded the natural leadership that had been the watchword of his forebears. And, she thought he might just provide an interesting counterpoint to the liberal northeast and the independent laissez faire west. It would be interesting to watch.

As she passed by another table with three young people engaged in a breakfast debate, her ears perked up. "Look, we start with the basics of the Bill of Rights and build something that defends and supports individual rights." This speaker was a ruddy faced young man wearing jeans and a T shirt proclaiming 'Terps are Tops'. She leaned over and saw the silhouette of Maryland on his badge.

"That's a short-sighted view. A central government must be an entity unto itself, superior to all others, including the individual. Some individual rights have to be subordinated to common need."

"Ben Franklin dealt with that thought a long time ago, my Razorback buddy. 'Those who surrender freedom for security will have neither freedom nor security."

"I thought we dealt with that 'states rights' crap last night, JR, not to mention a hundred and fifty years ago." The girl, blonde ponytail sticking out of a clean white unmarked ball cap, threw her napkin on the table. "No one individual, city, county or state can exist independently of all other external influences; and certainly not in utter subservience to the population. The Articles of Confederation put that to rest."

"Come on, Lily Mae, the liberal stance is always 'more government for all the people'. Do you know how trite that sounds? You're from the South where 'States Rights' is the motto. I don't understand it. And, I never have figured out why the 'Presidents Clinton', from Arkansas, too, as I remember, tried to use the government to beat the individual into compliance with some 'wealth redistribution' scheme. Look where that got us. We're up to our necks in debt, owed to countries that don't like us and the laughing stock of the world that we used to lead."

She could see the third member, a young man, 'JR' if she read his badge correctly and from either Alabama or Mississippi, she couldn't tell, was nodding his head in agreement. Ellen just couldn't tell with which stance he was agreeing.

"For starters Beau, not all southerners fly the 'stars and bars' in front of the courthouse or have gun racks in their 4-wheel pickup trucks. Get out of the 19th century! The 'Presidents Clinton', as you so cleverly call them, have done more to lift the lower middle class from poverty than any other administration except, maybe, Lyndon Johnson … and where was he from, huh? Texas, you 'copperhead'."

Ellen set her cup on the table. "Whoa!" Rapidly angering eyes shifted toward the source of the voice. She tried to smile to defuse the growing argument. "You're beginning to sound like Congress and that, continual unproductive bickering and name calling, my young friends, is exactly why you're here. There is as much fact in what both of you have said as there is fiction. However, you're taking the 'buffet' approach to political history; each one of you picking the facts you want to use and ignoring the ones that don't fit your program. Did any of the three of you hear anything that makes you want one of you to be a part of the leadership of this effort? That's what your assignment was. I'll check the calendar to see when a donnybrook can be scheduled." She picked up her mug and took a long slow sip while her eyes moved from one of the antagonists to the other.

Starting with the young lady, smiles began to appear. "Now, we're showing a C-SPAN reenactment of the Jefferson-Hamilton debates at 10:00 this morning. I'd suggest that you watch it. In one manner or another, it deals with the very same argument that you two just had; only 230 years ago."

JR spoke up. "Do we have to? I mean, like, is it an assignment?"

"No. It's a resource for you to use, just like the books in your tote and all the books and articles in both the library and online. We've got a huge job to do in the next two months and we have no time for recriminations or arguments."

"Oh, okay."

"Look. Do you know the difference between a loud argument and a heated discussion?"

Lily Mae, bit first. "No, what?"

"In an argument, both sides are shouting but neither is listening. In a discussion, both sides may still be shouting, but they're also listening. Try to keep those definitions in mind during the next few weeks, please." She picked up her mug again. "Ten o'clock. It's on channel 16 or on the screens in the theater. Bye."

#

Ellen sat on a bench in the sun outside the theater. She had her head tipped back and her eyes were closed.

"Meditating or napping?"

Ellen's head swiveled to upright and she opened her eyes. "Oh, hey, Joyce. Nope, just grabbing some air and hoping that an infusion of Vitamin D comes with a helping of patience. Pull up a bench."

The young DA sat. "Getting to you? It's only the first day. You're not scheduled to 'go postal' for at least a week."

Ellen laughed. "I've always heard of the difficulty of herding cats. Now, I know."

A laugh. "I don't care what the selection criteria was, these are still kids. They can't even comprehend the breadth of the problem, much less formulate a solution."

"That's exactly what this is all about. They have no preconceived notions. It's the diversity of conversation that I'm hearing that flabbergasts me. I'm hearing everything from 'impossible and too complex' through a selection of minutiae like 'immigration', balanced budget, defense, welfare, entitlement, legislation and 'checks and balances' to at least one serious discussion of the effects of any substantive change on the current national and international perceptions of power. Yikes!"

"Actually, that sounds pretty good. As for that last one, I hope you got names."

"I did, and it wasn't from any of our ivy leaguers. It was a kid from Idaho and another from New Hampshire, at lunch." She reached into her back pocket for a flip book. "One, Arthur Little, from New Hampshire and a, David Ingalls from Idaho. His dad, it seems, is a history prof at Idaho. Kid's got a better grasp of cause and effect than most of the population and he almost blew off a scholarship to Idaho State to enlist in the Marines."

Joyce laughed out loud. "Well, the Marines are always looking for a few good men. So, why didn't' he enlist?"

"Of all the reasons, his girlfriend told him that if he 'threw his future away for some perception of heroic sacrifice', she'd break up with him."

"Damn! I want her on the team."

Ellen shook her head. "Think maybe we recruited the wrong one?"

#

June 18, 2017

Lena's cell phone buzzed. She picked it up off the desk and looked at the screen. It was a text message from George.

This is an EVERYONE message. Please come to the theater at 1:00 pm. This is a mandatory meeting. If you meet anyone who does not have a cell phone or whose phone is off, please inform them of the meeting. Thank you. George

Lena looked at the clock on the phone and set it down on the desk. Then, she picked it up and set an alarm for 12:50pm. Phone in hand, she walked out and across the hall to room 205 and knocked.

"Yeah?" sounded through the door.

"Roy, it's Lena from across the hall."

"Hang on. I've got to put on my pants."

Lena smiled to herself, fighting the visual image. Then, the door opened and the tall muscular farm boy from Nebraska, stood barefoot in a pair of jeans. "Sorry, Lena, I just got back from a run and was almost in the shower. What's up?"

"I know you said you don't turn your cell phone on until evening. Everybody got a message from George about a meeting at 1." Her thumbs sped across her phone recovering the text and she handed the phone to Roy.

"Huh. Wonder what's up? Okay, thanks. I suppose I'd better shower before my room throws me out."

Lena giggled, took her phone back and turned back to her own room.

#

The noise level in the theater was exactly what you would expect from a hundred and a half teenagers, as Joyce opened the door for George, Dr. Elliot, Harold Gilbert and the other DAs. George stopped inside until one or two interns saw them. Movement reminiscent of 'the wave' at a ball game swept outward from the door and the noise level dropped markedly in only a few seconds. Then, they walked to the stage. Dr. Elliot, Mr. Gilbert and George mounted, while the DAs sat in five reserved seats in the front row. George approached the lectern and motioned to the projection booth. The lights went down, with only the stage lighted.

George put his hand to his brow, as if to peer into the back rows. "No napping in the back row." Then, he grinned and waited. A light laughter spread through the hall, significantly reducing the stress.

"Better. Now, there will be no executions following this meeting, so, to quote my kids. 'Just grab a chill'." He waited a few moments for another wave of respectful laughter. He held up his hands, palms out. "Okay, now. Again, welcome to Camp Donelson and the Initiative. The kitchen assures me that none of you are off your feed. But, you've had a day and a half to get acquainted on your own. The fun's over. Ladies and gentlemen, Harold Gilbert, initiator of the concept that brought you here." He stepped back as Mr. Gilbert stepped up.

"I think George missed his calling. Anyway, the DAs have watched you for the last day and a half as you met and sorted each other out. As far as I know, there have been no fist fights, street demonstrations or hunger strikes, so that's a good start. We've watched you individually and we think we know who the leaders are ... today. But, we're not sure you've decided who you want to follow.

This afternoon, we want to put you in a deliberate team development exercise, but very very free form. Call it a final exercise, if you wish. But, have fun in the effort. You're meant to enjoy the afternoon and the steak and lobster cookout that will follow."

Applause and few cheers erupted. Gilbert raised his hands for quiet and the room quieted.

"Tomorrow, you go to work in earnest. Always remember, that the task we've set for you is serious, meaningful and truly important. George?" Mr. Gilbert stepped back, and George returned to the lectern. He separated the microphone from the holder and stepped to the edge of the stage and, in turn, the light. He sat on the edge of the stage.

He turned toward the two founders and pointed stage left. "You guys can leave now." He turned to the audience of young people and grinned as the two men waved and left the stage.

"Okay." He looked right and left. "We're alone." He paused for effect. "Alright, seriously, we're having a sports fest this afternoon. There are 155 of you, six softball fields, six basketball courts and four volleyball courts. How you divide into teams, who you pick as captains, as well as whom and how well you play, are all part of the program. The DAs will serve as referees and umpires. Oh, I should warn you that the founders, Dr. Elliot, Mr. Gilbert and the two you've not met, Marion Dixson and Eric Leary will also appear and participate as YOU see fit. You may ask them to play, coach or referee. Me? I'm taking the afternoon off." He grinned again. "Not really. I'll be with the founders. Be kind."

"But, remember that 'Big Brother is Watching'. While you're having fun, look for the people you want to work with and who you want to follow. Find like minds and philosophies and determine potential doctrinal adversaries. You've got until 2 o'clock to change into sports gear and head toward the sports fields. The cookout starts at 6, okay?" He hopped back up onto the stage and put the microphone back in the holder.

"And your time starts NOW!" He walked off stage left, leaving the interns to their own devices, as the DAs observed.

Form and Function

The Sorting Hat

June 18, 2017 - Camp Donelson, Kentucky

Lena stacked Roy's dishes atop hers and took both trays to the scullery window. She glanced at the clock on her cell phone. Then, she refilled her coffee cup and returned to the table. "We've got twenty minutes before the first session, Roy. I've got to go get my notes and laptop. You want to get us a couple of seats?

"Sure." He pushed his chair back. "I wish I had your organization skills. I've figured out who six people are here, so far. You and I are two of them. I have no idea how I'm going to be of any use in this effort."

"Don't knock yourself, Roy. You're an 'A' student headed to the University of Nebraska."

"Yeah, on a partial football scholarship."

Lena shook her head. "Well, if nothing else, it means you know how to be a team player. Now, just go get us two seats, not too far back. I'll be there in five minutes." Lena turned and headed to the door, leaving Roy standing.

Mike walked up to Roy. "Quite a young lady."

Roy turned and, after reading Mike's name from his ID, responded, "I've only known her for two days, we have rooms across the hall, but I've learned one thing about her." Mike tipped his head and raised his eyebrows. "She could talk the Israelis into playing a soccer match in Mecca. And she'd get the Saudis to pay their way."

"And what skill does that give her. Is she a leader?"

Roy thought for a moment as he looked at his watch. "I'm not sure. She didn't want to play any of the games yesterday. She finally joined a volleyball team. Hey, don't we have a meeting? I'm supposed to save seats for Lena and me."

"You are correct." He headed toward the door. "Let's not keep the lady, or George, waiting." As they strolled, Mike drew out Roy's thoughts on Lena. Mike had seen her on the sports ground and, while she didn't excel at the sport, she did, twice that he saw, arbitrate a dispute over a call. In fact, she won a reversal on a decision made by George. Mike smiled to himself. George's decision was wrong, but he was unwilling to admit it and Lena had manipulated him until he came around.

His thoughts were interrupted by Roy. "She told me she'd learned how to resolve conflicts by working with challenged kids in her town. They were always getting into spats over 'turf' or some other item, trivial or important. She's, I guess, part mentor and part ... crap! Here comes Lena and I don't have seats yet, sorry." He hurried down the aisle before Lena entered the theater and grabbed two seats on the aisle in the fifth row. As he headed down to the stage, where he and the other DAs were to sit, Mike chuckled at Roy's need to keep his promise; even for such a small item, as seats. He mounted the stage and sat between Ellen and Joyce; his assigned seat, for some reason. Ellen handed him a printed agenda, as the Institute folks, all four this time, walked in from stage left; followed by George, who stopped at the edge of the proscenium at the lectern.

As the lights dimmed the noise level settled. "Good morning. Welcome to Day Three and what you think is the first day, when you'll earn your pay." He looked over the audience and noticed that interns were still coming in, in small numbers. He raised his voice slightly. "One of the first items on the agenda is punctuality. As you age gracefully in life, you'll quickly realize that most bosses like to know that their workers understand that 8am means 8am, not 8:10. We have too much to do in a short period, to let the schedule slide because we can't be on time."

He paused for effect. "Nuff said?"

"Okay. Now, a show of hands, please. How many watched the Jefferson-Hamilton debate on C-Span on Saturday?" Better than half the hands went up. "Good. I always enjoy those debates. They give good insight into how the Framers had divergent views of a central government and, in fact, the relationship of a government to those governed. Remember that when they wrote the Constitution, there was no right way. And, they explored many ways, as they moved toward the final document. That document was the result of weeks of negotiating and compromising. Keep that in mind, please, as you work.

"Now, as a reinforcing, and we hope amusing, few minutes, we have a short cartoon for you to watch. It's entitled 'The Parable of the Six Wise Men' and is based on a fable from twelfth century India. Enjoy it. When the lights come back up, it's time to make your first decisions, negotiations and compromises. Lights, please."

The lights went down, and the two large screen displays illuminated.

> 'In an exotic land far way and long ago lived a king beloved by his people. As in all kingdoms, there were problems aplenty and the king had a council of six wise men to aid him in ruling the kingdom ... *(The parable in its entirety is contained at the end of the chapter.)*

#

When the lights came back up, the lectern had been moved to center stage along with an audio/visual stand. Dr. Elliot was there with an overhead projector. He flipped the switch and a blank organization chart appeared. "Well, folks, it's time to earn your keep. First, it's time you officially meet the DAs. We've been very careful not to use the full term until this morning. It means 'Devil's Advocate' here." He swung his hand to point at the five. "Stand up, please."

He introduced all five but gave no amplifying information. "Each of these five staff members has an academic or professional specialty and special tasks to perform during this project. These specialties or tasks are not secret, and you'll eventually discover them. But, for now, they also serve as the 'adult supervision' for the Initiative. They will help when you get stuck, jar a creative thought or idea loose, insert a critical thought or help resolve any problems you have. They have no vote and will make no decision toward your final product. After all, they're all over twenty and they've all been contaminated by reality." A chuckle ran through the audience. "Don't hesitate to ask when you need them. They know the resources available to help you in search of your pursuits.

"The next item on the agenda is the selection, by you, of the Executive Committee. I hope you were paying attention over the weekend." His hand swept grandly over the audience. "Somewhere out there, are the interns in whom you will entrust the reins of leadership, to form and guide you all, as you go forward in the next two months. Remember that they must perform to keep their chair on the committee. They may be replaced, without recrimination, I hope, by majority vote, if you find someone more suited to the task, at hand, at that time. So, I suggest, that, for now, you pick organizers and negotiators. So, lights up please, and let's see nominating hands. Oh, you may not refuse a nomination, sorry." He grinned.

"Sir?" The intonation was distinctly Southern. It came out 'suh'.

George failed to locate the voice. "Stand please."

Dr. Elliot turned his head when he saw a young man stand. "Yes? Do you have a name for us?"

"Well, sir, I suppose that depends on whether we can nominate ourselves."

Dr. Elliot, somewhat taken aback, looked at the other three Institute members. A universal set of 'Why not?' gestures was the response. "Virginia, or perhaps North Carolina, right? Nominate yourself? I suppose so, but I sure hope you've been lobbying for the task. Are you standing for the committee?"

"Oh, heck no, sir. I'm not talking about me. See, I'm from Virginia and we're trying to get one of ours on the committee. He ought to be there but keeps saying 'no'." There was a distinct murmur from the crowd; even on 'Smart man' comment.

"Why not just nominate him?"

"Well, sir, there is one family in the old dominion that you never go against. It just isn't done."

Joyce jotted a note, stood and took the note to Dr. Elliot. He looked at it, glanced briefly at her and tucked the note in his pocket. "I don't suppose that that family would be the Lees, would it?"

The young man grinned, "Well, sir, it sure ain't the Grants." General laughter spread throughout the audience, at the Civil War allusion.

Dr. Elliot and the other Founders also laughed. Elliot held up his hands for order. "Please let the rest of your fellow interns in on our little secret. Oh, your name, too, please."

"I'm Rayford Louis Montroy, sir, from Winchester, Virginia. One of us from Virginia is a direct descendant of the Lee line, Alvin Lee of Staunton. Alvin is on his way to Mr. Jefferson's university with a full scholarship."

"And why should Mr. Lee serve on the Executive Committee? Better yet, why does he not wish to?"

Another young man, tall with red hair, stood. "I'd like to answer that question, if you don't mind?"

"Would I be remiss in presuming that you are the aforementioned Alvin Lee, FFV?"

"I have the honor being a part of that historic family, yes. And, it is exactly for that reason that I wish to work in the background. My name and family lineage should not be the focus, nor serve as guidance for selection."

Dr. Elliot walked toward the edge of the stage, taking the microphone with him. "Mike, would you please take the portable microphone to Mr. Lee?" There was a shuffle and some scattered sidebar conversations as Mike picked up the microphone and turned it on. He walked up the aisle and passed it to Alvin. "May I inquire as your intended course of study at UVA?"

"Pre-law, sir."

"I see."

Rayford jumped back into the conversation. "Ask him what his senior thesis was, Dr. Elliot. It won him an award and the scholarship to UVA."

"Ray, just shut up will you!"

"Mr. Lee. Please. We do not silence discussion here. However, would you enlighten us as to the subject raised, apparently to your dismay, by Mr. Montroy?" Lee hesitated, looking uncomfortable in the spotlight." You may as well, son. I can dispatch one of my staff and waste an additional five minutes, that we don't have to waste."

Lee sighed in surrender, "A comparison of the Framer's intentions, with respect to a strict versus a liberal interpretation of the Constitution, as a governing document." The noise level rose and fell as if a wave of murmuring had broken on the shore.

"Well, now. I, for one, would like to read that paper. Have you a copy or shall I search it out?"

"I didn't bring one, sir."

"Pity." He twisted his head to the right. "Ellen?"

"Done." Ellen made a note on her pad.

"I believe you have just boarded the train, Mr. Lee." His voice raised slightly. "Mr. Montroy, I believe the cat is out of the bag. Have you something to say, or should I clarify, suggest?"

Despite the glare from Lee, Montroy stood tall. "I nominate Alvin Lee, sir, on the basis of his intimate understanding of the document we are here to replace."

"Have I a ..."

A voice from the other side of the audience; a female voice. "I second the nomination."

Dr. Elliot walked back to the overhead projector and wrote 'Alvin Lee – VA' on one of the lines. "Thank you, Mr. Montroy, for our first nomination. Mr. Lee, my apologies for the apparent 'railroading', you might say, but we will require the very best for this project. I, for one, believe you are among those." A smattering of applause ran throughout the room. "Well, now that we've broken the ice, let us see who our next nominee will be.

#

Alvin Lee - VA
Beau Williams - MD
Tom McGinlay - WA
Kathy Greer – CT
Millie Dickinson – OH
Juan Morales – NY
To Wan Lin - CA

The name 'To Wan Lin' filled the bottom line on the display from the overhead projector. Dr. Elliot looked out at the audience. "Seven nominees. At least we have a horse race. You, the committee of the whole, will have to decide which five you wish to serve you." He looked at the clock hanging over the screen. "We've ten minutes before the kitchen opens for lunch. A quick review and some homework. These are the seven interns you've nominated for the Executive Committee. There are only five positions. I suggest that, during lunch and the hour after, that you talk among yourselves and with the nominees. Get to know how they might manage the project. You will want to know what they think of the organization and structure of a central government. Most of all, what do they say about organizing and managing large projects and groups of people?

At 2:00 we'll gather again, and you will vote by a show of 'nays'. It's the easiest way to count in a case like this. Oh, no record of who voted in what way will be kept. Once the 'nays' are counted, the records will be destroyed. Now, go to lunch. DAs please linger a moment."

The auditorium cleared in a routine noisy fashion as most of the interns headed immediately to lunch. A handful headed back to their quarters and a few clustered about the nominees. "I want you to watch the interaction between nominees and other interns during lunch and in the hour after. Try to get names, if you can. It's important to know who is really interested in how this project will go forward. Those who ask questions or simply listen are likely to be the involved interns. Those who simply eat and hang out with each other, may be talking about the nominees. Or, they may be talking about football. We need to know." He grinned at them. "Enjoy your lunch."

#

"A show of 'nays'? What the heck kind of vote is that?" Lena all but slammed her tray down at the table where Jane Abrams sat with Emelita Garcia.

"Querida, relax. This is an old politician's trick and one which I know well."

"What in hell are you talking about?" Lena snapped. Jane also turned her head in curiosity, placing the forkful of salad back on the plate.

"Look. It's an old trick in Mexico. The alcalde, the mayor, of the village, he holds a meeting to decide an important issue. Important yes, but not the most important, do you see? It looks like he is listening to his people. Everyone wants it to pass, except of course, the alcalde and his amigos. So, he calls a voice vote and counts the 'no' votes. These are few, of course, and the issue is adopted. Everyone is happy; even the alcalde. He now knows who his friends are among the people."

"What does that have to do with picking an Executive Committee?" This time, it was Jane who asked.

"The Devil's Advocates will take notes. We know this. But, those who are elected will also see who is against them, if they are smart, and watch. The alcalde knows his friends and the Executive Committee knows who does not agree with them. It is a clever way for the staff to let the new 'leaders' know on whom they need to concentrate as the work goes forward."

"Do they think we are that gullible?" asked Lena.

"Actually, most of the kids will not even see that coming, Lena." Jane leaned her elbows on the table. "It's clever politics in action. Of the seven interns nominated, I think only Al Lee, Tom McGinlay and Millie Dickinson will take notes. Beau and Kathy are smart, but not politically astute. I honestly don't know about Morales and Lin."

"How'd you figure that out so quickly?"

"My dad is one of the Quorum of Seventy; that makes him a leader in the Mormon church. Not only is he a deeply religious man and I love him to death, but he's smart, sharp and a political whiz. I've learned a lot growing up in our house."

Emelita finally asked, "So, if you're that politically savvy, why aren't you nominated for the Committee?"

"I really don't know. I do know that I'm a Mormon, a black and a girl. That's a hard combination for this collection of people to accept, quickly. I do know that I've got a lot of ideas and some of them are going to wind up in this, whatever it is, that we're building."

#

On the other side of the room Al Lee, Ray Montroy and Denise Walters, the three VA interns were talking at their table. They had piled their dirty trays at the fourth place at their table to discourage company.

"I'm not sorry, Alvin. You should be on that committee."

"Dammit, Ray, you just don't understand. I can do more for the family and the country 'working the district' as we say than sitting at the head table. Now, I'm visible."

Denise supported Rayford. "No Al. It's because you're a 'Lee', a true southern aristocrat, if not a First Family of America, that the others will listen to you. Ray is right. We don't have time, just two months, to do a lot of backroom politicking, for what we think America should be. We have to put the right ideas out and have people agree with them because the right people say they're the right thing to do."

"Denise, the Lee family has never sought to be a Kennedy, Roosevelt, Bush or Clinton. We're not rich and we don't seek power for power's sake. We've always fought and worked for what we felt is best for America."

"Sounds like you've just convinced yourself, Al," Ray said. "You get my vote."

"Mine, too."

Lee sighed and wished he'd deleted that email when he got it.

#

David Ingalls and Art Little had cornered Millie Dickinson as she walked toward the theater. "Art and I are trying to figure out how this is going to work. What's your plan?"

Millie looked uncomfortable. "Is that a trick question? I'm not even selected, yet?"

David supported Art. "Millie, we're not Fox News. We're all here to do a job we didn't have identified when we accepted it. You've got a five in seven chance of being elected. Personally, I see a 1:1 relationship. So, repeating the question, yada yada."

She sighed. "Okay, let's presume I'm on the committee. We can't just start writing. We've got some issues the Framers didn't have to face and some serious groundwork to lay." None of the three noticed Mike and Bill walking just fifteen feet behind and listening intently.

"Look, get out of the weeds. The Executive Committee must define not only the structure of the project and sort out resources but define the areas of concentration and the schedule. Are we going to waste time as a committee of the whole, break up into firm committees and subcommittees or assign specific problems to individuals? How are we going to validate, select and integrate our work? And the thousand-pound elephant in the room is how do we shift from what we *have* to what we *want*. 315 million people are sort of used to it being the way it is. Are we defining evolution or revolution?"

"Shit! I didn't think of half of that."

"What I'm worried about, guys, is convincing 150 interns to think of all of that fast. This is day 3 and the sun is not going to take a biblical stop in the sky."

Mike tugged on Bill's shirt and held him back until the three turned the corner toward the theater. "That's one smart girl. She nailed all but two of Ishmael's critical path items."

"I'm worried about both the conservative and liberal sides, Mike. My notes say that this girl is a solid middle-of-the-road independent thinker. She's gonna have to sell both sides."

"My over-educated guess is that she only has to sell the alphas on each side and let them carry the load. In the meantime, I'm going to let Ishmael know that he's got his protege."

#

Ellen knocked on the jamb of Harold Greer's open door. "You wanted to see me, sir?"

"Ellen, come in. Sit down and stop calling me 'sir'. We've known each other since the founding of the Institute and you've been a major part of this crazy scheme of ours."

"Force of habit, sir." She grinned.

Greer shook his head slowly, grinning in response. "Well, break it. I know a good psychologist, who can help."

"Funny, Harold, funny. Okay. It's 'Harold' in private. But, you still have to be aloof when we're 'out there'."

"Deal. Now, what's your 'big picture' take so far?"

"Unfair question, boss. I've had two weeks to study personal files and only two days to watch those people interact. I can't make valid evaluations that fast."

"I know it will change, Ellen. I just want a first impression."

"If you insist. An easy half or two thirds are, to put it bluntly, sheep or maybe lemmings. They're all great kids and the clear majority will do the U.S. proud. But, they don't have either the breadth of understanding or the mental toughness, fortitude, if you will, to handle hard questions and the harder answers. They're followers. Let's say one third are willing to work toward an end but need good leadership. We've already decided that they must lead themselves to enable a clean execution of the process, so the natural leaders must step forward. I think we've identified ten or fifteen that will serve that purpose. The question is whether they are sufficiently diverse to handle the diverse issues. And, fifteen IS ten percent. Not a bad haul from this fine kettle of fish you and George hauled in."

"Got any favorites?"

"Yeah, but I'm not going to tell you. It's still too early. The five DAs are meeting tonight to talk about the Executive Committee and what we can do to keep them on the right track; well at least within boundaries. Unfortunately, we don't know that track." She glanced at her cell. "And, don't we have an election to hold?"

#

Beau Williams - MD   5
Tom McGinlay - WA   13
Kathy Greer - CT   7
Millie Dickinson - OH 4
Juan Morales - NY   9
To Wan Lin - CA   21

"I believe that is a pretty clear result. Mr. Lin and Mr. McGinlay, thank you for participating. We hope to see you actively leading in the effort. And, with only 4 dissenting votes, Miss Dickinson will serve as nominal Chairperson of the Executive Committee." He looked over his shoulder at the clock. "Well, we did that in record time; only 30 minutes. Please relax for a moment or two while I speak with the Executive Committee. May I ask the four of you, Mr. Lee, the DAs and George to join me 'in the wings'?"

After some shuffling, twelve people gathered at one end of the stage. Everyone looked at Dr. Elliot. He gestured to George.

"Now, the Initiative really begins, Millie. When you walk back out there, you are in charge. Madam Chairperson, you have unlimited access to the Founders, as necessary, the DAs and, of course, me. The other four of you have unlimited access to me and to the DAs. I would advise all of you to do as much as you can, by yourselves. That is the secret to success. It also will increase the confidence the 'century and a half' have in you.

"Now, I suggest you spend this afternoon putting together a straw organization and schedule using the people that you know have skills and asking others, as needed. Rule by 'fiat'. Appoint, rather than ask. Time is of the essence. And modify or change as you see the need."

He looked at the five Devil's Advocates. "I think your first task will be to help these young people from being overwhelmed with personnel actions. I ask that you advise them, as needed on how to manage expectations. The first day or so is going to be interesting as the size and shape of the elephant is defined.

"Miss Dickinson, I recommend that you, personally, undertake the task of scope definition. It will help your committee in assigning areas of responsibility and tasks. I've got reliable reports that you have already defined nearly all the 'dangling threads', if you will. That is a remarkable feat for one so young.

"Are there any burning questions?" George did a silent count to five while looking at the five baffled youth. "Good. Then, Dr. Elliot, the DAs and I will leave by the stage door and leave you to your task. Dinner is at six."

Dr. Elliot paused as he walked toward the door. He turned and looked at the newly elected Executive Committee. "I cannot stress just how important this is. You have a very hard job ahead; but not one of which you are incapable. For all of us and, in fact, for 315 million Americans, Good luck."

The Parable of the Six Wise Men

In an exotic land, far away and long ago, lived a king beloved by his people. Even in a well-ruled kingdoms, there were problems aplenty and the king had a council of six wise men to aid him in ruling the kingdom. As happens from time to time, the problems of the kingdom began to overwhelm the king, for he wished to find only the best solutions to the problems.

One day, he saw that his council was becoming fractious and argumentative. They would scream at each other, tell tales and prevent any suggestion of one from being accepted. Jealousy and pettiness were their only counsel. The king could depend upon them less and less and became more and more tired, as he tried to resolve all the problems in the kingdom by himself. And, because of this, the people became less and less happy.

One day the king's jester, distressed by the discord and dissension and its effects on the king, whispered to the king an idea. The king tipped his head from one side to the other, wrinkled his brow in hard thought and then smiled. The next day he called his counselors to the throne room. "I wish you to help me analyze a problem. I have it in the next room. But, the problem is one unknown in the kingdom and it must, therefore, be kept a secret. Each of you will be blindfolded and gagged. You will have 15 minutes to form your analysis and opinion. Fail to give me a workable analysis and you will all die, and I'll find new counselors."

The counselors looked at each other with some trepidation, for each was jealous of the other and wished only to be individually recognized, as the greatest among them. The king's guards stepped forward and bound the eyes and mouths of each. They were led to a doorway and shoved in. "You have 15 minutes until this door opens again." And the door slammed shut behind them.

Nineteen minutes passed, and the door opened. Six soldiers entered the room and, moments later, led the six counselors out. They were led before the throne and their blindfolds and gags were removed. Each blinked and looked around at the others, unsure if he should speak. The king, his jester witting quietly at the foot of the throne, entered and sat.

"Counselor William! Your analysis."

The Counselor whose name was William stepped forward. "Your majesty, I searched the room and found the shaft of a spear, smooth and hard."

"Counselor Inmay!"

The Counselor, whose name was Inmay, looked at William strangely. "Your majesty, I found a great and immovable wall."

"Counselor Simeon, do you agree?"

"Your majesty, I don't know what potions my brothers are partaking in, but I grasped the sail of a great vessel of war."

The king looked at his jester, who looked back with an enigmatic smile on his face. "Counselor Dominic?"

"Your Majesty, these fools should be cast away. I was assaulted by a great snake. I battled it and brought it to heel at long last."

The king began to chuckle behind his hand. "Counselor Odeon are the rest of my councilors fools?"

Odeon was an old and clever politician. "Fools? Nay, sire. But, I'm not certain of their powers of observation. I kept to the walls and, at last, felt a breeze. I reached out and felt a whip strike my hand. I tried to seize it, but it continually swept by my hand. I regret that I did not trap it."

The jester choked back a laugh and the king cuffed him sharply, but with a twinkle in his eye. "Lastly, I call upon my old friend, Melchior. What discovered you?"

"Majesty, we need new laws for intoxication. These men are unaware of their surroundings. When I entered the room, I walked straight ahead and encountered the trunk of a great tree; around which I wrapped my arms."

The king stood, and his counselors fell to their knees. "It appears that you, each, have discerned my problem differently. Can you reach and agree on an analysis or shall you all die? I know I can find six more men in the streets who can argue with each other endlessly."

The six men cowered and shrunk back. Only Melchior, long a friend of the king, found voice. "Liege, how can we find agreement or solution if we all have found different truths?"

The king laughed out loud. "Truly have I the need of a new chief counselor. His wisdom is greater than all of yours. I will spare your lives, never fear. Each of you is wise in his own way. Only my new chief counselor understands. Jester, as my new chief counselor, explain the test that you asked me to put forth."

The six old men looked at the jester in fear. How had he bested their wisdom and knowledge? "My colleagues, I do not hold myself greater than any one of you. In fact, together you are far greater than I shall ever be. Let me display before you, the king's challenge. Come." He walked to the door, opened it and beckoned them to follow him.

Within the room was a huge elephant. The Councilors looked at each other in dismay. How could they have so misjudged? "My friends, each of you considered only a small part of what you encountered, that which you believed to be the whole truth. William, you grasped a tusk, Inmay, you stumbled into the body while Simeon grasped an ear. Dominic, you struggled with the beast's trunk while Odeon was bested by its tail. And friend Melchior, you grabbed its great leg.

None of you were wrong in your analysis. Yet, each of you failed to allow that your fellow councilors might also have been correct in theirs. You failed because you did not join your individual knowledge together to form wisdom. Let us work together as a team. Individually, the challenges facing the king are daunting and formidable. Together, nothing can prevent us from besting them in our joint wisdom."

The king, with his chief councilor and a team of wise men, ruled well and for many years.

Forming the Convention

Herding Cats

June 18, 2017 - Camp Donelson

Millie watched the door close behind the staff. She felt a shiver of fear. Then, she took a deep breath and turned to the other four. "So, where do we start?"

Alvin Lee was the first to speak. "We have to get their attention shifted from George, Dr. Elliot and the DAs, to us, quickly. I suggest that we make some immediate assignments at the highest level and see where discussion goes right now. We can get a lot organized before the shock wears off."

Kathy looked unconvinced. "We want to be sure they don't think we're dumping it all on them. There are a lot of egos out there."

"I don't have time for egos." Millie had the bit in her teeth now. "We know that we have three big areas at the highest level. We have the structure of the document, the structure of the central government going forward and the transition from what we have now."

Beau questioned. "Are you sure either of the infrastructures, present or future, are in our charter? I mean, we're just supposed to rewrite the Constitution, not redesign reality."

"If we don't pay attention to what has grown from the original document and, more importantly, *how* it grew from the original document, we're just spinning our wheels. If we don't have a clear path from now to then, our design is nothing but an academic exercise."

"Al's right, Beau. Alvin, is it okay to call you Al? I mean Robert E. Lee wasn't 'Bobby' when he was alive, and Richard Henry Lee was certainly never 'Dick'."

Lee laughed. "And, I'm none of the above. I'm just a Lee. Al is fine."

"Thanks. Anyway, Beau, we must do something decisive, and we have to do it right now. We can change courses within the next week if this doesn't work, but I'm going to pull rank right now. Barring a better plan, right now, this is how we start."

She took a deep breath and outlined her plan. Each of her committee-mates added and commented, but within five minutes, a revised basic plan, agreeable to all five, was in place.

#

The Executive Committee walked back onto stage; Millie in the middle. They lined up at the overhead projector. Millie picked up the microphone and stepped forward. "Alright, settle down please. We've got work to do." The noise continued, if at a lesser decibel level.

Beau took the microphone and looked at Millie. She nodded her head. He stepped to the edge of the stage and in the best voice his eighteen years could muster, "KNOCK IT OFF! This is not a high school assembly. We are being paid to do a job and 315 million people are paying the bill. Now, be quiet, sit down and listen. Let us demonstrate that we are adult enough to tackle an adult job in an adult way." He looked back at Millie and before handing her the mic, he made sure his words carried. "Madame Chairperson."

Millie gave him an appreciative smile and mouthed 'thank you'. "Alright then, it's us against the Constitution, the bureaucracy and the status quo. I, for one, think we can lick this sucker that's been kicking our parents' asses for years." She paused. To her relief a few cheers were accompanying the laughter.

"Okay. I'm Millie. You just heard from Beau. You know Al Lee. Also, here are Kathy and Juan. I think you can tell them apart. Juan wears glasses." Another laugh encouraged Millie. "Okay, your Executive Committee, now known as the 'head shed', has had a whole ten minutes to solve the ills of the world. So here is the solution to all our problems."

"Right, Millie!" an anonymous voice in the audience egged her on.

"We're going to take the rest of this week, four days, to define what we have. To do that, we're going to break up into three groups, for starters.

"Al Lee will head up the analysis of the Constitution itself; not the words, but the intent of the Framers with respect to each section and each amendment. Kathy and Juan will take a stab at what rights and responsibilities a central government should have; meaning what they expect from the citizens and what the citizenry should expect from them. Beau will analyze the current Federal government and how each section relates to the Constitution and/or amendments. I will take on integration, how the Federal government relates to everything else, state governments, foreign governments and responsibilities, etc. and, how they relate to the Constitution, as written.

"I want Oy Palomuto, of Guam, to work with me. Tom McGinlay, please assist Beau and To Wan Lin, please assist Al. When we break, I'm asking that Al and Lin go to the library. Beau and Tom, go to the cafeteria and Oy and I will be in the Company Day Room, the big room in the BOQ where we're staying. Kathy and Juan remain here. I think your crowd may be large. When we break up, everyone makes a choice, a non-binding choice, but a choice to work with one of the five teams and go to that location. Spend the rest of the afternoon putting together goals and a plan to accomplish those goals. Leaders will meet at 7:30 in the morning in the Day Room. Everyone else meet here at 8am.

"Sally Jamison, you doomed yourself in the opening meeting with a simple question. You are now the Administrator of this project, whatever its name is."

"Millie! What about a name?" Millie didn't recognize the voice. She made a private promise to quickly learn 'her population'.

"Why not? Any suggestions?" The next minute or two were punctuated by all manner of suggestions; few worthy of recording. Millie was close to regretting giving a voice to the question, when Al walked over to her and whispered in her ear. Millie's eyes lit up and she grinned. It was all she could do, not to hug him. She handed him the microphone and stepped back.

Al stepped forward and held up his hands for quiet. Eventually, he held the microphone away and, with two fingers in his cheeks, gave a shrill whistle. "People settle down." It took a moment, but the joking about a name subsided. "I think we already have a name. It was given to us by the Framers and it's just been waiting to be used. I suggest that the name defines this project better than any other name ever could. It comes from the Preamble to the Constitution. I suggest 'We the People'.

There were a few seconds of silence and then a single pair of hands clapped, followed by an explosion of applause. Al handed the mic to Millie. "Madame Chairman, I give you 'We the People.'

#

Millie downed a bottled water while the crowd dispersed. She was gratified to see Kona had elected to stay; probably because of Oy, but no matter. Her group was small, but that was okay with her.

Sally had also remained. "Just what does an Administrator do?"

Millie laughed at the ease of this answer. "Guys, give me a minute. Tell you what. Oy, take everybody over to the Day Room, please. I'll be right there." She walked Sally to the edge of the stage. "Sally, we need someone to keep us on track, to make us keep schedules, to make sure we have places to be, to transcribe reports, fill out forms, order supplies, keep track of any budget and generally keep the project moving. I know it sounds mundane, but as it goes forward, you could easily become a major player. You are now the official contact with the non-project staff with respect to entertainment, menus, extracurricular events, etc. As you work, define help you need, and I'll seek out and assign it."

"Does that mean I don't get to contribute to the project?"

"Heck no. Be a part of whichever team or teams you wish. You have as much right to contribute as anyone else."

Sally smiled. "Where do I set up shop?"

"Hmmm; executive decision time. Set up in the office, next to the Company Day Room. I'll get with George and see that you have everything you need. Okay?"

"Absolutely."

"Okay. We're both headed to the same place, so let's get out of Kathy's way."

#

George looked out the window of the Foundation office assigned to Harold Gilbert. Behind him, Harold asked a question a second time. "George!"

George turned. "Sorry, I was watching the interns leaving the theater."

"And?"

"For the first time since they began to arrive, I think we may actually see some sort of useful work." He pointed at the window. "Look at that. They're not just leaving the theater, but whole groups are going to specific places. I wish I had been there to hear what went on. We should have recorded it."

"No, that would violate the trust we're placing in these kids."

"Oh hell, they'd never know."

"Do you have kids, George?"

"No."

"Then you don't know that kids are amazingly perceptive. One wrong word, and they would know we are monitoring them. It would be over."

"If you say so. Hey, there goes Millie, our heroine of the day, with that young lady that wanted to know about the menus. I don't remember her name. I wonder what that's all about."

#

Millie looked around. She counted eleven interns other than herself. Oy had set up three tables in a squished "U" shape with twelve chairs around the outside. No one person was more than six feet from everyone else. She took the legal pad she had commandeered from George and ripped off five sheets for each person around the table. She had only eight pencils.

"Thanks for taking on this challenge. Eleven of us did it voluntarily. Only Oy had no choice. I have no idea what Chamorro is for 'Thank You', but thank you, Oy. In fact, thanks to all of you a lot. We have, in these first few days, the most challenging task, perhaps, in the entire project. What I want you to do for the next", she looked at her cell, "two- and one-half hours, is come up with every conceivable roadblock you can think of for a successful change of foundation documents; key word 'successful'. Write down every question. Even keywords, if that's what makes you tick. Taxes, treaties, language, commerce, defense relationships, banking, international ownership, state lines, states' rights, voting, all of it. The best question starts with 'How do we ...' The worst answer is 'We can't because ...' So, any questions?"

"Some of our questions and comments will conflict, or at least be the concern of one of the other groups. What do we do, then?"

"You are?"

"David Marion from Pennsylvania."

"Hi David, I'm Millie. Thanks for joining our crazy team. Good question. Work as though there are no other teams. Our job is to integrate. Those other teams can't work together without us. Our goal is to have answers before questions are asked. Break every issue down until it can break down no farther. Does that make sense?"

"Millie, how did you figure that out? It makes sense, but nobody ever talks about solving problems that way." Oy leaned forward as he spoke; almost in awe of the diminutive teenager.

"Think about what you just said Oy. Politics is, almost by definition, about defending or espousing a specific point of view or program for a specific constituency. It's never about making everything work together in the most effective, efficient or fiscally responsible manner. That's anathema to any elected official. They have to make only as many people as it takes to be elected, or more importantly, reelected, happy."

"Man, that sounds cynical."

"I guess it is. I get so tired of, supposedly intelligent 'leaders' mouthing projects, issues and solutions that make absolutely no sense, if you stop and think about it. Right now, I've got a chance... No, *we've* got a chance to actually espouse a future for our country that makes sense for as many of that 315 million people as we can; and, sacred cows be damned."

June 19, 2017

Kathy was the last Executive Committee member to appear. She had a folder of yellow paper under her arm and carefully squeezed it to her side as she grabbed coffee and a pre-made breakfast sandwich and set it down on the table. "Sorry all. I was up late trying to make heads or tails from my piece of this project and just plain overslept." Millie started to speak. Kathy held up her hand. "I've already dealt with it and added another alarm in the mix. It won't happen again."

Millie smiled. "Sorry. I guess punctuality is my trigger. I'll try not to be a pain. Sit down. We hadn't started yet." She looked at the wall clock. "Let's put it all aside for fifteen minutes and enjoy breakfast as friends, before we dive into the piles of paper I see at everyone's place."

"I can live with that. I'm hungry." Juan unwrapped a breakfast burrito, cut it in half and squirted in hot sauce from a plastic envelope. After a chomp or two, he tried to say something but, without success. He covered his mouth with a paper napkin and swallowed. "Sorry. You guys need to hit some burrito trucks in New York City. Man, this is lame."

Millie chuckled. Take it up with Sally. Food complaints are her area."

Burrito poised, Juan said, "I was kidding, but I just might. From what I see the menu won't kill us, but it won't make us happy either. These guys forget we're teenagers and need real food."

The conversation stayed in the same light vein until Millie's allotted time had elapsed. She put her silverware on her plate, picked up her tray and put it on the table next to theirs; intending to bus it later. "Okay, finish up, but we need to get started so we can look like we know what we're doing in", she glanced at the clock once again, "fifty-five minutes. I'll start. I set my folks, I have a dozen by the way, to dissecting every conceivable point of conflict, contention, problem that they could think of related to the Initiative. I've got nearly forty pages of things from tax conflicts to how to deal with existing Civil Service employees, continuing to pay for the military, the Library of Congress and federal prisons. We may not have it all, but we've got a great starting point. I'm setting Oy and the group to breaking it down and organizing it into an indexed database.

"That brings me to the first project-related personnel issue. Sally is going to head up our administrative group. We're going to need an 'IT' team to manage this database; starting with two people right now. I have no 'geeks', to use a derogatory term, in my dozen, so I'm putting out a call to the rest of you, to find me a couple of computer 'really literate types', who want to swap to Sally's group."

Kathy wadded her napkin and tossed it on her plate. She picked up her notes. "I might be able to help you. For starters, I've got all the wild-eyed liberals who want to defend every right for every life form on earth. Of the 139 left after this committee and your eleven, I have fifty-four. At least, right now, there isn't enough meaningful work. Janice Montesano, from Oklahoma, is a self-described database freak. She's got menu programs, library lists, phone logs and indexes of her indexes; and all on her smart phone and in the 'cloud'. You want her, she's yours."

"Sold. I'll have Oy transfer her. I suppose I'll need to recruit a personnel type admin, too. What did you get done yesterday?"

"Pretty much the same, except Janice was up half the night, putting it into a spreadsheet. That girl's scary."

#

The theater was full, and the doors closed when Millie led the committee in from the wings. She was more than gratified that there were no latecomers. A table had been set on the stage with five chairs facing the interns in the audience seats. The noise level remained high, so Al Lee stood up and walked toward the front, with one of the hand-held microphones.

The noise immediately died. He chuckled and took a mock bow. A few titters ran through the audience. "Thank you. I'll be here through the summer." He returned to his seat.

"Sally, will you come up, please?" Sally, seated in the front row, stood and mounted the stage. "Oy, see if there's another seat in the wings, please." She held up her hands. "Okay. Good morning. This will be the last 'daily' meeting of the entire group. For now, we will gather here on Monday mornings at 10:00 am for a review of the previous week and to talk about any details of interest to all. Obviously, not a lot of substantive work was done yesterday, but each team leader tells us that a great deal of scope definition was done. For that good start, I thank you." A change in the lighting at the back of the room caught her attention. She noticed that a door had opened, and the DAs had entered, along with George. They all sat in the back row. "Good morning, George and friends. There are a couple of details. I've asked the leads to find me two IT types to put together files and databases for our work." She saw Oy open a folding chair and return to his seat. She motioned Sally to sit and then continued.

She looked to the back of the room. "George, does the Institute have an IT staff that can help my folks set up server space and stuff like that?"

A disembodied voice came from the darkness in the back. "I think so, I'll get back to you, or should I talk with Sally?"

"Me, for right now, while we try and sort it out, thanks." She shifted her attention back to the audience. "I'd also like to see if there are folks who would be interested in the extra task of managing the organization, personnel sorta stuff, I suppose. If you're interested, tell your lead, please.

"Now, we agree that' all work and no play, etc.'. So, we'll see about putting a subgroup of interested interns together to plan entertainment, sports and other diversions, as our time permits.

"Finally, I'm going to ask George to have a mass email set up, so we can publish information, personnel needs, etc. every day.

"And that's about it for the group. I know that individual team leads have already started their own organization and tasks, so we can break up now and head to our team locations. Thanks, again and have a great Tuesday. It's usually better than Monday, so always remember S.H.I.T … So Happy It's Tuesday." She clicked the mic off and sat back down.

She swiveled her head and looked at both sides of the table. "Well, how did it look to you?"

Al Lee spoke first. "You saw what they did when I stood up. It appears that they accept us as the leadership. We just need to keep them believing that we're in charge."

"I think the newsletter is a great idea", said Sally. It will help me keep organized. I can also publish movie suggestions from the library, menus and other items of interest. It may help keep the overwhelming fact that we're trapped here, from becoming an issue. But, who's going to write it?"

Millie slumped slightly. "I didn't think that far ahead. It just popped into my mind. You for right now. You and me, actually, I suppose, until we find more people for your staff."

"Millie, you can't do it all." Her head swiveled and found Beau. "You're the chairman. You should have input, but delegate. I've written church bulletins and newsletters for a couple of years. Let me take it on, until Sally gets help. If you keep niggling little stuff for yourself, you'll get none of the big stuff done."

She looked relieved. "I know you're right, Beau, and I appreciate the gesture. I'll try and get it off your plate by the end of the week."

"Anything else?"

#

Jay strolled down toward the sports fields until he was out of sight and then ducked behind the abandoned scorekeepers tower. He pulled his cell phone from the pocket of his jeans and pressed the speed dial for his bishop.

"Hello?"

"Bishop? Jay."

"Hello, Jay. I suppose this call means you have discovered something about your project that upsets you?"

"Yes, sir. We broke up into teams and I picked the one that I thought might give me the best input to the final document. But, that team is packed with liberals who see the church, any church, as interfering with their rights, including nearly everything we stand against. I can't be a part of this, if I can't help keep God's word."

"Jay, settle down. It can't be that bad."

"Oh, yes it can, sir. I heard one of them say that the government shouldn't recognize any religious holidays, since it can't afford to recognize all of them."

There was a long pause and Jay heard a sigh. "Jay, listen to me. Don't do anything to draw attention to yourself. I'm going to contact Salt Lake and see what they want to do about it. Give me a few days, oh say, until Friday night. Okay? Can you do this?"

"Yes, sir. I guess I can, if you want me to."

"It's not me, Jay. You are a great asset to the church, right now. You are our only protection, until we can stop this Godless pursuit. I'll talk with you Friday."

"Good night, sir."

June 21, 2017

The phone on his desk rang. George looked at the display and answered. "Good morning, Dr. Elliot."

"I'm not sure about the 'good', George. We may have a problem. The monitoring service has trapped a suspicious and unauthorized cell call and turned it over to me."

"I'm not sure I understand, sir."

"The service analyzes all phone calls from our cell tower for keywords. Most are innocuous calls from the kids to their home contact. This last call, the one that triggered the report, used 'church', 'bishop', 'document' and 'stop' and was the second call made to the same number since check-in. I've no idea what algorithm they used or how they do it, but they think someone is leaking information about the project to a religious contact."

"Do we know who made the call, Dean?

"They trapped the cell number. Got a pencil?"

George reached for a pad and pen. "Yup."

"928.555.0267"

George read it back. "I'll have the staff go through the information we collected when they checked in to identify it. What if it doesn't look like an intern?"

"Then it would have to be the support staff, but I don't see that. Let me know what you find out, please? We need to stop this right now. The risk to the project is too great; especially if the' religious right' starts 'inventing' horror stories and floods social media."

"I'll get right on it."

#

"Hi. You're Beau Williams, right? From Maryland?" Janice sat down at the table. Beau was alone, two interns from Idaho had just finished and left.

Beau looked at the young woman across the table from him. She was pretty enough in a plain way. Her brown hair was short, but styled nicely, and she was dressed just a bit more stylishly than the rest of the girls he'd met on the compound. He wasn't surprised that she sat down across from him. It happened a lot back at home. He seemed to be a 'chick magnet', even without trying. "Guilty as charged. You are?"

She held out a hand. "Janice Montesano, Tulsa, Oklahoma."

Beau took the offered hand. Aside from being wet from the soda cup that she'd been holding, it was warm and soft. "You're the young database person that's going to help Sally, right?"

"A guilty plea from me, too. Janice 'M', geek-on-call." Her smile showed a mouthful of well-tended teeth. "Can I keep you company on the way back?"

Beau looked at her again. She had a nicely shaped body, too. He thought to himself, 'what the hell.' "Sure. Tell me about Oklahoma."

June 22, 2107

"Good morning and TGIF, I suppose. I'm not sure if this is the end of week one or just the first Friday. I suppose George will tell me. I'm meeting with him at 10:00. I've got some admin stuff from Sally before we dive into the swamp." Millie gave each of the leads a report binder. "She finally got her database up with all the information she has on every intern. In the binder is a master list by name, as well as a data sheet on each intern. Please do not let anyone, but your assistant, see the entire list.

"What we need you to do is check off the interns on your team, from the master list. Sally well make sure that we have accounted for all 155 of us and what team we're on. Then, give each intern his or her data sheet and ask them to verify it. It includes basic information, but also their room number, 'contact' email address and name as well as their cell phone number. I cannot imagine someone not having one. Once we have all of this we will test the 'reverse 911' application. We need this back on Monday morning, please. How you do it is your business; except for the personal privacy and security of not letting anyone see someone else's information. If they release it, that's their problem. I don't want it to be ours.

"Sally is still looking for one more IT type, but no more personnel types. We have three volunteers for that slot and the 'entertainment' team has more than enough to provide enough and diverse diversions for two months.

"Okay, that's the adminis-trivia. Al asked for some time, right off, this morning. You've got the floor, Al."

Al Lee pushed his chair back and tipped it back on its back legs. "My team's charter was to analyze the Constitution, for what it was designed to do; not the wording or what has happened to it since, but what did the Framers really intend. Now, there are those who say my family has always been special, but I'm not so special that I think that I, or the two of us, or the 30-odd interns who showed up for my team, can do a better job of analyzing that document than the politicians, scholars, lawyers, barbers and bartenders who have tried over the past 230 years. That *would* be ego-to-the-max.

"But, we have done our best in a week. We've read it, discussed it and tried to understand it from a citizen's level ... in 1780. That means that we recognize that the Framers lived in a different time; different by a mathematical magnitude. Virtually nothing that the Framers knew is recognizable today; not communication, transportation, education, demographics, population density or even food and drink. Recognizing that, we also recognize that the original document was never intended to be as robust as it has been forced, by time and necessity, to be.

"What I would like to do is 'game' the analysis. Basically, I want to set up three teams of ten, to put the analysis together, as they deal with day-to-day events. We want to reverse engineer it, in a sense. Ishmael said he thought it was creative and he'll mentor, as needed. He and I, along with one other intern, will pose the questions and scenarios and let the teams work to a solution independent of each other. I'll give them no guidance as to how to set up their game or how to run it. I'll give them the weekend and until Thursday afternoon. Friday, we compare notes. Ishmael and I both think we'll discover what sections are common and what are not. It's a modification of the 80:20 hypothesis. We should find out where the 'hard spots' are. We know they're there, we just don't know for sure, what they are." He let his chair fall to its front feet, with a sharp clump. He held his hands out, palms up, and tipped his head in question.

Millie looked at the other three committee members. Kathy spoke for the group. "Why not? At least they want to stop shredding and start building. My crowd is still parsing individual rights down to their choice of underwear allowed to be seen in public. At least the Framers could drink!"

Al laughed out loud. "I suppose having a tavern next door did have its compensations. Too bad we're all under age. I don't suppose you'd ask George ..."

"That would be 'no'." Millie was grinning. "Kathy, what do you and Juan need from us or our teams?"

"For starters, we can immediately use a network laptop for each team; mostly for notes, at the outset. And, Juan had a good idea. Starting, whenever a team is ready to begin building its prototype, we could use one of your dozen to sit in on the sessions. They can only ask questions and the only questions are for understanding. He said it would shorten the time frame for your folks, or the DAs to understand the prototype. You would have a resource on hand, with no ownership, who understands what the team proposed."

"Makes sense. You'll only need 'em for a day or two?"

"Just until we bring the report to the Executive Committee and maybe, if you think so, to the Committee of the Whole."

"You'll get them. I'll ask my team who wants to be an 'interested observer' and I'll ask Sally to talk with George about the laptops and sign-ons by team. Great idea." She shifted her gaze to Kathy. "Okay, Kathy, you spoke up. How is your team of rights advocates doing?"

"I'd like to say we're making ground, but they just keep making lists."

"You need to get control, Kathy. You haven't established boundaries for your group. That's why you're leader." The voice had come from behind Kathy. Millie looked behind her and saw Mike Eaves. "May I join you, Madam Chairperson?"

He didn't wait for permission, but sat across from Kathy. "Group dynamics; especially among young people, is amorphous at best. To generalize, you people listen in 'last in, first out' order. To put it bluntly, the loudest voice is the leader by default."

"So, how do I fix it?"

"Turn the mob on itself. By that, I mean, put the loudest voice in charge of a part of the job. Give him or her ownership. They'll find themselves on the inside, instead of the outside. You *will* see a change. Just make sure that you choose a 'loud person' who is trying to make a point and not just make a noise. Those exist in any sample. It's their raison d'etre."

"They get their kicks disrupting?"

"Yup. Mob mentality. It worked for Lenin and Hitler. Uh, sorry for the comparison."

Kathy giggled. "That's okay. I hardly think I qualify as either. Thanks for the help."

"Well, that's what the DAs are for in some sense. I have a suggestion, though. Take it or leave it. Find three 'team leads', if you will. One for individual rights, one for state's rights, so to speak and one for governmental rights."

"Governmental rights?"

"Sure. We just don't call them that. A government must expect a modicum of obedience, also known as law enforcement. A government must expect to be able to pay the bills accrued because of tending to the requirements of the governed. That would be taxation, no? The government must expect the governed to step forward, when needed, to protect themselves. I think we would call that defense. See what I mean by governmental rights? You might call it citizen responsibilities, if you wish to look from behind the mirror."

"Wow, I never thought of having responsibilities to the government."

Mike leaned back to soften the comment. "In some ways, that is a part of the problem today. Our citizens view that they have a 'right' to be fed, educated, defended and housed, with no return on the investment being made in them, by the government."

"You mean like 'how long will your car get you where you want to go if you don't change the oil or put gas in it?'"

"Excellent analogy, Beau. Just how long will it go? One of two things will happen, neither good, but one far worse than the other."

"Yeah, I know. You either run out of gas or you burn up the engine."

"Absolutely. And, right now, we're not sure which is going to happen to our country."

Compromise and Controversy

Torches and Pitchforks

June 26, 2107

"Look! We can't do that. Ben Franklin said, 'He who surrenders liberty for security, will have neither liberty nor security'."

"Gene, I've read the 2nd Amendment. I know how to shoot. My dad has a rack full of hand guns and rifles. I've no problem with handguns and rifles; even semi-automatic rifles. I have no idea why a private citizen should own one, but that's a my own opinion. But, fully automatic weapons with high capacity magazines have no purpose in private hands. And, that's the question under discussion. Stop trying to paint everyone who wants to limit military weapons in private hands as anti-gun. And, hauling out Ben Franklin is as ridiculous as Charlton Heston's theatrics with a flintlock musket."

"You're not changing my mind and I'm not supporting anything less than my 'right to bear arms'." Gene plopped his hat on his head and stomped out of the theater.

Beau shook his head and muttered beneath is breath. "Like trying to convince lead to change to gold; a worthy goal, but scientifically impossible." Janice, sitting next to him, giggled, as she keyed furiously into her phone.

Kathy smiled and shook her head. She looked at the five rows of interns. "My apologies for the disruption. I want to move on down the list of personal rights. Is there any dispute with that?"

"What are we going to do about gun-owner's rights?"

"Dave, we're going to table it, for right now. If we get wrapped around that axle, we'll get nothing done. I, for one, do not wish to resemble Congress in any way."

"Dammit, Kathy! If we table it, we ARE resembling Congress in absolutely *every* way."

Kathy was exasperated. "Dave, I just want to get through the issues we CAN resolve before we burn cycles seeking solutions to the hard questions. Gun control, abortion, gay rights, religious tolerance; these are the questions the Framers could not have foreseen. Let's put the ones we can to bed and then tear our hair out. Okay?"

Olivia, a young black girl from Mississippi, piped in. "Kathy, the Framers tabled slavery. Look what that got the nation; 600,000 dead and a hundred and fifty more years of racism. We have to deal with gun control or we may well face the same outcome."

"I doubt that the nation will face another civil war, Olivia." Kathy's voice was steady and lower, as she tried to defuse the emotions of her team.

"Maybe that's the view in Ohio, but the vote is still out in Maryland."

"Beau! We don't need that kind of talk."

"Kathy. America is in crisis. We are divided along economic lines, cultural lines, religious lines and racial lines. We are anything but the 'united states', right now. Beau is right. Wake up!"

A cold shiver ran down Kathy's spine. She had never experienced such vitriol from kids in her own age group. The group she was leading, or supposed to lead, she thought, was made up of kids she didn't know well and whose views of her country, its needs and its future, were completely foreign to her.

It was disturbing. Even more, it was scary. "Look. Let's take a break. We're shouting. If we're shouting, we're not listening." She looked at her cell. It's 10:10. Let's get a soda or coffee or something. I hear you, okay? Come back at 10:30 and we'll take one element of gun control at a time. We need to try and find a common platform. If this small group can't do that, there is no hope for 315 million people to do it; and I don't want to think about that." She closed her folder and, without looking back, walked quickly from the theater by a side door.

#

"Ellen? We've got a serious problem in our group. I just don't know how to handle it."

Ellen saved the document on her screen and minimized the word processor on her monitor. She spun her chair. "That sounds ominous. Okay, what's up? Your group is defining rights and responsibilities, right?"

"Close. We broke up into some subgroups and I'm heading up personal rights. We almost came to blows over details of gun ownership as a citizen right. No surprise there, but a whole lot of hidden anger came up, including racial and economic inequalities. This is w-a-y over my head."

"I'll get with Mike and we'll come talk to your folks. My first bit of advice to you is to not let them get into the weeds; especially on the trigger subjects. Your task is basic identification and assignment. It's much too early to try and define 'what' gun ownership is, or to define abortion or what 'religious freedom' is. Keep them at 50,000 feet or we're dead in the water." She reached for her phone. Kathy got up to leave. "Hang on a sec."

She waited for a few moments, with the handset to her ear. "Mike? Hi. Ellen. We've got our first 'crisis'. The individual rights folks are in full 'torch and pitchfork' mode. How about coming over to the theater at" she looked at Kathy and held up one finger. Kathy nodded. "right after lunch, 1:00. With luck and crowd control, it shouldn't take more than 30 minutes. Yeah, I know, 2:30. I'll be there. Thanks. See you at 1:00" She placed the handset back on the receiver.

"Thanks, Ellen. I'm sorry about this."

Ellen shook her head and stood. "Kathy, you're 18 years old and just graduated from high school. If you were able to manage this kind of 'uprising' with ease and experience, I would be really surprised. You did the right thing by coming to me; well, especially me, since I'm a psychologist. Mike Eaves is a specialist in Group Dynamics. The DAs are here to handle the 'too hard' situations and to teach our leaders the skills they need to handle them the next time. Now, go get 'em, girl. We'll see you after lunch."

#

Ellen and Mike entered the theater from the back and sat in the back row without being seen. They had expected to walk in and find a continuation of the arguing and disruptions described by Kathy Greer. Instead, they saw Kathy and Beau sitting on the edge of the table that held the overhead projector and two of the interns conducting the discussion. The overhead was turned on and showed a three-column display. The titles were 'citizen', 'state', and 'central gov'.

Kathy looked at Mike and whispered, "She's got them back at work. Do you know the two hosting?"

"I don't know the young lady. They guy is David, Oh, what's his last name? He's from Wyoming. 'Heretick ', David Heretick. He's from the 'Leave me the hell alone' school of government."

"Mike, look at the third line down under 'citizen'. I can't make it out from here. Can you see it?"

"Not clearly. I suppose we should announce our presence. It doesn't look like Kathy needs us, but you promised a 'come to the light' moment." He stood, followed by Ellen, and they walked down the aisle toward the stage.

As they approached, David was concluding. "Any other 'freedom's'?"

Kathy had seen them and was playing to the crowd. She stood and spoke up. "Hang on, Dave. We have visitors." She had timed it so that Ellen set foot on the steps at stage right, just as he said 'visitors'.

"Hello, all. Mike and I were just wandering aimlessly ... "

"Yeah right!", came from the center of the rows in which the interns were seated.

Ellen chuckled, "as I was saying, we were in the neighborhood. But, as long as we're here?" A chuckle ran through the audience. "We want to make sure that you're focusing on the right objectives. While we've asked you to write a new government document, we're not implying that you write the body of law intended to implement that document. Don't get hung up on trivia, details or minutia. After all, lawyers need employment, too." The chuckle became a laugh.

Olivia set the marker down on the overhead stand. "I have a question, though, about law, detail and minutia."

"Okay. What's up?"

"IF we write this and IF it is adopted, WHO will be responsible for writing and implementing this new structure?"

Mike walked over, took Olivia by the shoulders and turned her toward the audience. "By the time that happens, YOU will. You and those your age and maybe a bit older. Some of you will have gone to law school. Some will be in business. Others will be in the military. You will have to be the 'experts' we call upon to lead us forward. You will be the most important citizens your new nation will be designed to serve."

"That's scary", Dave said; his eyes wide.

"If you think it's scary, how do you think the 'old guard' will feel, when they realize that you may well be the nation's last chance to survive, with any resemblance to the United States they know. They … we … do love our country. We're just unable to save it."

"Damn!"

"We hope not." He tried to give the audience a reassuring smile. "Now, I have a question for Olivia and Dave. You're grouping any number of rights under a heading 'FotC'. I see First, Second and Fifth Amendment rights, along with some that came along later. What is 'FotC' and why the regrouping?"

Kathy interrupted. "May I, Olivia?" Olivia, rather uncomfortable being questioned by Mike smiled and nodded. "It means 'Framers of the Constitution'. When I got back from the coffee break we called to cool tempers, I was met by Dave, Olivia and two or three others. What they wanted to do, was go at our definitions and, beyond that, our document from the standpoint of a contract between the citizens and the government they were chartering to 'govern'."

David jumped in, "The way we figure it, the Framers went at it differently. They created a governing framework and then relinquished rights to the citizens. Of course, their citizens were, for the most part uneducated and very centered on survival, in a potentially hostile environment. The few educated, wealthy and powerful took it upon themselves to design and define a structure that, well, was built for them to govern."

"We don't want that to be the structure going forward. We view a population of educated individuals contracting with a 'government' to, well, manage our affairs, if you will. In so doing, we think we should lay out specifications for performance."

Mike looked at Ellen. "We need Ishmael." He turned to the four interns on the stage. "That is, perhaps, the most profound definition of 'government by the people' I have ever heard. I have no idea how that might work, but we, The Institute, did give you virtual free rein."

"And, the Founders. I think the 2:30 just had its agenda adjusted."

#

The Founders, all four of them for a change, the Devil's Advocates, George and Millie were gathered around a set of four tables in an open 'O'.

Mike had the floor. "I'm serious. This collection of 18 and 19-year-old high school graduates has completely redefined the way we think about the relationship between citizen and government. It may well be the first truly 21st Century governmental entity."

Joyce held up her hand. Mike held out his hand, inviting her to join in. She turned to look at them. "Dr. Elliot and other Founders, I have no idea what is working here, but it is something that may never happen again, in our lifetime. Ishmael and I sat in with Al Lee, as he and Lin outlined the high-level framework that his group is discussing. I heard keywords that will cause cardiac arrest, among those in charge today. I heard 'term limits'. I heard them design a whole new thing called an – I've no idea what it is - 'economic-geographic entity' to support a reinvented upper house. At least they left the legislature bicameral. I don't even want to see the final design of the Supreme Court. It's constructed along the lines of the Federal Reserve."

Dr. Elliot looked at the other Founders. Erick Leary was first to speak. "Dean, we don't have much choice. The contract 'we' have, says to give the kids free rein. Personally, I think some of what we've heard is intuitive and as perceptive in resolution of today's problems as the Framers faced two and half centuries ago. When do we have to report back to ..." He stopped, not mentioning the contracting body.

"Some will be here for the July 4th celebration. We'll give them a briefing on the next day. Only the four of us know who they are, and it *must* be kept that way. So, all the guests will get the briefing." He chuckled and grinned. "I'd sure like to be a mouse in the corner, when they have a chance to talk about this, behind closed doors. Let's just say that market stability and political careers would be shaking." He looked out to find the face for which he searched. "Ishmael. You're our Constitutional scholar. What's your take?"

"Well, from a, using your term, Constitutional scholar standpoint, what they're defining, designing and ultimately writing, is completely 'extra-constitutional'. In other words, it sets our current body of law on its ear. That's the bad news."

"Ishmael, I'm still trying to figure out their Supreme Court idea. Don't play with me. What's the good news?"

Joyce took the floor without asking. "One of the interns, a great grand-something of Robert E. Lee it appears, has kept them 'between the lines' – his words. He did his senior work on the Framers and seems to be sort-of idiot savant about the Constitution. He thinks, and Ishmael is still digging, that nothing they are imagining, will cause a single law to become instantly invalid. He's designed a 'sunrise' clause – again his words, that transitions old statutes to fit the new framework." On the 'gooder news' side, he thinks it also causes virtually every 'executive order' to be invalid, since it is illegal in the new framework, for the Executive to override legislation by 'administrative caveat'."

Marion Dixson, Founder and an economist with Harvard, spoke; almost for the first time since the Institute had executed the Initiative. "I always thought teenagers only watched MTV and the Kardashians. These kids have been paying attention in class."

Ellen chimed in. "Sorry to interrupt, but what these kids, and I think we'd better be calling them young citizens, have really been paying attention to, is the news. As much as we don't believe it, I think they really do care about their future."

Dr. Elliot looked at Millie. "Miss Dickinson, you have a very special group of new friends here, you know."

Millie gave him a grin. "I learned that the first weekend, sir. Al Lee and I were watching one of the volleyball games. He told me 'Millie. Your great times a few granddaddy didn't think we had the right to declare independence from the crown, yet fought for us anyway. My great times a few granddaddy helped give birth to our nation. Here we are, together, doing it again. It's historic, Millie." Then, he got a glint in his eyes that I've learned means he's being silly. "He said, and do you know why I know it will succeed? I said no. He said, not a one of us is a lawyer. We're not being paid by the obfuscation."

Dr. Elliot just shook his head, a giant grin on his face.

June 29, 2107

George picked up the handset. "George Hanover."

"Mr. Hanover, Marv Miller, NSA-D."

"Hey, Marv. Got the week's stats?"

"Nope. They'll be along later this afternoon. We finally got a trap on that spurious cell traffic to Arizona. We have both ends. The receiver is a Nelson Benson in Flagstaff. He's a Mormon minister. The number at your end is 928-555-0992. Any way you can trace that."

George smiled. "I do believe we have that technology without having to have you 'officially' trace it. Thanks."

"I'd say my pleasure, but, in this case, I doubt that it is. Good luck."

"Thanks, and you're right. One of ours is about to be really unhappy."

June 30, 2017

George knocked on the door to the Day Room. "Sally?"

Sally looked up from the screen. "Oh, hi, George. How've you been?"

"I'm great." He walked in and sat on the corner of the desk. "Listen, I need a favor. Well, more distinctly, the project needs a favor."

"Sure. We're all one project. What do you need from the lowly interns?" She liked George and grinned at him.

"I know you have a database with more information on the interns than we have. I need you to search the intern cell phone numbers for the series of "555" anywhere in the number. I need a list of the phone numbers and associated names. Can you do that?"

"Sure, I've got two interns that are 'super geeks'. When do you need it? But, it sounds to me like you already know the number you're searching for."

"I do, Sally, but we don't want anyone else to know what we're looking for. I'm sorry for the obfuscation, but that's the way it has to be. I expect you and Millie, at least, will figure it out soon enough."

"Uh, okay, I guess." She looked at the clock on the wall. It was 8:33. "How about right after lunch?"

George looked a bit uncomfortable. "We really need it, Sally. Who do you need? I'll go get them."

Sally pondered for a moment. "Janice Montesano built the database. She's on Beau's team. They meet in the back of the cafeteria. Since you're being so, 'secret agent', do you want me to go get her?"

"Would you mind, terribly?"

#

Sally returned with a young girl. George looked and tried to picture the petite girl wearing shorts and a T-shirt that advertised a great figure, as a 'geek'. She looked like she should be at a football game or on a beach, not in a room with a monitor. Then, he read the text on her shirt: 'It's all fun and games until someone divides by zero.'

Sally stepped back a half step, "Janice, this is George, Stage Manager and occasional PITA."

"Hi, uh, George."

"Hello, Janice. Don't let Sally's description get to you. I only eat interns on Thursday and only grilled with ketchup. Any chance she explained what we need?"

The girl visibly relaxed. "She said something about scanning the phone number fields in the database, but I don't know what template you need."

George shook off the feeling of being 'digitally challenged' and explained again.

"Aw, heck. I could have done that from my tablet and never left the meeting. We were just getting into the Executive Branch. What a can of worms. Who designed that thing, anyway? Can I use your laptop, Sally?"

"Sure. Let me log off." She sat down and closed the file she had open. Then, she logged off and stood.

Janice flopped into the seat and logged in. As soon as her user profile came up, her fingers began to fly. George moved to watch over her shoulder. "Hey! You'll see my password."

"Oops. Sorry." He moved away and sat on the edge of a table, while he waited.

She brought up a screen and typed in a search term. "You said any occurrence of '555', right, and you just want names and numbers?"

"That's right."

"Okay. It'll be on the printer in a minute. Do you need me to save a template of the SQL?"

"Huh?"

She giggled. "Do you want me to save the search?"

"Oh, uh, probably not. Thanks, though."

The printer spun up and a single sheet of paper flopped into the tray. George walked over to pick it up.

"Is that what you wanted?"

"He saw the number he wanted."

"Yes, it is, thank you."

Janice quickly shut down the application and logged off. "That all?"

"Yes, it is."

"Great! Gotta run. See you later, Sally. Meeting Beau for lunch." She shot out the door, as if she had been ejected and strode out of sight.

George watched for a moment. "Intense?"

"You have no idea."

#

George set the piece of paper on the desk in front of him and rechecked it, for the fourth time, against the note he had made, when Dr. Elliot had called him.

Brigham, Jay	9285550992
Horton, Kathryn	7555977231
Lawson, Albert	8042355590
Ramirez, Reynaldo	2135015556

Then, he picked up the handset and pressed a preset number.

"Dr. Elliot?"

"George. I have the name of the person making the cell calls."

"And that would be?"

"Jay Brigham. He's from a ranch outside Flagstaff, Arizona."

"I've asked the monitoring organization to set a flag for any more calls from that number. I'm going to have to make a visit to the good Bishop Benson to obtain his 'cooperation'. The question of what to do about young Mr. Brigham, remains. Have you any suggestions?"

"Well, sir, the risk here is really high. IF the bishop cooperates and keeps quiet, fine. If not, he becomes a leak, that we don't need. But, I've got half an idea. I'm not sure it's particularly ethical, but ..."

"Let me decide on the ethics. What's the idea?"

"It's kind of multiple choice, I guess. If the bishop cooperates, we tell Jay that the Bishop not getting in trouble for knowing 'classified information' without authority, is dependent upon his not contacting him, while Jay continues with the project. And, Jay doesn't get charged with violating his 'non-disclosure', if the bishop stays quiet. Some of this, I suppose, depends on what the bishop knows; or thinks he knows."

George, you are a devious sort of person. Are you sure you're not a lawyer?

#

"George? I've got Jay Brigham with me."

"Thanks Millie, come on in." George stood up and pointed to a small table. "Pull up a chair, please." He walked to the door of his office and closed it.

"Now. Jay, do you have your cell phone?"

"Yeah, why?"

"Place it on the table please."

"I don't have to. It's private."

"Jay, this can be easy or very hard. Put it on the table."

Jay, looking angry and confused, slipped it from his back pocket and placed it on the table. George reached out and picked it up. He verified that the number displayed matched the number on the report and then turned it off. Then, he stood and walked to his desk and picked up a small lock box. It had two keys dangling from the lock. He placed the phone in the box, locked it and removed the keys. He took one off the split ring and handed it to Millie. Then he gave the ring and second key to Jay.

"What the heck are you doing with my phone?"

"Right now, I'm making sure that no one uses it without my knowledge. Also, I'm guaranteeing you that no one, including me, will be able to get to it without you or Millie knowing. Those are the only two keys. The box stays in my possession. So as long as keys and box are not joined, the phone is secure."

"But, why, George?"

"Well, Millie, Mr. Brigham here has made two calls to, I presume, his minister, or bishop, as the Mormons choose to refer to them. Certain words in those conversations triggered the monitoring program that you all were told about. Jay? Do you deny the calls?"

"No. I needed to talk about this, whatever it is, project, with my bishop."

"You remember signing a non-disclosure agreement, don't you?

"My loyalty to my church and God, supersede anything I promised the project, George." Jay tried to look stubborn and righteous even as his wavering voice betrayed him

"Jay, really? Render unto Caesar? Come on. You and I both know that this project, in no way, imperils your church; or any other, for that matter. If anything, we hope it will clarify the relationship between every religion and the state. Now, you've gotten the bishop in hot water by giving him information to which he is not entitled; and incomplete or even incorrect information, at that. That knowledge carries criminal and civil penalties."

"Hey, he didn't do anything wrong. I called him. He just listened and said he'd check with Salt Lake ..."

"What!?"

"He was going to see what Salt Lake City wanted to do." The revelation hit Jay. "Oh, crap."

"Indeed, Jay. Crap indeed. Deep ... deep ... crap."

Rocks, Reefs and Rainbows

The Angels Intercede

July 1, 2016, Flagstaff, Arizona

Dean Elliot stepped from the cab and looked at the church front. It was an imposing structure for a city as small, and to his East Coast mindset dumpy, as Flagstaff. It was 90 degrees, but at least dry. He walked up the walk and steps to the nine-foot bronze doors and opened the right door. It swung open, effortlessly, and he stepped into the dim, but air conditioned, entrance.

"May I help you?" Dean looked to the right. A middle-aged woman in a dark high-collared dress stepped from an office.

"I'm Dr. Dean Elliot. I would like to speak with Bishop Nelson Benson, please."

"May I inquire as to the nature, sir. Bishop Benson is very busy getting ready for the Independence Day celebration."

"I'm sorry, I'm not at liberty to discuss it with anyone, but the bishop. However, I assure you that it is important enough to interrupt him. You may tell him that I am from the project which has employed Jay Brigham."

"Oh, Jay. Really a nice young man. He's due to go on his mission in September." She turned to walk away and muttered. "Australia, I think. I'll tell the bishop you are here, sir. Just a moment."

Dean was looking at the murals on the walls when he heard a male voice. "I'm Nelson Benson. How may I help you? I hope Jay is okay."

"He was fine when I left Kentucky yesterday. I suspect he is fine today."

Bishop Benson motioned toward the lighted door. "I presume that you are not a member of the church, so please, my office is this way." They passed through the office guarded by the woman. "My assistant, Delores Kemp." Dean nodded and followed. They entered an office, not sumptuous, but neither was it austere. "Please take a seat."

"Would you mind closing the door, sir?"

"I have no secrets from Delores."

"Perhaps not, but I may. The door, please?"

The bishop gave Dean a hard look and then closed the door. Instead of sitting in the chair opposite Dean, he took the psychological high ground and sat behind his desk. "Okay, you've got a secret."

"Alright." He took a deep breath and stepped into deep water. "Have you spoken with Jay Brigham since he left for his summer internship?"

A darkness shielded the bishop's eyes. "Why do you ask?"

"Bishop Benson, we can dance around in this rice bowl until it spills, or worse, breaks or we can be up front and solve a problem. Have you spoken with Jay Brigham?"

The bishop crossed his arms. Dean recognized the defensive posture and sighed to himself. "Yes, I have."

"And, during those two calls", revealing that he knew how many times Jay had called, "did Jay tell you anything about the project he works for?"

"I don't remember. He may have. Why?"

Dr. Elliot leaned forward and lowered his voice. Two could play at this game. "Mr. Benson, this doesn't have to be this hard. If Jay discussed, *in any way*, the project he is working on, he has violated the terms of a nondisclosure agreement. He may be, therefore, subject to both criminal and civil penalties under title 10, USC 2742(e)3.71. In so doing, he has also imperiled you by giving you information to which you are not entitled. So, I will repeat the question. Did Jay tell you anything about the project he is working on?"

"Jay's just a boy."

"He is over eighteen bishop. I will not repeat the question. But, I *will* call the local FBI field office."

Bishop Benson looked deflated. "Yes, he did. He's afraid that whatever you are doing there, and he really didn't tell me much, will hurt the church."

"He said you were calling Salt Lake to discuss it. Have you done that?"

"I, uh, well, I did place a call, but had to ask that they call me back."

For the first time since Jay had mentioned that call, Dean breathed easy and leaned back in his chair. "Well, bishop, I suggest you find a mundane subject to discuss with them when they return your call, because, if you repeat anything, and I mean anything, that Jay told you, your next service will be at the Federal work camp in Pennsylvania. Now, let's find mutual middle ground here.

"Now, since it appears that you have told no one what Jay told you, and I've no reason to doubt the word of a man of faith, I will ask that you say nothing to anyone. I will consider Jay's indiscretion under control and take no official action against him, or, by inclusion, *you*. Is this idea of interest to you?

"I remain concerned by what Jay revealed about this project."

"Since I am trusting you, I ask that you trust me. I assure you that, within the design of what we're doing are guarantees for all religious entities. I can't tell you any more than that without violating my own non-disclosure agreement. Can a gentleman's agreement serve?"

"Dr. Elliot, you really give me little choice. It appears that I have been given Hobson's Choice, at best."

"I regret that appearance, but it is easier to believe me as I believe you than to face the legal reality of spreading what is, most certainly, incomplete and harmful information; harmful to both nation and church. Have we an agreement, Bishop?"

July 2, 2015 - Camp Donelson, KY

The knock on his door startled Jay. He slipped off his bed, set his Bible on the desk and went to the door. He peeked through the peephole and saw George. He opened the door and saw that George had the lock box under his arm. "May I come in?"

Jay stepped back. "I probably don't have a choice, do I?"

George stepped in. "Actually, you do, but this is more private. Do you have the key we gave you?"

"Yeah." He opened the desk drawer and withdrew the key, still on its split ring.

George set the box on the desk. "Your bishop has decided to say nothing about whatever you talked about on the phone. Now, it's time for you to make the same smart choice. Will you abide by the terms of the non-disclosure agreement and make no more comments to him, *or anyone*, about the work you are doing here?"

"But, what if I don't like what's being designed?"

"You have that right, but may only express your concerns to those in this camp. You are a part of a team that is doing an important job. For now, only the team members have input to the output. If, someday, this project is in the public domain, you will then have the right to voice your opinion; but, not about what went on this summer. I cannot make that clearer. If you can't do that, I will have to report your violation to the appropriate authorities. Your bishop understands that. I need to know that you do. And, I need to know it now."

"And, if I do, I get my phone back?"

"Unlock the box. You get your phone back regardless. But, your phone calls are being monitored for 'those words' that got you in trouble in the first place. That is the only action taken if you agree."

Jay looked relieved, but was still unhappy. "Okay. I don't have a choice. I agree." He unlocked the box and removed his phone. "For what it's worth, I'm sorry."

"I accept your apology, but leave you with the warning. It's Damocles' Sword, Jay. You're smart and are contributing. Don't let your imagination get you in trouble. Speak with me or one of the DAs if you have questions. We *will* listen." He closed the empty box, picked it up and walked to the door. "Good night, Jay."

The Plot Thickens

"Do you think you've put a lid on it?" The question came from Marion Dixson. She had been out of town and returned in time for the weekly meeting; this one including the briefing on their brush with a potentially embarrassing public disclosure. Dr. Elliot had briefed the Founders, DAs and George on his visit with the bishop, followed by George's follow-up on his conversation with Jay.

George looked at Dr. Elliot who motioned for him to field the question. "Unfortunately, we will only know we've succeeded, if there is no release. If there is, it will be too late to stop it a second time. The most dangerous point is the bishop. He's outside our control, whereas Jay is here, where we can track his calls. We won't know if Mr. Benson calls his superiors until we hear about it from a Congressman or, worse yet, the Salt Lake media. I think we got Jay's attention, plus we have his phone on our radar. We can only hope that Dr. Elliot scared the bishop into enough silence.

"I'm certain that we share your hopes, George." She looked to Mr. Gilbert. "I'm done. Thank you for letting me hijack the agenda."

"No problem, Marion. Now, we all have the same information. A special thanks to Dean and George for the extra stress and work. Next on the agenda are the preparations for the July 4th celebration. George has invited Millie Dickinson, the surprisingly successful Chairperson of the Executive Committee, to join us for this planning session. I need remind no one that the only subjects to be discussed, while Miss Dickinson is in the room, should relate to the 4th of July celebration. No information about the attending guests is to be revealed. George, you may ask Miss Dickinson to join us.

George stood and walked to the door, opened it and leaned out. "Millie, come on in, please."

He stood at the door as Millie walked in. He introduced her to everyone at the table, even though she was familiar to all but two of them, and then held a chair for her on the side of the table. "Welcome, Miss Dickinson. May we call you Millie?"

She smiled shyly. "Please do. I'm nervous enough here with you. Calling me Miss Dickinson only makes it worse; like I've been called to the office."

Harold smiled at her. "You are here as a complement, Millie. The only reports we've had on you and your committee have been good ones. We want your help to make a key event work to everyone's benefit. July 4th, just two days hence, is more than our nation's official birthday. It is also exactly one-third of the way through this project. It will be a 'holiday' for the project. The time is built into the schedule, so there should be no impact.

George will share the event agenda which includes, I'm told, a staff versus intern softball game. Given my condition, I hope it's very slow pitch." A respectful chuckle ran around the table. "There will be a number of invited guests later in the day. All of them are aware of the general reason for the project. Some are responsible for our location, others for funding and infrastructure. Only a few are fully informed.

That being said, we would like you to give a very generic presentation on the work accomplished to this point."

Millie was surprised. "Wow. Just how generic do you want it? I mean, one or two of my teams are deep into the detailed analysis and nearly ready to summarize."

Dr. Elliot interrupted. "We don't want you to brief on anything that might give away any specific elements or direction you are taking, Millie."

"Well, that definitely leaves out Kathy and Juan. I've seen their stuff and it's going to be central to the new document." But, they might like to hear some of what Jay is doing. His team has been diligent in researching the writings of the Framers and in dissecting the Constitution for 'original intent', if indeed there was one. Al thinks there was.

"That sounds good. It's insight into the reasoning behind what we're, no, what you're doing," said Erick Leary.

"Beau's group on the current structure of the Federal government and from which sections of the Constitution it is derived, might be enlightening, too." Between them, and with some generic information, we can probably use close to an hour. Is that too much?"

"I think what you've outlined is marvelous. It's enough to let them know progress is being made and give them some insights into the swamp, into which we've thrown you. George, will you work directly with the Executive Committee on any requirements for equipment or services?

"Of course."

Millie and Ellen had eaten together as they discussed elements of the upcoming celebration. Ellen took their trays to the scullery as Millie sought out Beau. She spotted him at a table away from the rest of the crowd. She sat down at the table with Beau and Janice Montesano. "Hey, Beau, Janice." She noticed that Beau had pulled their chairs near one corner of the table, placing him and Janice closer together. "Ellen and I need to talk with you, Beau."

Janice leaned away from Beau. "Do I need to leave?"

"Naah. Strictly project stuff," Ellen said as she neared the table and sat down across from them. "Come to think of it, he'll probably need your help. You guys can work together on it." Janice's eyes sparkled, and her position relaxed markedly. Ellen's psychologist training perked up; as did her eyebrows at the cues the pair was putting out. Ellen laid out the high-level plan for the 4th. "Everyone else will learn about it in the morning, but we needed to give you time to flesh out the skeleton that Millie has given us."

"Beau, what I have told them is that your interns have done a great job of pinning the Federal org chart to specific sections of the Constitution, or, in some cases, to nothing more than Congressional or Executive whim. I'd like you to summarize your findings for the visitors in, oh say, 25 minutes. Can you do it?"

The young man didn't even hesitate. "Sure. We've got it in a database already. In fact, Janice did the design work and she can do searches that would violate the fifth amendment." Janice's head fell slightly, and her neck colored, but she had a grin on her face.

"Do you want charts and stuff?" Janice, her eyes sparkling at a challenge for 'her' information, spoke up. "I've got some software that will blow your visitors away."

Millie giggled at the enthusiasm from one of the project's identified geeks. "Make the numbers sing and dance, Janice." She looked at Beau. "Do me a favor though. Give Jay a chance to use her services, as well. I don't want his presentation to look unimportant because he doesn't have dancing spreadsheets."

Ellen made a mental note of Millie's inclusive leadership style; keeping all teams equal, as best as she could.

"We got this one. Jay's analysis is in tables in the same database, right Janice?"

"Absolutely. I can run SQL unions to pull down indexed data ..."

Beau's hand descended on hers. "Back, Simba! You're scaring the tourists."

Janice giggled, "Sorry. Got carried away. We can do it, Millie. We'll get with Jay and come up with an AKC pedigreed dog and pony show for you."

Millie beamed at Ellen. "Told ya."

#

Ellen and George were taking a walk after lunch. They passed the Day Room. "I think I've spotted our first liaison."

"What?"

"Beau Williams and Janice Montesano, the IT wonder, seem to be a thing."

"Oh, hell, Ellen. These kids are 18 and 19, trapped in a wire enclosure, working and living together. I'd be really surprised if there weren't' a half dozen sets of squeaking springs every night. Remember the first day when one of them asked about 'visitors'? We told them to act like adults. I think they are. Do you see any problem with this pair?"

"No, just making an observation."

George laughed out loud. "Don't observe too closely. Kids today could probably give us lessons." Ellen punched his arm.

July 3, 2107

Lena had just put her coffee and danish on the table when her cell phone buzzed. She pulled it from the back pocket of her jeans. It was an 'Everyone' text from George. She set the phone down, spread butter on her danish, cut it into three pieces and picked one up, as she keyed the text message open.

> Good morning. This EVERYONE text is to inform you that tomorrow, the 4th of July, is not only the official birthday of the United States, but marks the end of the first third of the project. We are declaring a holiday for the project you have named 'We the People'. Please take the opportunity to sleep in, but don't miss the events beginning with the Institute vs Interns softball game at 10:00. First ten sign-ups (dining area) are the first string. I'm refereeing. Please review the rest of the agenda. It will be in your email by noon today. Oh, yes, there will be fireworks. - George

Lena closed the message and looked around for the softball sign-up sheet.

#

"Okay, what's the guest list look like?" Dr. Elliot and Erick Leary sat across from George's desk.

"You want the VIPs or the whole shebang? So far eighteen of the thirty have responded. Twelve will be here, including all five VIPs."

Erick looked at Dr. Elliot. "Dean, I'm still concerned with the Vice President coming. That means Secret Service and his staff. That's a lot of potentially loose lips."

"I know, Erick, but he's also the driving force. I can't tell him he can't come to his own party any more than I can keep the Minority Whip off the list."

"Yeah, but she doesn't have a security detail."

"We have to depend on their normal 'need to know' procedures. I think it will be great for the interns to see just how much real support this project has."

"If it's such an occasion for the interns, will they be allowed any access to the Vice President? In fact, the Whip will have three constituents here. Will she be able to meet with them?", George asked.

"You know. I hadn't given thought to that. Great idea, though. I'll put out the word to remember their cameras for the 'ceremony'. I just don't want word about the Vice President released in case he doesn't come."

"Ah, uh, you might want to rethink the cameras, boss. If just one photo is sent home, the potential for uncomfortable questions to be asked of outsiders, exists. The number of potential 'leaks' goes up exponentially."

"I suppose you're right, but the kids will be disappointed in not being able to have a souvenir of what, for some, is a once in a lifetime opportunity."

"How about ..." George paused and thought, "If this went on in the outside, everyone would pass through a metal detector, right?"

"Sure. The Secret Service is delivering them this afternoon. We're using the theater, so the number of entries is limited to four."

"Okay, then. Tuesday is a holiday, so Kathy's group won't be there. How about we put out the word that no electronics of any kind are permitted, including film cameras, for security reasons. They'll understand when they see the VP. Then, we have our photographer there to take lots of shots, including photo ops with the intern leadership. The constituents of the Whip can have their pictures taken, too. We promise them packages at the end of the project, along with other memorabilia photos. That should keep the outcry down and prevent digital leaks."

"That's devious, but clever, George. Publish that in the agenda announcement. We only have to keep it under wraps for 37 more days, anyway. Of course, the proscription must be enforced for everyone, including us, at least in the theater."

#

Millie entered the dining hall as soon as the doors opened. She looked around and spotted the small table by the other door. She hurried over and picked up the pile of holiday agendas and the sign-up clipboard for the softball game.   Then she headed for the window table that had been dubbed 'the head table', where she would meet the other four members of the Executive Committee. She had thought about the announced holiday for an hour or so and then had an inspiration. She sought out the others and asked them to meet for lunch; when she was certain the announcements would be out.

Jay was first to arrive. He waved at her and went to the serving line. As he did, Kathy and Juan walked in the other entrance. Juan headed over to the serving line while Kathy walked over to the table and set her backpack down. "What's up, girl?"

Millie gave her a conspiratorial look. "Wait for the others. Go get your lunch."

Kathy looked at her for a second and then shrugged. "Sure. You want anything?"

"If they've got a Cobb salad, bring me one with ranch dressing on the side, please."

"As you wish, Madam Chairperson."

Millie grinned and blew a raspberry at her friend and fellow worker as she walked away.

Beau and Janice walked in as the others set their trays at the table. The smell of pizza in various incarnations assaulted Millie as she dipped a bite of salad in the bowl of dressing. "Go ahead and eat, guys. I want to wait for Beau." She popped a cherry tomato in her mouth.

Beau carried a tray with two plates on it as Janice brought napkins, silver and drinks. He looked questioningly at Millie. She thought for a moment. "Janice, this is an impromptu Executive Committee meeting. It's nothing earth-shattering, though. Can you sit and ignore what you hear?"

"Uh, you sure? I can sit somewhere else." Beau didn't look happy at that.

Millie shook her head. "I'm sure, and I expect that Beau trusts you. Besides, given what you do, we have very few secrets from you, anyway. Sit down. Beau, grab yourself a chair."

Beau scraped a chair from the next table and flopped into it. He picked his plate from the tray and pushed the tray to Janice.

"Okay." She held up the clipboard and an announcement. "I intercepted the signup sheet and announcements because I have an idea that I want to run past you. If they want to have a them vs us ball game, let's pack the house. By now, we know who the athletes are in the Interns. Let's build a dream team and have them be the 'first ten to sign up'."

Beau laughed, covering his pizza filled mouth. "Oh, you're cruel. We would have beaten that crowd of old folks anyway, and you want to pack the team with ringers? Priceless!"

Kathy looked around the table at the faces. "I think that pretty much is the consensus, kid. Go for it."

Millie beamed. "We've got about ten minutes before the crowd arrives. They'll be looking for these. I want the clipboard to be filled before they start volunteering." She flipped an agenda over and handed it to Jay on her right. "Okay, write down the names of your athlete nominees. When it gets back to me, we'll pick our 'dream team'."

#

Joyce walked into the dining facility thirty minutes later through the door closest to the table. The announcements and clipboard were back on the table. She noticed that the clipboard page on top was completely full. The pile of agendas was seriously depleted, as well. Then she did a quick double take as she looked at the list. She smiled and shook her head as she headed for the serving line.

"The kids are trying to pull a fast one, George." George looked up from his dish of ice cream as Joyce set her tray down.

"How so?"

"They packed the ball team."

"And you know this how?"

"The handwriting on the first ten names is the same. Somehow, I doubt that a bunch of guys would all have the same handwriting. Besides, I know what Millie's looks like."

George chuckled. "You have to love a conspiracy. They've really become a team in 19 days, haven't they?

Firecrackers and Fireworks

Casey at the Bat

July 4, 2016, Camp Donelson, Kentucky

George turned on the microphone in the scorekeeper's box. "Good morning and welcome to the first and only "We the People" championship softball game." The bleachers held a large contingent of the interns and they cheered and shouted in the best spirit of the game. Twenty-five or so had begged off to play a team of non-project workers at basketball. "As at all softball games, I ask fans and players alike to stand for the National Anthem. Today, the anthem will be sung by your very own Devil's Advocate, Joyce Sheridan."

At the end of the anthem, George put on a black ball cap, bill backward. "As the officially sanctioned umpire for this game, I declare the interns as visiting team. Staff take the field. Oh, and interns, I've been informed that you've packed your roster, so, rest assured that the staff has canvassed for anyone who played ball in college to be on their team. According to Dr. Elliot, 'You're going down!'" He was met by jeers and cheers from both benches. "Play ball!"

#

Ellen left the bleachers at the end of the fifth inning and drove to the former dispensary. David Barrow, a logistics specialist supporting the Initiative, was entertaining the invited guests; all but two. She stopped at the end of the lounge area and waited until everyone knew she was there. "Welcome to Camp Donelson. Thank you all for surrendering your Independence Day with your families to be here with ours. Dr. Elliot and the other Founders regret not being here, but when I left, they had the field and were only down by 5." There was a chuckling and laughing among the audience, that knew of the ball game. She turned to look at her staffer. "David, any word on the flight with our special guests?"

"Just before you got here, they reported ten minutes. They had just entered Fort Campbell air space."

She glanced at her watch. "Okay, great. Thanks." She turned back to the small audience. "The chopper is almost here. Please remember that the interns do not, or at least should not, know you. They will be briefed not to divulge any details of their work and we ask you not to pry. I *can* say, however, that their progress is both phenomenal and creative. You and most of the Initiative staff will be dining with the interns, a sort of holiday cookout, but inside. It's hot, hazy and humid out there with lots of flies and mosquitoes. Feel free to mingle with the young folks, but remember the rules about info. Anything else is fair game. I'm certain they are hungry for contact with anyone they haven't been staring at for 3 weeks.

"Right after lunch, we will all gather in the theater for a one-hour familiarization presentation, where two of their teams will present some of the findings that can be revealed, without divulging direction or final product. We regret holding back, however, the slightest inadvertent leak could well be disastrous and we all know just how important the work we're doing is." The sound of rotors could be heard approaching. "Are there any questions?"

Would You Care to Dance?

The fifty-year-old air conditioning in the theater was struggling to keep up with nearly two hundred people. The guests were seated in the front two rows of the center section. The DAs were seated at a table near the wings on the left, and there was a similar table, this one empty, near the other wings; awaiting the Founders and George. Trying not to be obvious, and failing in the effort, were two men in windbreakers standing near the backdrop. Their concentration was on the audience. Then, the back doors opened and two more men, also in windbreakers, despite the heat, stepped through to hold the doors. They looked down the aisle and caught a signal from one of the two matching bookends on the stage. The agents stepped aside, and the Founders walked down the aisle. Harold Gilbert mounted the stage and approached the microphone as the others walked to their seats on the right.

"Good afternoon, Interns, staff and honored guests alike. Happy 4th of July to all. I'd, first, like to comment on the ball game. Congratulations to the staffers for coming in second place in the tournament. I only wish the interns had done as well. Regrettably, they came in second from last." The moans overshadowed the laughter and jeers, at the use of an ancient piece of humor. "Yes, I first heard that joke when I was your age. Congratulations Interns. Your team of ringers beat our team of ringers 9 to 4."

When the celebratory noise had settled down, he continued. "Although the 4th of July is only an arbitrarily selected date, it does recognize the impact made by a small group of men determined to make changes to a firmly established structure. Today, you 155 are attempting the same, but in a much more different and difficult environment, than existed 230 years ago. Your progress, to date, is no more laudable than the very fact that you believed you could do it ... and simply began. Our invited guests represent the organizations, both within the government and from the public sector, who believe that we have no choice but to complete the work you will complete in 37 days; for complete it you must.

"I understand that some of you wonder where the impetus for this project originated and just how much support you have. Without knowing that, it is sometimes hard to be confident that your work will be recognized and have some chance of making a difference. I believe our honored guest will put an end to the questions. We are honored to have with us the representative of the primary sponsor of, what you now call, 'We the People'. Ladies and gentlemen, the Vice President of the United States."

The audience stood, and applause started as the VP entered the theater, accompanied by the Minority Whip and, of course, two Secret Service agents. At the front row, he turned and waved before mounting the stage, to shake hands with the five Devils Advocates. He then shook hands with Mr. Gilbert. Harold left the lectern to take his seat with the other Founders, while the two agents took station at both sets of stage steps facing the audience. After a few more moments of applause, he held up his hands to quiet the crowd.

"Good afternoon, staff and most of all, Interns of 'We the People'. I love that name. You have no idea how pleased I am to see all of you out there, and to celebrate our nation's birthday with each of you; especially given the seemingly impossible job we've asked you to perform. I'm going to start my remarks by being a shameless plagiarist and ripping off Winston Churchill. 'Never has so much been owed by so many to so few.' He was, of course, referring to the efforts of the Royal Air Force to keep the skies over England free from the Luftwaffe during the Battle of Britain, in 1940. It was, for Britain, a struggle for the very survival of the nation. What you 155 have been asked to do is, while far less bloody, no less important to the survival of this nation.

"You've gone down this unknown highway with no knowledge of who was driving the bus. You know it's not Mr. Gilbert or Dr. Elliot, but you took it on faith that it wasn't a false start or, I hope, some underhanded revolution. Of course, the last time we did this, it WAS a revolutionary turn of events. Well, now, the cat is out of the bag. If you listened closely, Mr. Gilbert said I was the 'representative' of the primary sponsor. You've been studying the Constitution, rather closely I suppose, so you know for whom I work. But the President is only one among the group of people, who are working to support your efforts." He motioned toward the center front rows. "The folks sitting in the front rows are among them, as well. I know you don't know many of them. In fact, the only one with any official government imprimatur, other than myself, is the Minority Whip of the

House. The others represent, or are, from departments of the Executive, Judicial and Legislative branches and private industry. And, we've ensured that some very vocal private organizations are recognized, as well. I'll leave you to try to divine who is who and who they represent; mostly because it's safest that no list be made until your job is done, but also because I have a sadistic sense of humor and can honestly say, *I know something you don't know. Nyah nyah!*" A laugh spread through the hall. "Thanks for the laugh. It was getting way too serious in here.

What the collective 'we' have asked you to do is let us know what you, the inheritors of our country, want to see it look like for another two centuries. We hear from you, but we listen through adult filters, your churches, your parents and your professors. In other words, we've listened but not heard. Each generation grew up feeling that they would inherit something good that they could build upon and make better for another generation yet to follow. I sincerely regret and apologize for, at least two past generations, when I say that we've failed you. You have nurtured a nearly unrecoverable debt, a damaged environment, a dysfunctional governing body and the mantle of 'world leader', held high for a century, that has become a tattered garment of sack cloth. We have become either a laughing stock or a symbol of hatred to most elements of the civilized world.

"I sometimes wonder why, if the rest of the world is so much worse that, even in our own self-made distress, millions still strive to come here every year. And, yes, now I'm whining. I have no answers and will make no excuses. I stand here, as close to the pinnacle of power as a single heartbeat, to tell you that you, 155 young Americans, are our last best hope to return our country to a positive direction. If I knew how to do that, I would roll up my sleeves and join you."

Ellen, sitting at the end of the table, watched the audience, as his address continued. The silence was deafening and there was no movement, no idle chatter or the expected squirming of young people forced to listen to the postulating of their 'elders'.

Her sense told her that the audience, intern and guest alike, was entranced, not so much by the speaker, but by the words spoken that confirmed the critical importance of what they were doing. She sought out the faces of the Executive Committee and others that were leaders in the effort. They sat equally spellbound. Her concentration on the audience was disrupted by the beginning of his summary remarks. She turned her attention back to the lectern.

"I cannot stress the importance of your task or the need that it be done in secrecy, until completed. It must be announced completed and in its entirety from the correct venue to better ensure its acceptance by the American people. Beyond that, I want to assure that you, each of you, is aware of the tremendous pride we feel that you, our youth, are doing what we could not. Thank you. Good Luck, Godspeed and God Bless the United States of America."

Ellen quickly returned her focus to the audience to gauge the response. For a moment, no one moved. Then, about ten interns, scattered throughout the audience stood and began to applaud. The applause grew as did the population standing until the standing ovation, applause and cheers reached a deafening level. The Vice President stood at the lectern, his head bowed.

George stepped onto the stage from the wings as the VP left the stage and walked up the aisle, a smattering of applause still sounding. He was shaking hands with those within reach of the aisle, as the Secret Service hovered at his side. As the Vice President reached the door, he turned and waved. Then, he turned and disappeared through the door. George gave him another few seconds of lingering applause before stepping to the lectern and raising his hands. "Please, quiet down. We have more ground to cover before the AC fails in here." He waited for another few seconds as the audience reseated itself. "On behalf of the Institute and the 'We the People' project, we were honored to have the VP stop to visit, if only for a few minutes. I'm sure you'll understand that, to maintain secrecy, he could only stop for a short time, taking a brief stop on a scheduled trip from Washington to Nashville, for a party fund raiser.

"We have two briefings for our guests remaining on the agenda. Two Executive Committee members and team leads, Al Lee and Beau Williams, will give high level briefings on their efforts. While these briefings are, primarily, familiarization for our sponsoring guests, I encourage all of you to remain and listen. It's one of the few times during this project, that you will have the opportunity to hear what the other teams have developed. I cannot help but imagine that any extra information will help you in the pursuit of your own team goals. So, if you choose to leave, please do so as not to disturb those interested in the information.

"First up is Al Lee. His group has been tasked with analyzing the symbiotic relationship between the Framers and the document they wrote. In brief, just what DID they intend the Constitution to do? Alvin Lee is the scion of the historic Lee family that has been involved in the political affairs of this country since its inception. He is FFV, that's First Family of Virginia, and a Constitutional scholar in his own right. Mr. Lee, the lectern is yours."

George stepped back to the wings, as Al mounted the stairs. He set his tablet on the lectern and opened the presentation. The screen remained on the Institute logo. A titter ran through his friends in the audience. He looked behind at the screen, then, he paused and covered the microphone with his hand, as he rustled papers beneath the lectern.

"Al! Here!" He looked up and saw Janice jogging down the aisle holding something up. Lee walked to the foot of the stage and took the offered item.

"The remote for the slides." A few jeers and cheers arose in the audience and he saw some smiles on the faces of the guests. He smiled and waved the remote. "The show must go on." He pointed he remote at the receiver at the foot of the stage. A split image appeared. On the right a copy of an historically contemporary painting of the Framers, including Washington's famous chair. On the left was an enlargement of the preamble to the Constitution.

"Good afternoon, ladies and gentlemen. George said I would give a 'high level' briefing. My introduction will be a simple statement. The very first words of the Constitution, 'We, the people', etc., were never the intention of the Framers. Bluntly, the Framers wrote the Constitution with the intention to create a government to be run by men exactly like them, entitled, privileged and rich. Now, before you grab your torches and pitchforks and storm the stage crying 'heresy', let me give you some statistics about the men who wrote our cherished foundation document."

A blank screen appeared, its background the same parchment they had just seen with the sacred words of the preamble written on it. "Let's consider what happened to the Framers after ratification. Two became President of the United States, George Washington and James Madison. Two others were nominees for that high office." As he enumerated history, names and positions appeared in line item order on the screen. "One served as Vice President and four in the cabinet of various early chief executives. Nineteen served in the Senate and thirteen as Representatives. There were four Federal judges and four Associate Justices of the Supreme Court, two of whom went on to be Chief Justice. Finally, another seven served on various diplomatic missions for the government." At the end of this summarization, the screen split between the list he had just given and the signature page of the Constitution with the associated names highlighted. A murmur swept through the audience.

Ellen, who had sat in on some of the group sessions that developed the information and statistics, looked not at the interns, but at the guests in the front rows. The Minority Whip looked uncomfortable, as if someone had discovered toilet paper stuck to his shoe. Most of the others were chatting among themselves. Most were somber faced. Two or three were rapt in their attention to information wholly foreign to them.

"No, the Framers wrote the document to ensure that they would govern 'we the people'. They were the landowners, the businessmen, the ship owners and the educated in a primarily agrarian nation, where communication was slow and undependable. Public education did not exist; and they intended that not to change."

Alvin went on, charts and lists flying across the screen, delineating legislation favoring perpetuation of a ruling class, wars to defend business interests and various legislative 'interpretations' that would ensure aristocratic rule. It would continue until the Civil War. As he did, more than a few note pads appeared in the hands of the guests and furtive notes were taken, along with occasional aside commentary between them. It was obvious to Ellen that much of this information was unfamiliar and uncomfortable. After all, they represented exactly the class that Al was excoriating.

"Oh, that was the bad news." Another chuckle ran through the house. He knew how to play to the crowd. "The good news is that the Framers, I'm not sure if it was inadvertent or providential, created a document with built in flexibility and extensibility. Despite their best efforts to hold the reins, when those reins were finally cut, the Constitution was robust enough to withstand the popular surge; at least until usurped by various and sundry special interests. For that, let's see what my compatriot, Beau Williams, has to say." He flicked the switch on his tablet and stepped away toward the stairs. As he turned toward his seat, one of the special guests approached him and the two spent a few minutes with heads together. Then, they returned to their respective seats as George approached the lectern.

"Now, that's a hard act to follow. Beau Williams, the Executive Committee member from Maryland, has the task of relating the current infrastructure, major areas of governmental function and recent activities to specific sections of the Constitution; rather like sorting a jumbled deck of cards into the order originally designed. Beau, the audience is primed and ready."

George returned to the wings, this time behind the DAs, as Beau mounted the steps on the opposite side of the stage. He approached the lectern, turned his tablet on and held up the remote to show that he had it. A short giggle from a few kids met his statement of preparedness. Then he aimed the remote at the receiver on the stage's edge. "Good afternoon. I suspect that if the AC in this building was still a function of the government, it might be working, but the likelihood of it being recognizable as a product of the original design is negligible. Let us build on this hypothesis. The Constitution has been chasing events since 1934, falling farther behind in continual, yet fruitless, attempts to be the 'guiding' document of this nation. It is so far behind and so hamstrung by bureau-crap and politics, that it will never recover."

Ellen saw shock, disbelief and immediate attention from the guests and, in more than a few instances, the interns. The Minority Whip looked angry.

"Let's spread the indictment among the co-conspirators." A bullet list appeared on the screen.

8. Congress is charged, by the Constitution, with producing an annual budget, yet has failed to do so since 2009.

9. The President has, in a de facto manner, declared war not less than seven times without the Constitutionally required Congressional legislation.

10. The Supreme Court has 'legislated' by judicial decision significant issues that are clearly 'extra-Constitutional' in managing the affairs of individual states and in direct contravention of the tenth amendment.

11. Using Executive Orders, numerous Presidents have violated the Constitution for their own 'policy' purposes; going back as far as Abraham Lincoln. Perhaps the most egregious unconstitutional Executive Order was the order for the unlawful imprisonment, without due process, and the seizure of private property of a single class of U.S. citizens, at the outset of World War II.

"Because the Executive branch of the government is the branch responsible for the day to day operations of the nation, the vast preponderance of extra-constitutional events may be laid at the doorstep of the Executive Mansion. Often, these violations are politically motivated. In the decades long power struggle between legislative and executive branches, they have been executed via the Executive Order, a presumptive right of the President. Legally, the Executive Order is used to ensure continued governmental function during a congressional recess. Almost universally, this was the case until the presidency of Abraham Lincoln.

"Of course, among the literally thousands of Executive Orders, of which FDR issued more than 3500 himself, are important and innocuous directives, such as the declarations of Thanksgiving and Christmas as holidays, the pardoning of turkeys and the establishment of National Monuments. The very first EO was issued by George Washington within three months of his inauguration. The fastest was by FDR on inauguration day. It would be hard to label the most egregious, although the Japanese internment order would be my front runner.

"Executive Orders have been overturned, such as most of the New Deal and Truman's Steel Industry nationalization. Some have been ignored 'for the greater good'; again, for President Truman and his unconstitutional desegregation of the military, in 1949. And conflicting orders have been issued. For example, President Eisenhower, by EO, ordered the expulsion of a million illegal immigrants. President Obama, conversely, by EO ordered thirteen million illegal immigrants to be ignored by competent authority. Go figure."

Ellen watched the scribbling by the guests and several side conversations; one of which became loud enough that George descended the stairs to hush the participants. The two thoroughly chastised and embarrassed gentlemen glared at each other, but kept their own counsel.

"My team continues to work on the number of times the Supreme Court has 'legislated', instead of dealt with mandated Constitutional questions. Perhaps the most recent is the Supreme Court's action to codify the definition of 'marriage'; a definition clearly outside the confines of the Constitution.

"Occasionally, collusion between all three branches, has resulted in the seizure of a sovereign state's rights and responsibilities to legislate perceived 'equality'. This activity has gone on since the inception of the Department of Health, Education and Welfare under former Cleveland Mayor, Anthony Celebrezze, in 1962, beginning with required curricula and continuing with 'Common Core'. Both were clear seizures of a state's right to provide for the education of the children of their citizens.

"In fact, there are those 'strict constructionists' that hold the Income Tax to be unconstitutional." A chuckle spread through the youth and several heads nodded among the guests. Beau grinned, "But, let's not go there. They may be listening in." A broad laugh passed through the theater, including the DAs and Founders.

"Congress is no stranger to legislating around the Constitution. We're still enumerating the number of times the second amendment has been 'fenced' by specific prohibitions. Example? For sure. We have a right to own firearms, but the government has banned ammunition and various accessories. I would be remiss if I didn't admit that the conversation surrounding these subjects is as heated, within our team, as it is in the nation. But, then, it should be. But, the fact remains that humans are ignoring the Framers words and, according to Al Lee, their intent."

Ishmael sat in his chair, grinning as the young people validated and exposed more than eighty years of, often politically motivated and always unconstitutional, government activity, including new departments, judicial decisions, property seizures and criminal activity. Yet, he was hard pressed to believe, much as he wished it, that such exposure would cause change, rather than recalcitrant backlash and persecution; as was so often the case.

Beau summarized at the end of his remarks. "I've given you none of the structure that we will recommend to the, yet to be formed, Framing Team. We don't know it yet. We're still trying to put all of this in some order, unencumbered by personal or corporate interest. Heck, we don't even know who will be on that team, either. We do know that we, as the citizens expected to 'soldier on', cannot do so, in good conscience or with any expectation of success, with the status quo. It simply doesn't work anymore. We've tried to give that status quo a name, but have failed. I do know that my grandpa, on the eastern shore of Maryland, would often remark when faced with an obvious fact, "'If it walks like a duck and quacks like a duck, dang it, it's a duck, sure as I'm a shootin' at it.'

"Soon, all the teams will meet to begin the task of defining a new skeleton. It's much too soon to flesh it out, but we hope the skeleton to be as strong, but wish it to be even more resilient and robust, than that which it may supersede. Thank you for your attention." He pointed the remote at the sensor and the screen went to a flag waving over moving scenic montage of wheat fields, mountains, streams and busy city populations. Polite applause began with the guests and spread throughout the theater. As he descended the steps, Janice flew into his arms and the applause exploded along with cheers from the audience, as they stood to exit the theater.

#

The five Executive Committee members assembled in the Day Room after the assembly. Millie high-fived Al Lee. "You guys blew them away. Ellen said she saw emotions ranging from shock to disbelief. Heck, some of the interns on Kathy's and my team hadn't heard half of that." Millie was beside herself with joy and pride in the two members who had validated the worth of the project. She high-fived Beau next. "Damn, you guys are good." She took a deep breath. "Okay, we've got the reception in five minutes. Let's go."

The five filed out of the Day Room and headed to the former Officer's Club, where the reception would be held. Kathy stepped next to Al Lee. "Who was the guy who came up to you after your presentation?"

"I'm not supposed to know, but he's the Dean of Harvard Law. He offered me, in his words, 'an opportunity to matriculate at the nation's oldest university. I told him thanks, but I was already accepted at the nation's best."

Kathy smacked his shoulder as she laughed. "You're hopeless."

Juan walked next to Beau and spoke. "You really gonna hold that President Obama was wrong in trying to bring automatic weapons under control? Dang it, why do you need an AK47?"

"Juan, that's not the issue. Whether I want an AK47 or not, isn't the issue. What's the issue is that the Second Amendment says I can have one and the President tried to stop me by saying I can't buy ammunition!"

"That's just wrong!" Juan's voice was becoming shrill.

"It's the law, Juan." Beau was unsure why Juan was getting upset. "That's why we're here, to defend the rights the Constitution gave us."

"It's stupid." His voice was now loud.

"Guys." Kathy tried to calm them.

"Shut up!"

"Juan! Enough!" Millie yanked him around to face her. "What is wrong with you?"

Juan's hand swept across his brow and he took a breath. He stopped in the street. "Just a minute. Beau!" Beau turned, a mixture of anger and confusion on his face. "I'm sorry, man. Gun control is a real trigger. I try to avoid talkin' about it, but, I guess it can't be avoided here. I'm sorry, you just got the blast and you didn't deserve it."

Beau relaxed a bit. "Juan, we've got to work together. Why is it a trigger?

A pain crossed his face. "A banger with a '47 ran a clip across a gang in Queens a couple years ago. He killed seven 'ricans from a rival gang and two civilians in a store behind 'em. My sister was in that store. She never came out."

"Shit, man. I'm sorry."

"Me, too. Asshole copped a plea. His lawyer said he had a right to own the gun." His hurt eyes looked at Millie. "He didn't have a right to kill my sister, Millie."

#

The reception was somewhat subdued. The restriction on discussing the project was the 800-pound gorilla in the room. The guests, for security purposes, wore a stick-on name tag with their first name. The staff and interns wore their IDs. For obvious reasons, Beau and Al drew most of the interest, although Millie, as chairperson, drew the attention of several the women guests interested in her experience as a female in charge of a potentially world changing project. For the most part, she simply smiled and talked about organizing, negotiating and researching in her own team's area of responsibility. Juan and Kathy retreated to a corner and observed.

"May I call you Jay? I'm David Kn... Sorry, it's hard not to give a name. I was impressed with your analysis of the Framers' intent. Where did you find most of that information?"

Jay knew the trap. His granddaddy had taught him this one. "Mr. Kn, We have access to the Library of Congress and, of course, Google and Wiki. I have a super team of interns who, like I, are being paid to do the very best we can. The facts and history simply structure themselves, as we uncover them." Jay smiled and took a drink of his soda.

"Excuse me. Everyone? I hate to break up a party, but the transportation for our guests is here and we need to be on our way. Several have flights and we have just enough time to get them to the Nashville airport." George paused. "On behalf of the Institute, thank you for coming and acquainting yourselves with the project you are sponsoring. I believe we have demonstrated to you that your trust is not misplaced. Thank you very much."

"George?" Millie walked toward him. "Just a minute." She turned toward the guests. "I'm sorry we were restricted in what we could say today. Let me assure you that 155 of the best young citizens in this country are working to save it, if not for you, then for us and, someday, our children. Thanks."

Holes in the Sand

The Gordian Knot

July 5, 2017 - Camp Donelson

Kathy and Juan were the last two EC members to leave the breakfast meeting. Millie glanced, again, at her notes. They didn't morph into a grand solution. The last of the good vibe left over from the previous day's celebration evaporated into cold hard reality. It was first day of what might just be the hardest part of this project. She thought back to the meeting with George and Dr. Elliot.

#

They had stepped up next to her as they bid farewell to the bus transporting the special guests to the main Fort Campbell complex. Sandwiched as she was, she felt hemmed in.

"Millie," George said, "Dr. Elliot and I need to talk with you about 'next steps'.

She turned to look at him, "Next steps?"

Dr. Elliot double-teamed her. "Yes, we're one third into this project and it's time to put together a time line."

"Uh, okay. Isn't that our job?"

The conversation ping-ponged back to George. "Yes, but we think you might need some help. The next section, if you are true to form, is going to be very contentious."

"I thought you were going to let us run this project? It sounds like you want me to be a puppet for the Founders." Millie took on a purely defensive stance; her arms crossed in front of her and her face taut."

"I told you she wouldn't take it sitting down, George." Dr. Elliot stepped in front of Millie. "That may appear to be so, Millie, but it's not. Can we go to my office and talk about this?"

"No. I won't do this alone. I want some of the other members of the Committee there."

Dr. Elliot looked at George. George's eyebrows were raised. He paused and then shook his head. "We don't want this to become a big thing. It should seem to come from you, as chairperson. How about one member?"

"If that's all I get, I want Al Lee."

"George seemed to chuckle. He looked at Dr. Elliot. "Smart lady. Good choice. I'll go bring him to the office."

Dr. Elliot was reading through a file and Millie was nursing a soda, as George returned with Al Lee. "Hey, Millie. What's up?"

"It appears that they want to drive the train, but make it look like we're in the driver's seat." Her voice had a cutting edge.

"Hey, that violates ..."

"Stop!" Dr. Elliot's voice was sharp. It softened, as he stood and walked around his desk to the table. "Just listen please." He sat. "We did this all wrong. Millie, I'm sorry. It is not what it appears. Really. Please, just listen. George sit down, but let me talk. Al, you just listen, too."

He signed. "Look, Millie. We're used to setting schedules, reading reports and subordinates who report to us. You aren't accustomed to either. So, let's try this again and we'll both be better off." Millie pushed her soda away and sat back in the chair. She stared directly at Dr. Elliot, but her arms were still crossed.

"Okay. I've read the notes all your groups have written. You knew that we would, so it's no surprise. What *is* a surprise is the depth of understanding and analysis that you have all done.

In fact, I'm glad you're here Al, despite the reason. Ishmael is so impressed with your work that he's trying to convince me to bring you onto the staff of the Institute, as an intern, after your freshman year."

Al didn't quite know what to say. "I, uh, don't think I should reply to that, sir. I haven't even registered for my first day yet, and UVA is one tough school."

"You are absolutely right, but I wanted you to hear it from me, before Ishmael let his mouth get ahead of his brain." He looked back at Millie. "Sorry for the sidebar, Millie. What we think you should do is accelerate the schedule. You know enough now, we think, to begin to line up the elements of a new document. Mind you, we're not telling you how to line them up. We just know that you're going to be up against some serious structural and legal issues that have taken 230 years to get tangled up in bureaucracy and personal interests."

"We've been talking about that, but no matter where we want to start, it's always dependent on something else. We can't find the end to pull."

"Welcome to the world of Constitutional law, Millie. But, are you open to a suggestion? And, I mean that. It is a suggestion ... only. But, it is the way I would tackle this, if it were mine to tackle. But, then, my ordered mind is colored by years of habit. Yours is open to creativity. That's why we brought all of you in."

Millie's arms dropped, and her hands fell flat on the table. It was a bare release of the tension, but George breathed a silent sigh of relief. She replied in a flat voice, "I always listen to suggestions."

"Thanks. I suggest you gather your team leads, and their assistants or recorders or however you've set up your groups. Start with an issue, or special interest, or some element, it doesn't matter which, and put it in its cubbyhole in the project. One element might be 'include', which means it will be dealt with in the document. Another is 'right', or 'freedom' and I know Ms.

Greer has a whole litany of these, some quite controversial. See where I'm going?" Millie and Al both were listening, but also trying to process in their own way.

George spoke up. "May I, Dr. Elliot?" He received a nod. "Do you remember the parable of the wise men? If they had talked together they would have been able to analyze their puzzle quickly. So, treat each line item, if you will, individually. See how, current infrastructure, its relationship to the Constitution, interrelationships with other line items and any future structure might work. Even if you leave a thread hanging for future discussion as you analyze a relationship, you will know what to do with that line item."

"I think I understand what you're saying." Al leaned in toward Millie. "Look Millie, do you remember how I first laid out the governmental organization, primary laws and the Constitution? I did it with a bunch of post-it notes stuck to the wall." He looked at Dr. Elliot as he spoke, now. "So, we take, oh say 'taxes' and we see what taxes are collected right now, where they're authorized, or not authorized, in the foundation document and how that revenue will be accumulated in the new government, for lack of a more inclusive term." Millie's head turned, but it was obvious she was thinking his words through. He turned to look at George? "Close?"

George shook his head. "Exactly correct, Al. Quickly reduce each issue to its smallest state; who, what, where, why and how? You'll be surprised how quickly it will clear."

"Yeah, clear like the Mississippi; fast, muddy and treacherous." Millie muttered, as she took a deep breath. "Look, I'm sorry I thought you were trying to take over, but it's been really weird being left alone to drive a project as important as this one. Yesterday's guests seemed to be skeptical, at best, and a couple in complete disbelief, that we could do this. I was waiting for the other shoe to drop. I think there is much merit to the way you suggest we do this. I do have a request, though."

"Shoot." Both Elliot and George answered simultaneously.

"I want a DA to work with each team. It really is time that we had some 'adult supervision'. If we're going to start breaking down things like 'religious freedom', taxes, term limits, 'checks and balances', immigration and the balanced budget, we're going to need more knowledge than we can dig up from Wiki in a month, and probably ringmasters and riot police."

Dr. Elliot chuckled. "Fair enough. You and your committee assign them, as you think their value lies. But, you don't have a month, either. You need to start writing no later than July 22 to stay on schedule."

Al Lee laughed out loud. "And I thought we'd be rushed. Hey, we'll have time to sleep at least a couple nights a week."

#

Millie shook the memory of the day before out of her mind. The meeting she had just concluded had been stressful enough. She was, however, glad that Al Lee had been there with her. His insight and support made delivering the news of the direction change much easier. In short, it was a 2 to 5 discussion and Kathy always went with whatever Al wanted. Beau and Juan were another thing, however.

She flipped over her copy of the list that Sally had written up in a table format.

Health Care	Budget	Defense
Veterans	National Resources	Entitlements
International Relations	Immigration	Gun Control
Taxation	Term Limits	Legislative Makeup

"My God what a mess! How will we ever make this into a cohesive document that we can agree upon, and we're only 155 out of 315 million?

Bites of the Elephant

July 6, 2017

Ishmael eased himself into the Day Room and sat in a chair.

"Look. The only way to keep out of debt is to write in the requirement for a balanced budget. I'm sure the Framers didn't intend a National Debt."

"You might be surprised. Start with history. Our first debt dates to 1781. The first Secretary of the Treasury, none other than Alexander Hamilton, felt that a National Debt was a good thing 'so long as it is not excessive'.

"He was wrong! You can't run a government in the red. State constitutions and city charters all require a balanced budget. So, should we."

Ishmael saw Jane Abrams stand up. "Hang on. Both of you sit down. You each have good points, but listen to me. The Federal Government is the funder of last resort. Try this simple example. A city must fund schools, so they use tax money. But, the state levies new requirements that the city didn't plan for. So, the state grants them money that they've raised through taxes. If the state needs money for federally required programs, the federal government funds them. But, there is no one to give money to the federal government. They have only taxation on the debit side of their ledger. If they plan well, a balanced budget will work."

The young man on that side of the argument grinned. "But, wait." She continued. "A hurricane sweeps the east coast and causes $500 million in damage. The federal budget doesn't provide for that much. Or, an entitlement grows beyond the original funding. Where does the central government get the money? Why they raise taxes, of course."

The advocate of debt piped up. "Most people won't support new taxes; especially when they don't see it directly benefiting them."

Jane tilted her head, "So flood insurance isn't paid, and cities don't get disaster aid. Aid to dependent children runs out and food stamps are no longer honored, or the unemployed don't get money for food or school lunches end or farm subsidies are canceled, and prices rise. Or, do you borrow money? May I have the envelope please?"

"It's not that simple, Jane."

Ishmael stood. "Actually, it is. A balanced budget for the funder of last resort is exactly that simple. Of course, congress has passed laws and made promises that caused spending that they never provided funding sources for. Therein lies the real rub, not whether there is a balanced budget, but are there controls on promises and payments for it."

"So, what is our approach?"

Ishmael smiled. "Now, that is not my job, guys. That's yours. See how it's been done by other countries or by other organizations. Check it against the document and design how to do it going forward that doesn't cause the same disruptions. Oh, and figure out a way to pay down the debt, at the same time." He turned to leave. Over his shoulder, he said, "But, you never heard it from me."

#

"This is nuts", Kathy said as she threw her shoulder bag on the floor and slumped onto the couch in the Day Room; now unoccupied by a team but beginning to be populated by the 'after dinner' crowd.

"Aside from everything, what is nuts, girl friend?" Olivia Carson closed her laptop and slid down, from the end of the couch.

Kathy rubbed her eyes and leaned back. "We've been dealing with 'entitlements' all … damn … day. All we want to do is sort them out and define them, but we're playing 'whack a mole'. 'Is it an entitlement?' 'What is an entitlement?' 'Who's entitled?' 'How's it funded?' I'm surprised half of Congress hasn't gone postal."

"Look. I come from Mississippi. We got more people on some Federal program than, probably, any other state. Heck, I don't know. Maybe the governor is drawing some check. Problem is that generations grow up with some government check as their revenue. They expect it. How are you gonna fix that? You can't just tell half of Mississippi, 'I'm sorry, but we're gonna stop all those programs. Just git over it'. Kathy, that just ain't gonna fly. This time they won't fire on Fort Sumter. They'll burn Washington to the ground. That is, if they can find money to get a bus ticket."

Kathy smiled. "Olivia, believe it or not, I heard that one today, too. Every possible defense of 'promised money' was on the table. I couldn't tell the players without a score card. I had North vs South, Republican vs Democrat vs Independent, Conservative vs Liberal, Poor vs Rich. I swear the only thing I didn't have at some point was Paper vs Plastic. Strangely, though, the race card was never on the table. I think everyone knew where that was going to go and just didn't go there."

The scoot of a chair brought Jay into the conversation. "Are you sure you weren't in the Citizen Freedoms discussion group today? I admit that I'm a solid Mormon, but I'm not sure St. John Paul II could help on this one."

"Freedom of 'fill in the blank'?"

"Absolutely. The simple words of the First Amendment 'Congress shall make no law respecting an establishment of religion, or prohibiting the free exercise thereof.' I heard more interpretations of those sixteen words than the sixteen factorial combinations possible. If they'd let me, I'd call my bishop and tell him to move the temple to Australia."

Kathy snorted and covered the laugh. Quickly recovering, "That bad, huh?"

"Oh man, you have no idea. The interpretations are painful. The problem is that, to me, they all boil down to 'Render to Caesar the things that are Caesar's, and to God, the things that are God's.' But, how do you write that into the document of a secular-by-design governmental structure? Just what does it mean?"

"Give me an example. Oh, I'm Olivia."

Jay looked at the young black woman, to see if he recognized her, then continued. "Hi Olivia, Jay. Example, huh? Okay. I'm Mormon. We believe that marriage is a sacred covenant between man and woman. We also believe that gays and lesbians are living in sin and damned to hell. Yet, the Federal government says they can get married and that living together is legal and okay. Both sides of the argument use the same words; parroting the Constitution. 'Prohibiting the free exercise thereof.' It just doesn't work. The Constitution can't be a Mobius loop."

A new voice entered the conversation. "May I join the melee? I see one space left on the couch."

"The more the merrier," Kathy said, scooting over. "You're To Wan Lin, right?"

"Indeed. And you are Kathy Greer." He sat on the couch, but sat ramrod straight with both feet on the ground and his hands on his knees. "If I may add a dram to the scales, we are all trying to solve all the problems, in a black and white way. My grandfather would say that black and white do not exist in nature. Black, like cold, is the absence, the vacuum. White, like heat, is the total, the collection of all, in one place."

"Nice words, friend, but how do they relate to our, what did you call it, a mobius loop; a two-dimensional object that appears to have only one side?"

"Let me try a very simplistic example. Take all the entitlements that relate to survival. Include food stamps, Aid to Dependent Children, Unemployment etc. What are these? They are piled in a basket labeled 'a right to live'. Now, I do not include, in that very close title the 'right to life' argument, for that is an entirely different item and not an entitlement, at all."

"Oh, an unborn child doesn't have a right to live?" Jay burst into To Lin's explanation.

"Jay, I did not say that. Let's not mix our apples and oranges, please. I said that, what is, gently, called 'reproductive rights', is not an entitlement, as that word is used in the current manner."

Olivia asked, "So, what you're saying is that we redefine everything, reducing it to a least common denominator and deal with that?"

"I think it is worth an attempt. At any rate, can we do worse than I have heard here, or, in fact, in my own group which, is hopelessly locked in a round robin discussion, and I use that term loosely, of immigration and citizenship. Even Confucius would be confused." His stiff countenance melted, and he collapsed into the cushions of the couch and closed his eyes.

"You guys got room for one more frustrated intern?" The voice came from behind the couch Kathy was sitting on. She, To Lin and Oliva all twisted around. Their heads tipped down, almost in unison. Jane Abrams sat on the floor in a yoga pose.

"Jane?"

The diminutive black girl unfolded her legs and flipped to her knees. "For the record, meditation doesn't help either."

"Sister, what are you doing down there?"

"Olivia, it's called 'Savasana'. It's a lot better than the translation, let me tell you. It's a restorative pose and after being deluged by term limits, checks and balances and legislative makeup, I definitely need to be restored." She grunted as she stood and stretched her back. "Would you welcome an idea from the most 'outside' member of this group of 'outsiders'?"

Jay filled the question. "What do you mean outside?"

"Jay, my fine Arizona native, I'm a black, female Mormon in Kentucky with a hundred people who think Mormons all have two heads and twenty wives."

"You're not the only Mormon here, Jane. We're all treated the same way."

"No, Jay, 'we're' not," she snapped. "But, we'll not air the laundry of our faith in this forum." She stared at him until he looked away, then she continued. "As I was saying, there may be too many people pulling too many strings in too many directions."

"No argument there. And, I apologize."

Jane dipped her head in acceptance, but didn't break stride as she walked around the couch and dropped into the lotus position, on the floor. "We are a representative democracy. Why? Because, even when there were only three and a half million people, there were too many people with too many opinions to make a success of running a country. So, we elect representatives to 'represent' our will and grant them the power to do so. Please write down 'grant them the power'. Even 465 of them can't do it well, so they break up into committees to deal with the details. And those committees break up into subcommittees. My guess is that parts of subcommittees break up into meetings to do the dirty work of governing."

"Okay, that's the short version of how we get nothing done, but where are you headed?" Olivia wasn't quite as quick as Kathy.

"No, wait. Are you saying that, even as we, broken into small groups, that we won't be able to refine this?"

"Well, the jury is still out, but how was your day? Mine sucked."

A thin smile spread over To Lin's face, despite his closed eyes.

Kathy beckoned for her to continue.

"Okay, just let me ramble for a bit. If the Institute guys want us to 'reinvent America', it must be because the problem is too big and complicated for the elected officials; all of whom have loyalties that they cannot violate without signing up for unemployment. I think we can understand that. So, they invite 155 'unsullied' minds to a remote location and toss the hot potato in our laps. Why?

"If we succeed, they look great and have earned their pence. We get our grants and go on to college, or wherever, as a footnote in history. Believe me, the headlines *will* go to them. There will be no cereal boxes or sneaker deals for us. However, I digress. If 465 of America's leaders can't do it, how can 155 of us? Because, we don't know that we can't. That's why. And, that's our greatest weapon."

"Jane. Even if you're right, we look just like them, only younger. We're going around and around the same philosophical merry-go-round."

Jane shifted her position, but didn't break her train of thought. "We're still too many and, more importantly, no one is 'in charge'. You cannot solve a problem, especially a complex one, by committee. I'll pause for anyone who wishes to dispute that. Long enough. I think, it was almost deliberate, on their part.

They created an organization for us and are guiding it toward their ends ... designed defeat.

"Kathy, I think you should talk with the Executive Committee and suggest that the 'committee of the whole' give them, or some other group the power to write the document and the authority to say, 'here it is'. They'll have the notes and they know where the resident experts are among the interns. When it's done, a larger group looks at it, a conference committee, if you will, to flesh out areas needing work. Finally, the entire group gets to discuss it in a non-destructive way. I want to work it with 'how can we', not 'why we cannot'."

"You want to build from the inside out?"

"Even the mighty redwood began as a seed."

A Palace Revolt

July 7, 2017

"That is the damnedest idea I've ever heard. It's positively brilliant." Al Lee shook his head as he let the ramifications sink in.

"What bothers me most, is not the idea. I love that. It's her supposition that we're being 'used'. I've gotten nothing but help from the DAs."

"I know. I tend to agree, but I'm going to be just a bit more aware. You weren't there last night. Ideas were flying around like Pennsylvania black flies in August."

"I suppose we could discuss it" Millie spoke up. "Heaven knows we're not getting anywhere now. We're three days in and everyone is just frustrated."

Kathy paused for a moment, then plowed right into it. "I want to suggest that Jane be put on the Executive Committee."

"Why do we need that?"

"I think the EC and a few others should write it, but she's got all the ideas. I think people are more likely to support her enthusiasm and ideas, if she's one of the 'leaders.'"

"You know that one of us would have to step down to bring her on. She would have to be 'elected' by the whole group."

"I know. In her own words, she's got the issues of black, female and Mormon."

Millie barked. "For God's sake those are defining characteristics, not issues. I think 155 of today's brightest high school students can be trusted to see beyond that."

Juan added, "At least enough for a majority. Look. I'll step down, if it helps. It's great being on the committee, but I'm viewed as a token, by most of the interns. Maybe Jane will be viewed as a better choice. Can't we use our own contacts to make the 'followers' follow? I'll still have input, anyway. I just won't have the private office, secretary or key to the executive washroom."

Millie giggled. "Let's let this stew until lunch. I'll see if Jane even wants to be on the committee. Let's have lunch together and see what we think. I can't make that big a decision without running it around a few times. Don't talk to the DAs about it and few, if any, of the interns. Right now, it's an Executive Committee thing. Okay?"

July 10, 2017

"Have a minute, George?" Ishmael had Ellen with him and was leaning in the door to George's office.

"Sure." He looked at the time, on his laptop. "A bit early for the meeting. Something up?"

Ellen took the lead. "Well, we're not sure. The attitude of the Executive Committee has changed a bit."

George stopped looking at his screen and turned to give the two lead DAs his undivided attention. "How so?"

"It's barely negligible, but they're easing us to the sidelines," Ishmael added.

George pointed at a pair of chairs. "Look, I've no desire to play verbal ping-pong. One of you take the lead and tell me what you think is going on?"

Ishmael pointed at Ellen. "She felt it first. You tell him, Ellen." George focused on her and beckoned for her to continue.

George cocked his head. "Felt it? You're a psychologist, Ellen, not a medium." He grinned at her.

Ellen stuck her tongue out at him. "It really *is* just a feeling, George. I first sensed it a couple of days after the 4th. We're still welcome, but if we sit in on a meeting or session, the subjects are mundane and routine. I'm not hearing any of the sparks and creative analysis, that I heard in the first trimester."

"I agree with Ellen, George. I checked with the other DAs and they're all getting the same treatment. To put it bluntly, I don't know what they're up to, but they're up to something."

"Come on, guys. What can they be up to? They're here to analyze, create and write. That's all. I think they're just in a different mode. I know that they're all upset by the sheer complexity of this thing. Isn't that why we brought them in?"

"I have to disagree. I don't know why. Hunches aren't admissible, but I've got a hunch. For one thing, the Executive Committee has met every day, for at least two hours, and Jane Abrams has been there."

That piece of information caused George to turn his head and look hard at Ishmael. "That's interesting. See if you can find someone to ferret out what's up. Dr. Elliot doesn't seem to want Jane too close to the top, for now."

Ellen asked, "Why is that? She's a darned good arbitrator."

"I'm not certain, but that's one reason. Why he wouldn't want her skills working out compromises to these polarizing issues, I don't know. Just keep an eye out."

#

The closing credits of the movie were still on the screen, as Beau nudged Janice. "Hey, I think you missed the big finish."

She mumbled and then stretched. "I know how it ends, hon. Sorry, I fell asleep."

"I don't know. Can I tell everyone you slept with me?"

Janice elbowed him. "You do, and you never will."

Beau leaned down to kiss her as the door knocked. "Crap. Hang on!" He untangled Janice from his shoulder, rolled off the bed and walked to the door. As he opened it, he looked at his watch and then at Al Lee and Millie. "What in the heck can you guys want at 11:30 at night?"

"We need to talk with you for a bit." Millie looked past him. "Hi, Janice. Beau can we come in?"

"There's not a lot of chairs, guys. Can we go to the lounge?"

"No. We'll sit on the floor. We don't want to give anyone a reason to talk about a late-night meeting between Committee members."

Beau shrugged and stepped back, pulling the door open. Millie and Al stepped in. Beau closed the door and turned on the overhead light. Millie looked at Janice. "I'm sorry to intrude, Janice."

Janice smiled. "Don't worry about it. You didn't bust up anything." She snickered and stuck out her tongue at Beau. "At least not tonight. Do I need to leave?"

Beau spoke up. "You may as well let her stay. I'll tell her everything as soon as you leave, anyway."

Jay smirked and shook his head. "Darned women. Okay. Janice, just keep everything between you and Beau. Okay?" She nodded, but had a quizzical look on her face. "Beau, you know that Juan is going to step aside. We want to put Jane Manning Abrams on the Executive Committee. She is really great at arbitrating and making conflicts understandable."

"Yeah, Kathy told me. So? I like Jane. She'll get my vote."

Millie picked up the thread. "Your vote is only one of 155. We need 78 votes to put her in."

"And that's where the problem is," said Al. "We think the DAs and, through them, the Institute, don't want her on the committee."

"First off, they aren't supposed to have a say in that. Secondly, why the hell not? We've got factions breaking into factions. If we ever needed a good 'negotiator', it's now."

"I know that. But, some of the kids are telling me that the DAs are talking up other possible candidates. The issue there is that they've not been told that Juan is going to resign."

Janice couldn't help it. "Wow. You mean we've got a leak somewhere?"

"That, or someone got sloppy. Olivia said that Joyce was sitting at a lunch table and commented that Jane didn't have enough leadership skills to be on the committee. Of course, she couched it in other words, but the idea was to discredit Jane."

"What kind of crap is that?"

"We don't know. What we do know is that we need a solid front to get Jane in, with no further interference. We've been careful not to talk about real issues when the DAs are around and Jane's idea to drive all the way to atomic level, seems to be working. But, the analysis is going to come out soon, and we need Jane in a position to lead, when we start putting it back together."

Beau sat on the edge of the bed. Janice scooted up and put her hands on his shoulders. "Okay, obviously, I've missed some of the stuff that's driving this, but it makes sense. What can I do?"

Millie took off. "All five of us, and that includes Juan, need to actively work with our separate groups to support Jane. Look there are about 18 to 20 of us doing most of the heavy lifting. That's more than ten percent and reasonable. There are 40 or 50 that work hard and follow. That's not the 78, we need. Try to get your involved interns to 'mentor' one or more of the others, when we announce the election. We're going to publish Juan's resignation tomorrow and have the election on Thursday. We can't wait any longer. We need to get back to work. More importantly, we need to make this a fait accompli before the DAs and Institute can counter with a different candidate."

Janice had a thought. "How do we keep 'the leak' from, uh, 'leaking'?"

"That we do not know. Other than impressing each person with the idea that this is an 'internal' thing and none of the business of the DAs. Just don't discuss it if one of them, or George, for heaven's sake, are around."

"Hey, I've got an idea on how to whittle down where the leak is." Janice flipped off the bed and stood up.

"We're listening." Al beckoned for an answer.

"Okay. In the book <u>The Word</u> by Irving Wallace, they had a spy. It's a book about the supposed discovery of a gospel that completely changed the story of Jesus. Anyway, they wrote twelve memos, each talking about a different disciple. When the leak surfaced, they knew who it was because he had leaked one of the twelve names. Get it?"

Al clenched his fist. "You know that might work in some way. Millie, how about this?"

July 11, 2017

Dr. Gilbert picked up the phone handset. "Gilbert"

"Harold, George. I've got some news. I just don't know if it's good, bad or just news. Juan Morales has resigned from the EC. They're going to announce it at lunch, in the dining hall. They've got two people in mind as nominees for the interns to select from, Jane Manning Abrams, the girl from Utah and, Mike tells me, the big kid from Hawaii, Kona Opana."

"What the hell? How come this is a surprise? And, why is he resigning?"

"Ellen and Ishmael came to see me a couple of days ago. They said they 'felt', they used the word 'felt', that the EC was up to something, but they weren't getting any good information, when they sat in or talked with the interns; even the ones that are really friendly."

"Let me guess. Al Lee and Millie?"

"They do seem to be in the thick of it, yes."

"I can ask them to meet with me, to see what's going on."

"I wouldn't do that unless you have to, sir. That would let them know that we have 'ears'. We told them that we would give them absolute freedom of action. If we seem to know what they're doing, it will make it worse and confirm what Ellen thinks."

"Okay. I suppose we're in charge in the end, anyway. We are the ones publishing any results. How do we keep the Abrams girl from being selected?"

"The only way I can figure is to push, gently, for the Opana kid."

"Push gently, George, gently. I do not want Miss Abrams on that committee."

"For the sake of my curiosity, why not? She's smart as a Whip."

"And just as unmanageable, George. So far, we've managed to nudge things the direction we want by using Ellen's experience with subliminal persuasion. She's had no luck at all with the Abrams kid. That makes her a loose cannon. No, get Opana elected somehow."

To Catch a Thief

The lead menu item was tacos and the smell of tomatoes, cheese and chili filled the dining hall. Millie looked up from the traditional EC table and saw that Ellen, Joyce and Ishmael were eating with various tables of interns. She looked at Al. He gave her a grin and a thumbs up. She smiled back, stood and picked up a pan cover that she had commandeered from the serving line a few moments before. She took her table knife and reversed it. Then she smacked the knife handle against the pan, as if beating a ranch triangle. It wasn't melodic, but its clanging first drew attention, and then drew quiet in the hall. "Sorry to interrupt lunch. I'll only take a minute. I promise that your taco won't be soggy. Now, based solely upon table count, we have a quorum, so I have an announcement to make that won't wait until Friday.

"Executive Committee member, Juan Morales, submitted his resignation this morning. His reasons are enough that the committee has reluctantly accepted it, effective immediately. He'll still be an integral part of our job, especially when representing the views of the unofficial 51st state, Puerto Rico, and a segment of the minority citizenship.

"That leaves a vacancy on the committee, at a very inconvenient time. Juan nominated his own replacement and, while that is certainly unusual, there's nothing wrong with it. He has suggested that we put the name of Jane Manning Abrams up for election. I so propose at this time."

Olivia Carson thrust her hand into the air. "Second the nomination." Ellen's head turned at the immediate response, to what should have been a surprise.

Millie continued. "We have one nominee. Are there any more from the floor? If so, we will assemble a slate of nominees and hold an election. If not, I'm going to call for a voice vote, just to get this off our plate."

"Has Jane agreed to run?"

The diminutive young woman stood. "I was asked earlier this morning. If my skills can be of use to the project, by my serving on the committee, I'll be happy to allow my name to be in nomination."

Across the room, Ishmael was sitting near Kona. "I thought you were also nominated."

Kona looked surprised. "Me? Oh, heck no, bruddah. I don't like being out in front of nothin'. I'm happy right where I am."

A cold chill hit Ishmael's stomach. Something was happening, and it was happening damned fast.

"Seeing no hands and hearing no argument, I move the nominations be closed." Oy Palomuto was serving well as Millie's shill.

"There is a motion to close the nominations. Do I hear a second?"

"Hey, I can second that one, too." Olivia's response brought laughter from her table and a comment, from a friend.

"Always number 2, huh, Olivia?"

She responded with a raspberry that brought another laugh.

"It is moved and seconded that the nominations to fill a vacancy on the Executive Committee be closed. All in favor?" A rumble of 'ayes swept the hall. "Opposed?" The obligatory dozen hands and 'nays were raised.

"There are always a few who just have to be different." A general laugh ran across the room. "Nominations are hereby closed. There being only one nominee, the chair moves for election by acclamation. All in favor?"

A generally loud 'Aye', resounded.

"Opposed?" She was thoroughly surprised that the naysayers saved the effort this time. "By acclamation, Jane Manning Abrams of Utah is elected to the Executive Committee. This impromptu meeting of the committee of the whole is adjourned. We now return you to your plates of rice, beans and tacos. Thank you." Millie sat down, a Cheshire grin on her face.

#

"I get the distinct impression that we were just had." The DAs were gathered in the Institute conference room, awaiting George and Dr. Elliot. Ellen bemoaned, "I just don't know how."

Ishmael chuckled. "That, my dear, was a classic piece of political railroading. We were left standing on the platform when the train left the station."

"What are you talking about?"

"When a caucus wants something done, but isn't sure about the opposition position, they meet in secret and plan it all out. Then, with no warning, a quorum call puts just enough votes in the hall, and a carefully choreographed script is executed; in this case the nomination and election of one Jane Manning Abrams to the Executive Committee with the full knowledge that we, nominally the opposition, were not in favor of same. I had forgotten that Miss Dickinson is the highly intelligent daughter of a state delegate, from Ohio. She's learned well at her father's knee."

"You sure it wasn't Al Lee?"

"Uh uh. Al isn't a political animal. His family is, historically, above political infighting. I'd say Millie inherited the very best political traits of the honorable John Dickinson of Pennsylvania. What I haven't figured out is that 'red herring' about Kona Opana. I know I was led to believe he would be a nominee."

"I was told it was going to be Lena Nordstrom, not Opana," Joyce said.

"I believe I can help explain that." George walked in followed by Dr. Elliot. They sat at the table and he began. "We just had a very interesting visit with the very Miss Dickinson you are discussing. I believe we may have underestimated our young leadership.

"She actually wanted to see George, so I sat quietly. She informed George that she was adding an 'archivist', I believe was the word she used, to assist Sally with records keeping and to help her with off-time activities coordination. The young man is a Michael Taylor, of Oregon. She wanted George to know that Mr. Taylor would not be participating in any of the analysis and authoring activities any longer."

Bill Walters muttered, "Crap!"

George showed a conspiratorial smile. "Would it be a reasonable assumption, Mr. Walters, that, based upon that utterance, that you are having a Van Gogh moment?"

Bill sighed, nodded and slumped back in his chair.

"Mr. Walters has just lost an 'ear' in the intern camp, my friends. I believe we were entrapped by the simple ruse of giving each of you the name of a different potential nominee, if you had someone in that group keeping you informed, 'sub mensa' or for those who attended less prestigious schools, 'under the table'. Apparently, the young Mr. Taylor has been found out and exiled to purgatory for the duration."

Dr. Elliot added the post script. "But, what the hell are they up to?"

Metamorphosis

Chrysalis

July 11, 2017

"Well, that worked like a Swiss watch. Welcome to the Committee, Jane."

"Thanks. For what it's worth, that was almost fun. Did you see Ellen's face?"

Millie chuckled. "I did. Daddy told me about that little gambit, but I never saw it. I'm really surprised it worked."

Al said, "The problem with silver bullets is that you only get to shoot them once. We are now in an adversarial relationship with our bosses. We need to remember that."

"I'm operating on the assumption that they still want us to do the job they gave us. All we've done is, sort of, notify them that we're going to do it our way."

"I guess since my skills as an arbitrator are what caught your attention, I should advise that the next step is in their court. Just have the guys do the job as we're laying it out. If they take issue with it, we'll know where we stand."

July 14, 2017

The Executive Committee met, by design, at 4:00 pm every Friday, to discuss the week's progress. This week, Juan, Oy, Janice and To Lin were also in attendance, along with Sally; ostensibly to take notes. But, she was often the lubricant that kept the meeting moving.

"Okay, this meeting is called to order. I'd like a quick consensus on how the DAs are behaving. I'll start. I've had Joyce, Ellen and Mike sit in at various time. It's amicable. Only Mike has asked about the new analysis process. I kept nothing back. His only comment was 'Ingenious'."

Al Lee raised his arm, from the elbow, to be heard. Millie nodded at him. "Interestingly, Ishmael cornered me and expressed a certain disappointment in what we had done. No. Strike that. He was disappointed in what I had done. His words, 'I thought we had a good working relationship.' I simply told him that we do and continued with the day's effort. Other than that, I've seen him, Joyce and Ellen. Oh, George did a drive-by on Wednesday, but didn't have anything to say."

"George stopped me after lunch on Wednesday and congratulated me on being elected. He asked what Juan's reason was for resigning. I told him I didn't know, since I wasn't on the committee then." She grinned.

"Nicely done, Jane. Perfect answer." Millie added. "Come to think of it, George pulled up a cup of coffee after dinner last night and asked me if there was any reason that Mike was chosen for the archivist position. I told him that Mike enjoyed doing 'planning kinds of things' and that it seemed a logical choice. He then asked if there was any problem with him. I told him that all we expected him to do is concentrate on his new job."

"I do believe they are aware of what we did." Al said.

"Too late to worry about it. Anyone else?"

All the folks present, except for To Lin, had had encounters with the DAs in the three days since the election. The consensus was that they were acting as if nothing untoward had occurred, but were very attentive to every detail of how the new analysis was going.

"Well at least, we're not in a hot war," said Juan.

"I'll take that and move on. Jane, how is the revised analysis going?"

"All told, pretty good. The guys doing what are now called 'Citizen Freedoms' are still sorting and resorting, but at least they're not arguing. It took me about two hours of working with them to get them to understand that definitions of a freedom do not include all interpretations. I tried to get them to list 'exclusions. That seemed to help."

"What are exclusions?" asked Kathy.

"Things that are *not* rights, but rather wants. Example. We have a right to seek employment in any field we choose, regardless of race, religion, etc. But we do *not* have a right to gainful employment in any field. That means that no one *has* to hire us in the field we desire; providing all other laws are observed. Another? We have a right to seek an education to any level and in any field, but we have no guarantee that we will be able to obtain the education desired or, more importantly, that someone else will pay the bill. Those sort of things help them to corral the real rights."

"Doesn't that impact public education?" This one from Oy.

"We're defining rights, not details, Oy. Legislation will have to speak to the details. There are a myriad of models from other countries that can be compared with ours. That's out of our scope, right now."

Millie observed. "That sounds great, but the unanswered question is whether they'll be ready to write on the 22nd."

"I wish I had that answer. Right now, it's 'que sera sera', what will be, will be."

"I guess we have no choice but to live with that for now. Al, how about structure?"

"The best I can say is that the consensus is to retain the original three branches. Beyond that it's 'Katey, bar the door'. The group is so far outside the box that they've got a team redefining the meaning of 'box'; term limits, length of terms, removability, how elected, eligibility, all of it. They decided that there would be no 'sacred cows', and the last I knew there were dead 'cows' all over the room."

"Graphic as always, Mr. Lee. Thank you."

"I'm not done, Millie. They seem to have adopted a mantra that intrigues me, 'Because we used to do it that way, ain't good enough today'. I'm still trying to figure out exactly what it means."

#

Leonard Bromberg and Dr. Elliot were walking back toward the residence hall, following the Shabbat service. Leonard still wore his prayer shawl. As they passed before the library, they noticed Al Lee sitting on a bench in the near darkness of the mid-summer evening. "Dr. Elliot, excuse me, I want to talk with Al for a bit."

"Certainly, Leonard. Shalom." He looked toward Alvin. "Shalom, Mr. Lee."

"Good evening, Dr. Elliot." Dr. Elliot walked on and Leonard sat down next to Alvin. "What's up Leonard?"

"I thought of your studies this evening, as we were at Shabbat."

"Why would that happen?"

"The discussion was about why the Hebrew people had different forms of government, as their times and fortunes changed throughout time."

"Did you reach any conclusions?"

Leonard laughed. "The one universal truth is that a Jew never reaches a single conclusion, my friend. We were six at Shabbat. We reached no less than seven conclusions."

Alvin laughed.

"Seriously, Al. We Jews have a history more than 4,000 years long. We've grown from a tribal patriarchy to kings, rabbis and now a genuine legislature in Israel. Each was defined by the differences in the driving environment."

"Okay, and you're headed where?"

"This country is a mere 230 years old. We Jews have had arguments longer than that. What is it that causes the Constitution, that is that young in the lives of men, to become impotent; apparently unable to function?"

"Let me try to put it into a couple of sentences. I should warn you, though, that these sentences are open to endless interpretation. Okay? At the highest level, the big five reasons are population, diversity, education, transportation and communication.

"Consider population. Two centuries ago this country had one percent the population we have today. The land area that stretched, at the greatest distance, 300 miles from the Atlantic, now spreads ten times farther west. Alaska is larger in square miles than the original thirteen colonies.

"Number two, diversity. The overwhelming population, specifically the voting population, of colonial America was white, male, Episcopal and of English extraction. Within narrow parameters, they all had the same background, beliefs and expectations. It would be safe to say that WASP, White Anglo-Saxon Protestant males are a negligible minority today. Measurable portions of our population are African American, notably from divergent cultures, Hispanic, Asian, again from a mélange of populations, Native American and a cornucopia of subcultures, and even more significantly, religions of all makes and models available world-wide.

"Let's keep going. Education. It would be fair to say, that the clear majority of the 3.5 million 'first citizens' were illiterate or, at best, could read the Bible. It was, in fact, the American Revolution that gave rise to universal and, more importantly, public education. Today, the percentage of illiteracy is a single digit percentage and the percentage of college graduates rises every year.

"Okay, grabbing a quick breath, I'll move to transportation. It took more than five days for John Adams to travel from Philadelphia to Boston and Jefferson packed an overnight bag to travel from Monticello to Williamsburg; a drive of four hours for Adams and ninety minutes for Jefferson, today. Trains, planes and automobiles didn't exist anywhere except in the folios of Da Vinci. I can bicycle in one hour the distance my forefathers traveled in a single day.

"Now, the piece de resistance, communication. Newspapers, brochures and broadsides were the rule of the day. That and, of course, the pastor, constable and town gossip. News did not travel fast, if it traveled at all. Books were expensive and, other than the family Bible, rare in the everyday home. Today, a 'selfie' sent from Rome, Italy is in Rome, Georgia in seconds and a New York Times best seller resides on your cell phone.

"It's simply not Kansas, anymore, Leonard. The seams of the Constitution, a container comfortably sized for 3.5 million homogeneous souls, are stretched so tight, as to be incapable of governing today's United States in any meaningful fashion."

"You paint an abysmal portrait of our future, Al."

"That's certainly not my intent, Leonard. Please do not misconstrue what I've said. I'm simply laying out the challenges facing the new Framers in renovating the framework, by which we govern. We need to use the rainbow of differences to strengthen the form and function. That is eminently doable; so long as we don't play Lot's Wife and look back. As a nation, we have no choice, literally none, but to move ahead and recognize the entirely foreign parameters within which we must work."

"I've never heard it explained that way."

"I'm sorry to say that the leadership is afraid to lay out the breadth and depth of the extremis, in which the Constitution lies. I would say that anyone capable of understanding it beyond the very rudimentary explanation I've given you, has a stake in the current game that they are unwilling to share or surrender."

"Can 155 High School graduates reinvent it?"

"Well, for one thing, it is highly likely that we have no stake in the past or current state. None of us is a 'trust fund' recipient. And, it is certain that each of us has a stake in the future. It is, after all, our future."

"You need to run for office someday."

#

"You're kidding, right?" George leaned forward toward Joyce.

"I wish I were. I asked twice to clarify. They want to write in, not only term limits for members of the lower house, but completely restructure the upper house, along ancient Greek lines. I tried to pry details out of them, but To Lin said they're not ready to say anything yet. I did get an inkling of huge changes to the Supreme Court structure, including true checks and balances on some decisions and defined reasons for impeachment. They were arguing term limits on that, too."

"Look, go find the other DAs and have them write up everything they've heard this week. We need to get a summary to the Institute right now."

Mike added, "We can do that, but it may be moot. The group working on transition is really hung up on how to ensure an orderly transition from old to new."

"It's easier than they think, but let them stew for a while. Just get me those summaries. Dr. 'E' says some of the sponsors are looking for an update with real information in it."

Mike snorted. "Good luck with that."

#

"You know that the original reason for the setup of the House and Senate, was so that the less populous states had the same representation as the more populous states."

Al, that is ancient history. The reasoning existed when the states still held their individual economies. Now, that system is not only redundant with respect to representation, but fails to recognize geo-economic entities. My idea recognizes both the old and the new. It also gives a more secure 'corporate knowledge' if you will, given the term limits imposed."

"David. I suspect that your opinion is probably shared by most of the mountain west. There's always been an inferiority complex that the Eastern states, and then California got all the contracts and press. Then, you turn around and complain that your space is being impinged upon by 'coasters'.

"Don't make it personal, Al. It's not. I'm from Wyoming, but our general needs are one and the same with Montana, Utah, Colorado, New Mexico, Arizona and Idaho. Our identity is similar, our cultures similar. Why shouldn't our interests be centrally represented, when needed?"

Al had noticed the Ishmael had walked in and sat down, but hadn't acknowledged him. Now, Ishmael spoke up. "May I ask you to explain what you meant by geo-economic entities?"

Lee sat on the corner of the table. "It's convoluted, if you don't understand the restructure, Ishmael."

"Give me the 'elevator speech' then."

"Okay. For starters, the fifty states retain their identity status quo. But, two segments of our population are not represented in Congress; at least with any vote therein. Those are the District of Columbia and the territories. Remember that, when the Constitution was written, we had neither territories nor the District. So, they became, so to speak, bastard step-children; seen but not heard. Well, we're not changing that in the lower house, but the geo-economic entities include them. For example, all territories, including Puerto Rico, the Marianas, the U.S. Virgin Islands, Samoa and all the other islands constitute a geo-economic entity. They all have roughly the same economic needs. They are not identical, but they are similar.

"The other side of the coin is somewhat more micro. Northern California has far more in common, economically, with Oregon, Washington and the panhandle of Idaho, than it does with the southern two thirds of the state. Others are easier. For example, New England is an entity, New York, New Jersey, and Pennsylvania, east of the Rappahannock, are economically similar. Get the idea?"

Ishmael was taking notes. "I see what you want, but it's going to be a hard sell."

Al laughed. "Hell, Ishmael, the whole damned idea is going to be a hard sell. But, coupled with the term limits, the geo-economic entities have the longest tenure of anything being written, save the Supreme Court. That's the selling point. We're still redefining the 'boundaries', if you will; stuff like Colorado splitting on the Continental Divide, with part being Mountain and part Great Plains. Some are still being looked at. The idea is still a 'work in progress'.

"How are you going to manage transition? Senior Senators are not going to go quietly into the night."

"Olivia is still working that out. The most I can tell you is that, right now, we're thinking three Senators, if that names stays, from each Geo-Economic Entity (G-E-E), each serving a six-year term, one up for reelection every 2 years. They may serve a maximum of six terms or until their term ends, after they reach their Social Security retirement age. A big item in the entire restructure is that those who write the laws must live with the laws they write. That includes social security, medical care and taxes; no free rides and no special benefits."

"How about all the special powers that the Senate has now, like 'advise and consent'."

Al smiled. "Now, if we gave away all of what we're planning, you wouldn't need us, would you, Mr. Devil's Advocate? Sorry, I'm not at liberty to divulge information of that specific nature."

July 19, 2017

"Hi, this is Sally."

"Sally, George. How's the Admin Whiz?"

"Well, I'd love to plan a party. Can we put a holiday in August?"

George laughed. "Hey, you guys are in charge. Go for it."

"Great, we'll get a team on that. Now, why did you really call?"

"Well, it's an administration trivia question. Are you sending out more postal mail than normal?"

"No. Nothing out of the ordinary. Your people do the heavy lifting on mailings and such, why?

"I'm not sure. We're just following up on a request from the base post office. They handle our postage, which includes yours, and they say we've gone from two to four pounds of mail a week, to fifteen and most of it is first class. I'm just trying to find out what's up. Thanks."

"You're welcome, I guess. Can I name that holiday after me? National Sally Day."

"You get my vote. Oh, who in your new design handles National Parks and such?"

Sally grinned. "Nice try, George. Bye bye," and she hung up.

George replaced the handset of his phone and looked at Harold. "You heard? For some reason, the interns are sending letters home at a rate of just over one letter a week per intern. They've got email. Why are they using 'snail mail'?

"I suppose that I can think of only one reason, George. They know that we monitor electronic traffic. We can't read their letters; at least not legally."

"Can't we see who is sending the letters?"

"I'll talk to the base postal officer, but I don't have a warm and fuzzy about that."

#

"Hello, this is John Seacrist."

"Hi, this is Harold Gilbert. I'm the head of the Institute project at Camp Donelson."

"Yes, sir, how can I help you?"

"Your folks in the postage group tell us that our mail has increased at least four-fold in the last couple of weeks. We're trying to figure out why. May we inspect the mail from the boxes on the camp to see who is sending what?

"Mr. Gilbert, did you say? Once a letter drops into that box it is protected by federal law from tampering. I can't let anyone touch it except my people. Even then, it's only to bag it for shipment to the sorting facility in Nashville, sorry. "

"I was afraid of that."

"I do have an idea though. It's not much, but it might work."

"I'm up for any suggestion."

"Well, if you can get the facility supervisor to go along with you, he can sort specific bags individually. The sorting machine will spit out the delivery zip codes of every piece of mail in that bag. He can drop you a report."

"That might just work. Do you happen to have his number?"

Seacrist laughed. "HER name is Harriet Dolan. She goes by Harry and don't cross her in a dark alley. She humped mail for thirty-one years before she landed this job. Her number is 615.555.0022. Good luck. Tell her I gave you the suggestion. We used to sort together in Knoxville."

July 21, 2017

"Thanks, Donny." George looked down the list of interns until he found the one he wanted. Then he picked up his handset and dialed a number.

"Harold? George. I had Donny go through the two inches of paper printed from that the file I got from the Post Office in Nashville. It appears that the interns ARE sending a lot of letters home, but one is either in love, homesick or communicating with the outside world. Two to three letters *per day* are going to one zip code, 21793.

"This isn't Jeopardy, George. My area of expertise is not postal zip codes. I presume that is not the North Slope of Alaska?"

"Sorry, it's a suburb of Frederick, Maryland. We have three kids from Maryland, of course. One from Baltimore, one from Easton, that's on the Eastern Shore and one from Frederick.

"And the winner is?"

"Beau Williams"

"Shit!"

"That, *and* Little Eva. A member of the Executive Committee."

"Damn. This is not good. Okay. I'll tell Dr. Elliot. You ask Millie to come see me at". he looked at his watch, "2:30 this afternoon. And, for God's sake, make sure he doesn't find out that we suspect anything."

"Harold, it would be far better if we either met with Millie in her office, or in a neutral location. We're still under some suspicion for our perceived meddling. She's not going to be happy to be summoned to your office and told that a member of her team is suspected of ... just what *is* he suspected of?"

He sighed. "Yeah. You're right. Ask her if she'll meet us in the library. We can get one of the study rooms."

"I think that's much better, boss. I'll call her now."

#

George and Harold walked up the walk to the library. Millie was sitting on a bench. "Hi, Millie. Thanks for coming to meet with us. I've asked for a conference room. Can we go inside?"

"No. At least not until you give me an idea of the subject. Once again, I'm outnumbered."

George spoke before Harold, this time. "There is no conspiracy, Millie. The project is threatened by something happening from inside the intern camp. We need to keep the risk contained and we want your help to do it."

"Fair warning, George. I will not betray my fellow team mates."

"Understood and therein lies the rub. One of your team mates may have betrayed you. Can we go inside and get behind a door, where we can't be overheard. It really *is* important, Millie."

Millie sighed, stood and walked up the three wooden steps into the library. George looked at Harold and shrugged his shoulders, before turning to follow Millie in.

#

"That's all we know right now, Millie. A lot of heavy mail is being sent to a zip code in the city he lives in. We need to know, first, if he's sending it and, then, what he's doing and why."

"Are you certain it's Beau?"

"As a matter of fact, no. Right now, it's guilt by zip code. But, we can't think of any seamless way to determine if it's him or not."

"I have half an idea. He's been getting chummy with Janice Montesano. Maybe she knows what he's up to."

"That's an interesting thought. But, she can't know we're really interested in his mail habits."

"George, you've grown up. High school kids, even geeks, love to gossip with their peers. Let me sick my geek on his geek and we'll see what shows. Can you give me a day or two?"

Harold spoke up. "I can't give you much more than that, I'm afraid. Each day, someone is sending a lot of something out of here. We've got to know what it is. Fortunately, today is Friday and the mail has already left. So, six to nine letters will sit in the mailbox until Monday. I can't stop them. The best I can try to do, is intercept them, and only if they violate the agreement that you all signed."

"I just don't think Beau would go against something he signed. What earthly reason would he have?"

"That's what we need to know. What earthly reason would any of you have? I can give you until Sunday noon. If you don't know anything by then, I'll have to call Beau in for a 'chat'."

Millie sighed. Okay. I'll try. I really hope it's not Beau."

"I really hope it's one of you sending recipes to a restaurant," said George.

#

"Alright, we've agreed that Supreme Court Justices do not serve' for life'. I know that the Constitution says that they can be removed for 'bad behavior', but that's never been applied and the one time an Associate Justice was impeached, he was acquitted. We know that was completely political. Here's my suggestion." The speaker was Tim Erickson from Wisconsin.

Janice interrupted, "Wait a minute, Tim. Do I need to record this or is it simple enough for my notes?"

"It's simple, Janice. You don't need to record it for posterity."

Janice flipped a page in a steno notebook and said, "Okay, go ahead, my friend."

"Let me get through this before any of you ask questions, please. Each Associate Justice serves a term of ten years. At the end of ten years, they must be renominated by the President and reconfirmed by the Senate. If so confirmed repetitively, they may serve 'for life', as it were. If the President does not renominate an Associate Justice, the question goes to the house. They may, by simple majority, renominate. This gives check and balance to the other two branches, that they've never had over the Court."

Emelita asked a question. "You've spoken about the Associate Justices, what about the Chief Justice?"

"Good question, Emmy. I'm still pondering two possibilities. One is, same rules as for the Associates, except that the President may choose to renominate only for membership and nominate a new Chief Justice at the end of his or her term. The other is a 15-year term, with only Senatorial confirmation; in other words, he or she is above the fray."

"What about removal?"

"I would write in detail of 'misbehavior'. Do we toss a Supreme for an extramarital affair or drunk driving? Or, do we wait for judicially unethical behavior, like taking a bribe to influence a decision? It's a slippery subject, and it's been ignored for 230 years. Today's citizenry won't allow a loophole, that big, this time. The reconfirmation process resolves much of the question of permanence."

Beau jumped in. "I like it. It may need some refining, but it's a good solution. In fact, it's well thought out by all. Good job.

"Have you given thought to public recall of a, as you said, Supreme?"

"We bounced it around, but wonder if the public can't be a bit too volatile? It wouldn't take much for a stack of recall petitions to paralyze the governmental process. I'd rather they send a million emails to Congress and let the House decide, if the behavior warrants impeachment. Oh, and that's the same with the President. We'll still be a representative democracy. We elect people to make those choices. Mob rule hasn't come across the border ... yet."

"I'm sorry, Janice, did you get all that. We just started rambling."

"I got the details I need for the records, Tim. When I transcribe it, I'll find you, to make sure I've got it right."

In the Weeds

The Melting Pot Boils Over?

July 21, 2017

The notice on the board in the dining hall intrigued Ellen.

> Informal and unofficial discussion of trigger issues;
> Saturday, July 22, 9:30 am - Library Conference Room 1
> No decisions. No notes taken. All opinions welcome!
> 9:30 - 10:00: Immigration
> 10:00 - 10:30: Entitlement Programs
> 10:30 - 11:00: Health Care
> The Truth is Out There

She walked over to the table where Beau, Maggie and To Lin were finishing dinner. "Is anyone invited? And by that, I mean, may any of the DAs or Institute come?"

"This was put together by a trio of Jane Abrams, Roy Tipton and 'RAM' Taylor, Ellen. When they asked me about it, they said it was an open forum to get as close to a representative consensus, as might be had on this compound. When I asked about the DAs, the answer was, I kid you not, 'if it breathes and has an opinion, that opinion is welcome to be heard." Maggie gave Ellen a cocked smile and asked, "Answer your question?"

Ellen laughed. "Save me a seat. I really want to hear this one."

To Lin reminded her. "No notes, Miss Haley."

July 22, 2017

Ellen all but ran from the DA meeting that ran late. Only Joyce had shown an interest, but said she would be there for the 10:00 entitlement discussion. Ellen walked in at 9:40 and the discussion was well underway and, surprisingly, civil. She walked across the back to the side aisle and noticed Janice sitting in the back row of seats. She seemed to be preoccupied with her cell phone rather than listening in on a voluntary discussion. Ellen put that discrepancy aside, as she sat on the side end of the 4th row of folding chairs. She thought to herself, that she had never seen a discussion about immigration, that did not dissolve into an argument.

"No, you don't understand my point." The speaker was To Lin. "Immigration in this country has come in two major varieties. Historically, the immigration was Caucasian. Each wave may have been from a different country, or a different ethnic or religious group, but until the first Chinese immigration, it was primarily white and, within a generation, easily assimilated."

"You left off a big immigration, To Lin, black slaves," Olivia added in a calm, but accusatory voice.

To Lin turned to face her and answer her directly. "Olivia, I would not consider the forced importation of unwilling humanity to be an immigration wave. All of the elements of a true immigration, among those being desire, hope for a better life and voluntary movement, were missing."

Olivia dipped her head and held out her hands, palms up, in concession of the point.

To Lin continued. "With the first Chinese importation, labor for the railroads, the first non-Caucasians arrived in measurable numbers. The result, as you well know, was discrimination on a magnitude that the Irish, probably the most ill-treated immigrants, never suffered. Subsequent measurable immigrations of 'non-Europeans', and I put that in quotes, because the Russian Jews are European, as are the Italians, suffered, as well, from anti-immigrant discrimination."

Emelita had been biding her time. "To Lin, that is an academic explanation that is altogether too simplistic. It does not reflect the cultural or environmental factors which differed with each wave of immigration. The early immigrants benefited from the opening of the west and the Industrial Revolution. They created enclaves of majority population such as Germans in Chicago and Milwaukee, Scandinavians in Wisconsin, Minnesota and North Dakota. Even the oriental populations centralized themselves in 'zones of comfort', like the big cities or agricultural centers; mostly depending on where, in the orient, they had migrated from.

"Each wave entered at a time of evolving and vastly different infrastructures of transportation, education, industrialization and communication. I will deal with my own cultural group. We didn't immigrate, in the beginning. We were here first!" She held up her hand to stop what she knew was coming. "Yes, my family came from Mexico … legally, I shouldn't have to add, and we are all naturalized citizens. But, most of the Hispanic population of the southwest was not immigrant; at least not until after World War II."

"Hey, this is all well and good, but can we cut to a discussion of the trigger points?" Art Little, from New Hampshire, seldom spoke up. He contributed research and ideas in groups, but was averse to 'being recognized'.

To Lin looked at Emelita. "I guess I'm done. I just wanted to point out that you can't put immigration into any clearly defined set of boxes. People, times, reasons and the world are all different."

To Lin turned to Art. "Your turn, Mr. Little."

"I grant you all of the aforementioned, but it's history, some ancient, some recent, but history nonetheless. The Mexican immigrant of your grandfather's time, Emelita, came for a better life, yes, but through labor and time. Today, the border is flooded with hundreds of thousands who come for the 'benefits', with being a part of America, second."

Emelita stood and nearly shouted, "I have to disagree! That's stereotyping …"

"Emmy! No arguments. Let Art speak, please." To Lin, nominally the moderator, admonished her gently." She was unsatisfied, but sat down. Ellen watched her arms and legs cocoon her into a defensive posture. "Art? Be careful to keep your remarks impersonal, please."

"Sorry. It wasn't intentional. I'll pick on just one then, automatic citizenship. We no longer seek huge increases in our population. Why should our most valued prize, citizenship in this country, be a reward based upon a set of GPS coordinates? I'm willing to let minor children ride along on their parent's road to citizenship, or even give special treatment to parents of those born here, but the automatic citizenship works against us, when the parents are not here legally."

Olivia added, "Good point, Art. Another is the immediate right to all the programs, education, Medicaid, and other entitlement programs to everyone in the country. Heck, an illegal can even get a social security number and driver's license; ostensibly so they'll pay taxes. We need some studies to determine if that is a positive cash flow for the nation."

Art chuckled. "I've never heard the economics put that way, but it's a good point. Immigrants come here for the 'benefits of citizenship', yet the only price paid is taxes. In most cases, those taxes, if any are paid at all given immigrant income levels, are far less than the tax dollars expended."

"That's a good point Art." To Lin looked at the clock on the wall, at the back of the room. "Okay, we've got five minutes before we change topics. Personally, I think we've shown that analysis, discussion, even arguments over trigger subjects can be informative. Now, with the kind permission of the audience, what do we do with anything we've heard?

Emelita spoke out before other's hands went up. "I don't want to see Art's thoughts lost. I think we should investigate 'return on investment' in the case of immigration; legal and illegal. And, do that analysis from both sides."

"I want to know if our immigration policies are 'fiscally neutral'." Olivia stood. "I know they're not, but I don't have the proof. Are they skewed by the laws and regulations; such as the laws in the early 20th century, that all but prevented Oriental immigration? Or, are they skewed by individual, or organizational bias? Let's remember that, at least from the 20th century on, immigration has been a political issue, and by that, I mean a vote gathering issue. Both skewed processes can be repaired, but in very different ways."

"Great. I know we're not supposed to take notes, but we can't lose this. I'm writing those two suggestions down and I invite any other suggestions to be emailed to me, or any other EC member, if you don't want to write to me. You can even send it to Sally. And, if anonymity is your thing, print it off, fold and staple it and toss it in the basket by the bulletin board." Another glance at the clock. "Okay, take a three-minute bio break and then this room becomes a discussion group on 'entitlements'. Great job, folks."

#

"I'm stunned and amazed by these kids. If the UN or Congress could discuss truly contentious issues with the courtesy and diplomacy with which that roomful of teenagers did, we would have world peace, clean water and cheap gasoline." Ellen set her tray down and sat at the DA table. George and all the DAs were there except Joyce, who was not there. Those kids have some truly innovative ideas about immigration and some of them have a better grasp of the benefits and problems, historical and current, than the last three administrations."

"Why bother though?" Bill picked up his empty fork and used it as a pointer; pointing into space. "Trigger issues will not be in the new document, so why waste time?"

"I'll field that one," Ishmael said. "Every trigger issue has its foundation in one or another section of the Constitution or an Amendment. If I understand Ellen correctly, they want to frame the foundation in such a way, that it precludes the trigger from being an issue going forward. Is that close, Ellen?"

"She had just put a bit of salad in her mouth, so hand covering her mouth, a muffled, "What he said" came out.

Mike countered, "The problem with that, and it's unavoidable, is the transition. The population is not going to change viewpoints or opinions overnight, and some of it will never change. I mean the FDA has changed the nutrition pyramid a dozen times, but Ketchup is still considered a vegetable and chocolate a food group, by most of the population."

"Mike, you're forgetting that the population deals very well with paradigm shifts. The small segments that resist change eventually die out by age or attrition. Give me an example of the most die-hard population segment you can."

"The Catholic Church."

"I can beat that one, but let's use it. In the past fifty years, the liturgy has gone to the predominant local language, divorced members are allowed the sacrament and illegitimate births are no longer a reason for excommunication. Gays and Lesbians are, if not accepted, at least tolerated. Heck, in WWII a service member discovered to be homosexual was imprisoned. Today, they can command combat units. No, the public will accept the changes; some over a longer period. Make the change even appear to be advantageous to them, and they'll change. Make it profitable and they'll claim it was the government that kept it from happening."

"Spoken like a true psychologist, Ellen."

Ellen tossed Ishmael a good-natured raspberry. "Help me out here, Mike. You're the specialist in group dynamics."

"She's actually pretty close to correct on a population response to a paradigm shift. It goes back to hunter-gatherer shifts to stable agriculture and to the domestication of animals. Think about it. If you stop and gloss history, you'll find them; good *and* bad. The discovery of the new world, manned flight, one-year tomatoes are poison, the next year a delicacy. In WWII, the government bought and gave away cigarettes. Now, that would cause an outrage among the voters. On the flip side, I remember an entire population who turned and persecuted a segment of its very own because they were told otherwise. Call it 'the Chicken Little' phenomenon."

"You're talking about Nazi Germany and the Jews."

Mike smiled. "No, I'm actually referring to the treatment of black Americans throughout our national history. Remember that they started out as property enumerated with a value 3/5th of a white citizen. In a specific instance, I refer you to the 1896 Supreme Court decision, Plessy vs Ferguson, which all but invalidated the 14th Amendment by making segregation, by the doctrine of 'separate but equal', the law of the land. You want a more modern example? Executive Order 9066 completely changed the way any person of Japanese ancestry, citizen or not, was viewed. No, my friends, we don't have to look outside our borders for an evil paradigm shift and subsequent mob behavior; oops, sorry group dynamics."

"Ouch!"

"I don't write the history. The winners write the history. But, then, history is not always the truth, is it?"

#

"Hey, Janice, what are you so diligently writing. I can hear you through these wonderful walls and you're burning up the keyboard."

Janice's head jerked up at the surprise interruption. She had ear buds plugged into her phone and hadn't heard Lilly approach. "What? Oh, hey, Lilly. I'm just writing notes up for the database." She hit a key on her phone and took out the ear buds.

Lilly walked in and looked over her shoulder. As she did, Janice minimized the screen to prevent her from seeing what she was working on. "I just try to get it in a record, while it's still hot. It's a pain to have to remember everything. I couldn't take notes in the sessions today, so I'm trying to remember it all."

Lilly glanced at the phone on the desk. "Whatcha listening to?"

"Huh?" She saw Lilly looking at her phone. "Oh, just a play list of stuff. Hey, I'm sorry, Lilly, but I need to keep my mind on this or I'm going to forget something. I'll see you at breakfast, okay?"

Lilly gave her half a smile. "Oh, okay, sure. Good night." She backed out of the open door and headed next door.

Janice put her ear buds back in and hit a key. Then, she maximized the application on her laptop and continued working.

Lilly was uncomfortable with that few seconds she had spent with Janice. First off, she had heard no music coming from the ear buds and the screen she saw was a word processing document, not a database document.

Hiding in Plain Sight

July 24, 2017

George tapped on the frame of Millie's open door. "Millie, may I speak with you for a minute?"

Millie glanced at her phone. "We're supposed to meet in 45 minutes, George. What's up?"

"I know, that. I wanted a private word with you. Can we grab a coffee?"

"I'm not quite ready. Give me 15 and I'll meet you at the dining hall, okay? Do I need anyone else?"

George smiled at the implication and shook his head. "Nope, this is just you and me."

"Okay. Fifteen then."

George had two mugs of coffee and a pitcher of milk waiting at a table beneath the window, when Millie walked in. She set her bag on the table and sat. "Okay, your nickel."

George didn't look comfortable, but he stepped off. "We had another batch of large envelopes in the box this morning. I made sure that I was there, when the mailman emptied it. He wouldn't let me look at anything, but I saw three fat envelopes with a bunch of stamps. Have you had any luck with tracking Beau?"

Millie shook her head. "You might be surprised, George, but I did take your request seriously. I've asked people who are in his groups to look for anything out of the ordinary. They've seen nothing. Jerry, his next-door neighbor in housing says, that aside from Janice, who spends a lot of time with him, he's seen nothing either, including mailing things."

"Have you asked Janice?"

Millie gave him a cynical face. "George. Really? I'm going to ask his girlfriend if he's doing anything he shouldn't? How long has it been since you were a teenager, George? I mean, I'm straight arrow and even I would be upset, if you asked my boyfriend, and no, I don't have one, what I was up to. Get real!"

"Sorry. It's just that important and the risk too high, not to tug on every string."

Millie shook her head. "I'll bet you still check under your bed for monsters. At any rate, you may add one intern buying grass from one of the non-project staff, one clandestine gay relationship and one intern so OCD that she's trying to write down everything that happens, to your list of 'high crimes and misdemeanors.'

George chuckled and then his face got serious. "Who is keeping notes besides the official record submitted to Sally?"

"I wasn't ratting out an intern, George. I was pointing out the fact that there are 155 teenagers here, trapped in a wire enclosure. Of course, they're going to do weird things."

"Maybe I do look for monsters under my bed, but someone may be sending information out of here, and that someone would be keeping lots of notes. Please tell me who?"

"It's ridiculous George."

"Millie, please? I'm serious."

Millie held her hands out. "Okay. But, it's ridiculous. Janice is Beau's girlfriend. Why would she be doing anything except keeping records. Hell, she's got access to nearly every official piece of information anyway."

"Janice. Wow. You don't need to give me names, but how did you find this out?"

"I won't. One of her friends happened to hear her typing like crazy late Saturday night and got some totally weird answers when she talked with her. For one thing, she claimed to be working on a database, when she clearly had a word processing screen open."

"Millie, I'm going to talk with Dr. Elliot, but I'm going to have her network IP traced to see what traffic is originating from it. If she's sending documents anywhere, including to print, it will show. In fact, the 'Stage Manager' is officially informing the chairman of the Executive Committee of this action and requesting cooperation and silence."

"George, come on."

"No Millie. This is serious, including potential criminal activity. By making it official, I'm keeping you and the others at arm's length, okay?

"That sucks, George."

"Which would suck more, to use your words, Millie; your not liking that we're looking into it or waking up with the half-finished project on Fox News?"

His only response was a long sigh as Millie stood and picked up her bag. She looked into George's eyes and turned to leave the dining room. "I'll see you at the staff meeting, George."

#

"Harold? George. I called the IT spooks, right after I talked with Millie. I asked them to trace the IP traffic from Janice's machine. They just sent me the first scan. I think we might have our leak."

"What have they got, George?"

"Well, they tell me, and this is all ancient Greek to me, that everything is wireless here, including printers. That means that anything attached to the network has its own IP address, whatever that is, and that means they know the movement of every file; although they have no idea of content. According to them, Janice's laptop, or rather her IP, sent eight documents to her printer, between 6PM Saturday and 9AM Sunday. Each document was large enough to be fifteen or twenty printed pages. She made no attempt to access the Internet or internal resources before, during or after that period. Whatever she did came from her laptop. I estimated that at 120 pages; certainly enough to account for several large envelopes. That would be 3/4" of paper printed one side; and the printer she accessed does not do two sides."

"And you think she's sending her notes, or whatever, out of the compound?"

"Well, I doubt that she's writing screen plays, boss."

"Do you think she picked Beau because of his access?"

"I don't think she's that devious. I think that was fortuitous, but not intentional. So, what do we do now?"

"My first thought is to put some of our security people to watching the mailbox. And, ask the base postal officer to have it locked, or whatever, so that no mail can be put in. Then, if or when she approaches with her mail, we simply ask her to come to visit us, mail in hand. That way, since it never went into the box, it's not mail … yet. My second thought is to take a rubber hose and bright light to an interview with her, but I'll go with my first thought."

George snickered. "I'm glad you can laugh. I'm not sure I can."

"We'll know after we hear her story. For the project's sake, I hope she *is* the one and we can stop looking for the culprit and start dealing with damage control."

#

Millie opened the Executive Committee meeting. "Good afternoon, all. Well, today is the first day of the final third of the project. It's time to start writing our masterpiece."

Kathy straightened her notebook and, carefully, placed her pen on it. "Are we certain that we have enough information to do this?"

"We most certainly have more than the Framers had, Kathy."

"Al, that's apples and oranges, and you know it."

Millie tapped her knuckles on the table. "Alright, you two. The point is that we must begin to write the first draft, regardless. Sally has indexed all the notes, as best as she can.

Janice helped her with some special indexes. All of it is ready to access."

Jane leaned in, "I have to bring this up. Creation by committee is a known trap. No two minds comprehend even a simple fact in the same way. Given that, two people, even two in total agreement, are going to envisage this document differently. Imagine the disaster of five co-authors."

Millie sighed. "So, you're telling me that one of us, and only one of us, must draft it?"

"I'm afraid so, if we want anything useful in the allotted time. There's plenty of time for revisions and to ensure that we've written down what we have decided that the nation wants, citizens and leaders both. But I'm afraid it will have but one author."

"I'm afraid to admit it, but I agree. The question is, ladies and gentlemen, who will be the father of our Constitution Redux?

Jane said, "There is only one real person who will be accepted by everyone, Al Lee."

Al leaned back in his chair. "History is often repeated. When the Second Constitutional Congress was debating the Declaration, they invited my ancestor, Richard Henry Lee, to participate. He begged off to become Governor of Virginia. Robert E. Lee, less than a hundred years later, refused to be a part of the Confederate government, serving instead as Commanding General of Confederate ground forces. Well, third time's the charm and I won't write it. First off, I have very strong feelings about many of the nuances that will be written in. Like my ancestors, I will work for its success, but I can't write it." He folded his hands, tipped his chair back onto its back legs and sat silently.

Millie was soft spoken as she said, "Wow. I think I followed all of that. I suppose it could be written by someone outside the EC. Are there any ideas? Who is a good writer and who has been in on most of the analysis?"

"How about that, instead of the father of our document, we have a mother of it?"

The feet of Al's chair hit the floor as he leaned forward. "You want a woman to write it?"

Kathy's voice hardened. "Do you have a problem with that idea, Mr. Lee?" Her emphasis on the 'Mr.' was a verbal confrontation.

Al recognized the potential conflict that his next statement could cause. "Kathy, I, personally, have no problem with a woman. What I'm afraid of is the acceptance by the general population. I think they'll get hung up on the author, instead of the document. Every crackpot with a blog will analyze the document looking for 'feminist' influence."

"Oh, that is so much macho bullshit, Al"

"STOP!" Millie stood. "I will not allow us to descend into petty arguments over viewpoints! Sit down, both of you!" She paused. They sat.

"May I say something?" Jane asked quietly.

"If it addresses our need to begin writing, yes, you may"

"Thank you." She took a breath. "Look, there is some truth to Al's perception of public acceptance. On the other hand, we can't pander to that by avoiding the use of every resource we have at our fingertips. Let's just use the best author, make the best edit and produce the best document to lead the best country forward. Let the Institute worry about marketing. That's all I have to say. Get out of the weeds and go to work."

Beau looked at Jane and then at Kathy, Millie and Al. "Jane, you've got the job."

"I wasn't volunteering. I was pointing out the error in the direction of the discussion."

Kathy joined in. "Beau is right, Jane. You are the best negotiator and arbitrator we have. You can see both sides of an argument, while imagining creative middle ground. I cannot imagine a more appropriate author and I call the question."

"Second", came from Al Lee.

Millie grinned. "All in favor?"

Four ayes and one moan sounded in response.

Jane's voice was sharp. "If I'm going to be the engineer of this railroad, I want Al Lee as my conductor and Kathy as my consultant."

Millie didn't even hesitate. "Done. Now, can we get to work?"

#

"Janice! Hey, wait up." Beau had just exited the library, when he saw Janice walking from the residence, toward the theater for a group meeting. She paused while he caught up. "I'll walk with you. "He reached for her hand, but found that her right hand carried her laptop case and her left arm was cradling three large envelopes. He leaned over and gave her a kiss on the cheek. "I missed you last night. What in the heck have you got there?"

"Sorry, honey. I got tied up typing up data. By the time I was finished, I figured it was too late for a visit."

Beau stepped in front of her and turned to walk backwards. "Late hasn't bothered us before. Early, either. What's going on? And, I'll ask again, what have you got in the envelopes?"

She didn't look directly at him, as she answered. "It's nothing important, just some stuff I'm sending home." She kept walking and tried to walk around him. "I need to get them in the mail. I'll see you in the meeting." Beau stopped, turned and watched her back. He was confused. He continued in the same direction, but didn't try to catch up with her.

As she approached the mailbox, she reached for the handle to open the chute. She tugged twice. It did not open. Two men stepped from the doorway of the empty postal building. One spoke. "Miss Montesano?"

Janice jumped; startled. She turned, a panicked look on her face, to face the source of the question. "Who are you?"

"Are you Miss Janice Montesano?"

"Yes, but who are you and what do you want?" She looked over her shoulder. Beau had stopped and was watching. Then, he began to walk toward her.

One of the men saw her look, and noticed the young man walking toward them. He walked past Janice to intercept Beau. The other man pulled out a folder and showed her a badge and identification that identified him as an agent of the National Security Agency. "Would you please come with us to Dr. Elliot's office?" Janice looked over her shoulder at Beau, a scared look on her face.

"Hey, wait a minute!" He started to jog toward the pair. The second man stepped in front of him "Sir, I suggest you leave them alone. This is official business."

"And that's my girlfriend and I'm on the Executive Committee, so I have an interest when someone hassles my girl or one of the interns." Beau was doing his adolescent best to appear forceful. It wasn't working well.

The agent, who was now holding Janice by the arm with the envelopes, overheard Beau. Without looking away from Janice, he spoke up. "Is he Beau Williams?"

The second agent looked at Beau, cocking his head. "I'm Beau Williams, yes. Why?"

"Bring him, too?"

"Yup"

The second agent showed his credentials. "Would you please accompany us, as well, Mr. Williams. We're headed to Dr. Elliot's office." He took a grip on Beau's arm and walked toward Janice. As they walked, he took out his cell phone and keyed in a preset number. "Willard. We have Ms. Montesano and a Mr. Williams. We're bringing them to Dr. Elliot. ... Yes, she was. ... No. The box was locked as we'd been told. ... No, no problems. ... Okay. Will do." He ended the call and put the phone back in his pocket.

As they approached the Institute offices, Beau saw George with Millie, hurrying from the theater in the same direction. Janice looked at her boyfriend. "Beau, what's going on?"

"I don't know, Jan, but Dr. Elliot won't let anything bad happen."

Prejudice and Pride

Tribunal

July 24, 2017

"Hello, Beau. Please sit down over there." Dr. Elliot did not acknowledge Janice yet. "Thank you, gentlemen. Wait outside, please. If we need you, George will fetch you." The agents left the room and closed the door behind them. Dr. Elliot sat at the center of a long table, George to his left and an uncomfortable looking Millie to his right. To Janice, left standing in front of it, it appeared quite intimidating; exactly the effect planned. Beau took a seat on alone folding chair behind Janice and to the left.

"Janice, please put those envelopes on the table." Dr. Elliot's voice was even and unemotional.

"They're private mail. I don't have to give them to you."

George looked at her. "Actually, they're not mail until they're dropped into an official mailbox, Janice. Right now, they're documents that we may examine under the conditions of the non-disclosure agreement that you signed. Now, please set them down," he pointed at the table in front of Dr. Elliot, "right here."

"Millie, what is ...?" Beau leaned forward and looked at Millie. Millie shook her head and held up her hand to stop him.

"Hush, Beau! I don't need your help." Janice an angry look beginning to form on her face walked forward and, holding the thick envelopes about six inches above the table, let them fall with an accompanying thud as they hit the table. "Fine." She stepped back and crossed her arms.

George leaned forward and, without touching them, read the address and then the return address. He looked up at Janice and then at Beau. Then, he twisted his head to the left. "These are addressed to Beau's parents with his return address on them."

"What?" Dr. Elliot drew the stack toward him. He read the top envelope and looked at Beau. "These are yours?"

"What the hell? No, they're not mine. Janice had them in her hands when she left the residence building, or at least she had them when I saw her. I was in the library."

"They have your return address on them, Mr. Williams."

Beau stood and walked forward. "May I look at those, George?" George spun the top envelope around for Beau to read. He picked it up and read it, then turned it over. He shook it. "I've no idea where this came from, but it is my return address and the address of my parents." He turned to look at his girlfriend. "Janice, where did these come from?" She turned her face away from him took toward the windows.

Beau's voice became insistent. He walked over and stood in front of her. "Janice? Why is my address on these? Her head swiveled away from him. He started to move in front of her again.

"Beau," Dr. Elliot said. "Go sit down." He paused, and his voice softened. "Please." Beau's eyes appeared hurt as he looked at Janice before he turned and returned to the chair. It squeaked as he sat, and Janice flinched at the sound.

Dr. Elliot pushed an envelope to George. "Open it, please."

Janice turned her head back. "Those are mine! You can't open them."

An even, cold voice spoke from behind her. "They have my return address on them, Janice. George, Open it." Janice's head Whipped around. She saw cold contempt on Beau's face, but tears were forming on his cheeks.

George withdrew a penknife from his pocket and slit the tape on the envelope. He dumped out nearly an inch of printed pages. He stacked them and handed them to Dr. Elliot. "They're printouts from the database of notes. The top sheets are dated last Friday."

Elliot looked at a selection of pages selected at random. Then, he re-stacked them and slipped the stack to Millie. "Janice, why are these working papers being mailed out of the project?"

Janice gave him a cold smile; almost a sneer. "How would I know? They don't have my name on them."

"Is that the way you want to play this? You put Beau's name on them in case they're intercepted?" Janice remained silent, her eyes cold. "You're not much of a geek if you think they can't be traced, you know. We have the, what did he call it? Oh yes, packet transfer report showing large amounts of files being sent from your laptop to your printer over the weekend. Do you still want to claim that these belong to Beau?"

"Janice! What are you doing? And, why did you put my name on them?"

She turned and looked at him. She smirked at him." Beau, you're a great guy, I kind of like you, but you're so naive. Don't you see what these people are doing? They're corrupting America; trying to make it something it's not. It was easy to use you. I've been using guys like you to get whatever I want since I grew tits. Grow up!"

"Janice?" Beau pleaded. She turned back to the table.

Dr. Elliot swiveled his head from George to Millie. "I'm satisfied that Beau had nothing to do with this. Anything from either of you?" Millie's head was down, and her hands were together and flat on the table. George shook his head from side to side. "Beau, you may leave if you wish. Thank you and I'm sorry for the suspicion."

"My name was on a bunch of envelopes, I take it. If I may, I'd like to stay."

"Millie, is it okay with you?"

Millie lifted her head. "Beau is on my committee and I'm responsible for him. If you're asking me, he can stay."

Dr. Elliot nodded his head. "In that case, Beau, would you please call home and see how many envelopes there are and ask how they knew they were coming and what they were supposed to do with them?"

Janice mumbled. "I used Beau's email and sent them an email telling them he was accumulating notes for a book he was going to write about the project after it was over. There are 27 other envelopes. At least, that's how many I sent, I think."

"Beau? Please make the call, anyway. If all the envelopes are there and unopened, please tell your parents to put them in a safe place and you will come get them. You may tell them that we know about the book and that it's okay, but we want the information kept safe here until the project is over."

"Yes, sir. May I go outside?"

"Certainly." Dr. Elliot raised his voice a bit. "Jim?"

An agent opened the door. "Yes, sir?"

"Please accompany Mr. Williams outside for a phone call. Stay with him while he makes a call and then bring him back in, please."

"Yes, sir." He beckoned toward Beau. "Mr. Williams?" The two left and the door closed behind them.

A pause ensued, and the Millie's soft voice broke the silence. "What were you going to do, Janice? I doubt that *you* were going to write a book."

"Humph! You're no smarter than Beau, Millie. I was going to give the whole kit and caboodle to some people I know in Philadelphia. They want America to be what it was before all the social programs and immigrants and politically correct crap. The IT security here is a flipping joke. It was so easy to grab every word written down. We're going to see that your 'document' never sees the light of day."

"Don't you think we're trying to make America great again, but the America that is today. We can't go backwards."

"What we had was great!"

"Only if you were one of the few on the top of the heap. Our greatness was built on the backs of people who had no voice. We want to protect them, as well. They deserve every benefit, too."

"That's Socialist bullshit. I will never believe it." Janice turned her face away from Millie and looked out the window.

The room was frozen in a depressed silence for a minute until the door opened and Beau came back in. The agent looked at Dr. Elliot who beckoned him in, too. "What did you find out, Beau?"

He looked at Janice for a moment. "All 27 envelopes are there, sir. They thought I sent the email and they've kept them in a box in my room. I told them I was coming to get them."

"That's good news," he looked at Janice, "for everyone. Okay, sit down please. Jim, you and agent Katey McGregor will escort Miss Montesano to her room where she will pack her bags. The laptop is Institute property. She is not to touch it. Leave Katey with her and return the laptop immediately to IT." He spoke to Janice. "Miss Montesano, please look at me."

Janice turned her head even farther away. "I doubt that you have anything to say that I want to hear."

Elliot sighed. "Very well, then. Jim is going to escort you to Washington, DC; to St. Elizabeth's Hospital, to be exact. You will be admitted there for a period of evaluation lasting exactly as long as this project lasts. Consider it paid leave. After that period is over, you will be free to leave. However, the non-disclosure agreement remains in effect, per your agreement. If you talk, write or, in any way, communicate anything about this project without the permission of the Institute, you will be subject to criminal and civil penalties. Do you understand?"

Janice said nothing, but she did nod her head. "Very well. Jim?"

The agent stepped forward and grasped Janice's elbow lightly, "Miss, please come with me."

After they had left, Dr. Elliot spoke again. "Beau?"

Beau looked up, tears streaming down his cheeks. "I'm sorry, sir."

"You have nothing to be sorry for, Beau. You were duped by a devious young woman who had an agenda different from ours. Now, you and George will fly to DC, as well, and then go to Frederick where you will recover all 27 envelopes, unopened, and return them here. After they are destroyed, we will put this unfortunate incident behind us."

"Sir, may I ask a question?"

"Shoot."

"Shouldn't someone write the story of what we're doing? Those notes are a piece of that story, as is what Janice did, or tried to do."

George spoke up in support. "You know, Doc. He's right. How about I keep the envelopes in secure storage. After the fat lady has sung, we can decide who will write our story."

Dr. Elliot rubbed his eyes. "I'm getting old. Okay, George. We won't rewrite the history of this project. We'll tell it like it is. Keep the envelopes. But, please keep them safe."

Solitude and Solidarity

July 26, 2107

Jane's neck jerked as she dozed, and she awoke with a start. She looked at the clock by her bed; 1:30 in the morning. She looked at the monitor. Her laptop had gone to sleep, just like she had. Two days. Two days and not a word written. She was depressed, confused and lost. She had ten days to write an, potentially, historic document. She spoke out loud. "I'm half the age of James Madison when he wrote the Constitution. How can they expect me to be smarter, more literary and more creative at eighteen? It's nuts! I wish Daddy could help. He'd know what to write." She slammed the monitor of her laptop closed and threw herself on her bed. In only a moment, she was asleep.

Her sleep was exhaustion working its way off, but there was one dream. She knelt before a monument, its structure was undefined in her dream, but she knew it was a holy and sacred monument. In her dream, the monument grew bright; almost too bright to see. She heard a soft voice,

> "In the beginning God created the heaven and the earth. The earth was without form …God said, Let there be light."

She awoke with a start. "Of course. God had a plan. We have a plan, too. I don't have to write the new Constitution. I have to follow the plan. I just have to remember what we've decided and write it down in clear sentences. I'm not the author.

I have 155 authors. I'm an editor, that's all. She looked at her clock again, 5:43. "Good enough!"

She sat at her desk and opened the laptop to the blank document. She typed the word "Preamble" and saved the document for the first time. She gave it a working title "redux" and pressed 'Enter'. She remembered a quote from a favorite author, J.R.R. Tolkien, 'It's the job that's never started that takes the longest to finish.' Now, I've started." She left the preamble blank and moved on to outline the document section by section.

12. Legislature

13. Executive

14. Judiciary

15. Central structure

16. Amendments

17. Fiscal Responsibility

She tried to give a more modern take on the structure. Then, she highlighted the outline, hit CTL-A to select it all and pressed Delete. 'That's not what we had in mind.' She started again.

2. Citizen Freedoms

3. Citizen Expectations

4. Citizen Responsibilities

5. Government Structure

6. Government Expectations

7. Government Responsibilities

She hit Save, closed her laptop and picked up her bag. "It is begun. I have a skeleton. Now, I need flesh, muscle, tendons and, most of all, a strong heart and a reasoning mind."

#

"Kathy, may I sit with you?"

"Sure, Jane. Where have you been? I haven't seen you since you got picked to write the document."

Jane set her tray down. "I need coffee. I'll be right back." She returned with a pitcher of coffee and a small pot of creamer and set them down. She sat down and poured a mug of coffee, creamed it and took a long sip. "I needed that." She set the mug down and leaned over her breakfast. In between bites, she explained, "I've been locked in my room staring at a blinking cursor. Talk about writer's block. Anyway, I had a minor epiphany this morning," she grinned, "or maybe I just needed coffee, but whatever. I made a start and now I need help."

"What can I do?"

"You can start by handing me the salt." She took the offered salt, shook it onto her eggs and continued. "I need you and your notes. The first section of my document is about Citizen Freedoms and Expectations. You're the resident expert. So, I need you to tell me what you've decided. I'll turn it into words on paper, well disk anyway. After you, Beau and Millie. Al is last. When I've picked your minds, I should have a document we can all work over. I'm giving myself four days to put this together. Then the Committee will review, and we'll be ready to 'face the mob'."

"That sounds pretty aggressive, Jane."

Jane took a bite of toast and egg, a quarter slice of bacon perched on top. She chewed a few bites and then covered her mouth. "Hey, I don't know I can't do it, right? So, I intend to do what I don't know is impossible."

Kathy tipped her head and wrinkled he eyebrows. "Uh, okay, I guess." Kathy grinned at her friend, "And, don't talk with your mouth full."

#

"Now, that is an interesting challenge, Kathy. You've listed education in all three categories. It's a freedom, an expectation *and* a responsibility?"

"Not so unusual. Health care falls into all three and to a certain degree so do self-defense, entitlements and taxes."

"I'm not sure I follow on self-defense."

"Okay. The Second Amendment, in 27 words, says, loosely, that we have a right to defend ourselves with firearms, both as individuals and as a 'militia'. That means a freedom to own firearms, an expectation of reasonable controls, and a responsibility to use those firearms in a manner best guaranteeing both our own safety and the safety of those around us, including our nation."

"I've never thought of it that way. Wow. Hang on, I want to write the gist of that down." She rapidly typed into a note taking application. "Okay, how does that work for education?

July 28, 2107

"Good morning, Millie. May I come in?" George leaned in the open door of the office.

Millie looked up from her laptop. "Sure" She saw that he was wearing a suit; unusual for the ever-casual George. "Hot date?"

"What?" Then, it clicked, and he looked down, his hand brushing his tie. "I wish. No, Dr. E and I are headed to DC to brief some of the sponsors. He asked for the latest progress report. How's Jane doing?"

Millie spun the desk chair around and leaned back. "She tells me that she's happy with the progress. She won't show anyone the draft, but that's not unusual for someone writing a long paper of any type. First drafts are notoriously amorphous, and you can imagine that this one, while shorter, is even worse. I spoke with Kathy and Beau. She's taking the Committee members one at a time to get their take on the areas of concentration. Kathy says that she's on to something, but won't tell me any more than that it won't look like the Constitution. Beau said, after he was done, that he was still trying to get a handle on the way she was going about it. At any rate, she says that she's confident she will have a draft on the 7th, as promised."

George glanced at his watch. "What then?"

"Right now, the plan is for the extended EC, meaning the five of us, To Lin, Oy Palomuto and Tom McGinlay, will meet to look it over. My dad calls it a 'murder board'. We'll try to find holes in it, but not in a destructive fashion. We picked her to write it, so we've decided, as a committee, that her version is what we'll start with. She will meet with Sally over the weekend before to do grammar and continuity checks. Then on the 9th, we expect to be able to call what we're calling 'the Convention'. It's a meeting of the Committee of the Whole. Sally will read the document, in its entirety for the first time. Copies will be handed out. No digital copies will be made, for security sake. On the 10th we begin debate and vote on the 16th."

"That's a very aggressive schedule, Millie.

Millie adopted a Cheshire grin. "It's not our calendar, George. It's yours."

George chuckled. "Touché."

"Assuming that there are no fist fights or walkouts and that a consensus is found, Sally will format and copy on the 17th. Her group is putting together a Farewell/Victory dinner celebration for that night. We'll present it to you on Friday; format to be determined.

"That does recall a question that most of the kids are asking. How and when will they be allowed to leave?"

George leaned back against the doorway. "Wow. Okay. When I get back, you, Sally and I will get together to make plans for Friday the 18th. Off hand, I would think that any time after noon, the Interns will begin to out process." He glanced at his watch, again. "I've got to go. We've got a plane to catch in Nashville and we didn't want to use a helicopter." You and I can meet on Monday morning after the meeting, okay?"

"Sure."

"Oh, what are the others doing?"

"To Lin and Oy have broken them up into groups to work on transition. You know. How do we go from this to that with the least disruption?"

"Based upon a document not yet approved? Gutsy."

Millie slowly shook her head. "Go catch a plane, George. Remember, you gave us the job and set the schedule. We're just trying to earn our meager pence."

July 28, 2017 - Alexandria, Virginia

"Harold. Is it, then, your opinion, then, that the product, for want of a better word, that your gross of teenagers is writing may be of more value than the simple research for which we contracted?" The retired CEO sat in a wing chair facing the two Institute representatives. The mate to his chair held the Minority Whip who, for the time being remained silent, his eyes shrouded.

Mr. Gilbert took a breath and tried to frame his answer carefully. "Sir, this isn't just a high school term paper to them. We've worked hard to give them the incentive and resources to produce a real-world product. We've asked them, in good faith, to rewrite the Constitution to govern the United States of today and tomorrow. I believe that they are doing just that. What I don't know is the format or content of it. This project is only funded for a million dollars and almost half of that is the salaries we're paying the interns. A properly bid project in the open market would have been exponentially more expensive and impossible to keep quiet. We're approaching the end of the project period. I'm asking that you let my team complete their 'contract' in their own way."

The Whip spoke. "Perhaps, but I need to see, no make that 'we' need to see the resulting document before it goes public; if in fact it ever sees the light of day. We can't let something that's too far out or too far to the right or the left, be construed as the direction this nation is taking. Get me a draft of this thing." His voice was insistent and bordering on angry.

Harold turned to George. "Can you get a copy of the draft?"

George shook his head. "I really don't think so. The only two people who have seen it in any form, to date, are Jane Abrams and Sally Jamison and they do all their work off-line. The Executive Committee won't see it until the 7th, the first time it's sent to a printer. I *might* be able to get a copy then, but it would require some subterfuge and the cooperation of IT."

The CEO almost shouted, "I don't care if it takes Tom Cruise and the Mission Impossible team. Get me a copy. We've got to be able to control and if not control, then spin this thing right from the start. I'm sorry the President ever authorized it. It's bad for stability and the market." The sponsor stood from the table, shook Harold's hand and completely ignored George before walking out. "And, I don't want to wait until the 10th. Do you understand?" He did not wait for an answer before he left the room.

"That went well." George remarked.

"Come on. We've got a plane to catch."

George and Harold settled into their seats on the plane for the flight from Dulles to Nashville. "Harold, did you sense a certain lack of enthusiasm on the part of the Minority Whip? I am not comfortable getting an advance draft of the document."

"George, we're being paid to do a job. I didn't like the way he talked to me, either, but he *is* paying the bills. See if you can get a copy of the draft without breaking the law."

"If we get caught, the EC will lock us completely out until they turn the document over. You know that, right? As it is, Millie is just barely talking with us."

"It's a risk we'll have to take, George. We work for the Institute, not the Interns."

"Are you going to tell Dr. Elliot what he said?"

"No, and I recommend that you don't, either."

George was silent as he leaned back against the acceleration of the aircraft.

The Clubhouse Turn

Potholes

August 2, 2017 - Camp Donelson

Jane walked into the day room where Sally was engaged in typing up notes from the committee, putting together the ceremony for the 18th. "Sally?"

She held up a hand. "Hang on a sec." Her hand dropped back to the keyboard and she continued typing for a minute or two. She saved the file and sat back, picking up a tall glass with a straw and sucking in a neon yellow liquid. "Okay, your nickel."

"What are you drinking. That looks hideous."

Sally laughed. "Dew and green Gatorade. This keeps me awake. I've been so busy, it's almost the only thing keeping me going."

Jane made a sour face. "Do you have any idea what that stuff is doing to your stomach?"

"My stomach, Jane. Whacha got? I've got fourteen more pages to enter before lunch. It's not the pure entry that takes the time, it's the meta-data, keywords and cross referencing that take the time. I can't get you guys trained to give me that information. I have to dig it out myself."

"Talk to Millie, hon. Have her jerk them up short. You're too important to us to make you do *our* work *and* yours. Oh, here's the flash drive with the next sections on it. I tried to give you all the reference material."

Sally held up her hand. "Hey, you're easy. First, you follow the template. Second, you're writing the document and that means it makes sense and that the grammar is good. I'll take one of yours to any two of the others. Hand it over."

She took the flash drive from Jane and recorded the number of the drive, Jane's name and the time it was turned over. "By the way, did George ask you if he could see the draft?"

Jane stopped and looked at her. "No. We agreed that only you and I would see the roughs. After that the Executive Committee. He won't see it until the 10th. Why?"

"He stopped in yesterday and asked if he could see it. He didn't really say he had your permission, but it was a loose allusion. I told him that I couldn't let him see it unless I talked with you. He told me not to worry and that he'd talk to you."

"Hmmm. Okay. Forget it, but no one will see it before the EC, okay?"

"Done."

#

Millie didn't knock. She entered George's office, closed the door pulled a straight back chair to the edge of his desk and sat down. "George, what's going on?"

George looked at the clouds on her expression and took a breath. "Hello, Millie. Come on in. What are you asking?"

She leaned forward and put her elbows on his desk. "Cut the crap, George. Why are you trying to get a copy of the CwC? We explained the schedule to you last month. What's going on?"

George ignored her for a second time. He simply asked, "What's the CwC? I've never heard you mention it."

"George, I'm not angry ... yet. First, you asked Jane for a copy of the document she's writing. Nice try. Next you try to convince Sally that you have Jane's permission to see it. Transparent. Finally, you send your 'geeks' to try and intimidate my 'geeks' into giving you access to our servers. Stupid!

"I will ask one more time, George. If you treat me like a kid instead of the head of your project, I will walk out of here and you and your DAs will spend the rest of the project drinking coffee." It was obvious that Millie was upset. She stood. "George, you have three seconds to tell me why you're trying so hard to get something you'll see in a week. That's one second!"

"George held his hands out in front of him in surrender. "Sit down, Millie. I need to talk to you."

#

"Oy, I just can't figure out how we're going to transition the Senate. The changes we're making don't give us any real path for the incumbents. I mean, we're not talking about a simple redistricting. We're talking about a paradigm shift for the upper house. Mac and I are in caffeine poisoning for all the coffee we've had staying up late. We're hoarse from talking with the interns about this and that."

"Did you reread Article 1, Section 3, as I told you?"

"Yes, but we didn't have Senators, then. They were all new hires."

"Then, be creative and follow the same basic line. Try something like this. Each Geo-Economic Area, or GEA, will be entitled to three Senators. At Ratification +1, the three senior Senators from the states making up that GEA retain their jobs. All others retire within a specific transition period; still to be determined. The junior of the 'keepers' is up for reelection at the next general election. Four years later, the second 'keeper' is up reelection and eight years beyond that, the final retained Senator must defend his job. How's that sound?"

"Jeez, man. How'd you think of all of that?"

Oy laughed. "Don't give up your day job to go into politics, Gary. You're still stuck in the old ways. This whole effort of ours only succeeds if we are creative, inventive and dogged in our pursuit of fair and effective solutions. If we don't, we fail. And failure is never an option. Just keep at it, Gary. "

"Hey, Oy? Don't leave."

"Yeah?"

"Remember that we decided that the new legislature minorities couldn't use fancy rules to block legislation? We think we should soften that a bit."

"Well, I'd be breaking the rules if I said 'no', so enlighten me, Bruddah." He grinned. "Kona taught me that one. Like it?"

"Yeah, but, I'm a bruthah, not a bruddah."

Oy shook his head. "Oh, brother. Make your point, Dean."

"Okay. If we don't allow filibusters and super majorities and committees to 'not report', we give all the power to the majority, with no check on them. They can block legislation that favors a minority opinion forever."

"Or until the next election, anyway. Well, that was the intention. Majority rules, right? It causes the minority party to be a 'loyal opposition', something we had before the Vietnam mess and Watergate."

"Hey, man. We're both minorities. What do you think the majority is going to do for us if we have no way of stopping them from railroading us?"

Oy smiled, "Dean, where I come from I'm the majority, so your comparison is flawed. But, I hear you. So, what have you in mind?"

"I don't know, yet. It should be the job of that house to keep itself in motion, so intervention from the Executive, the Judiciary or the other house doesn't work. We're thinking there should be a class of legislation that can't be blocked. The rest is open for political in-fighting."

"That's a fairly harsh statement."

"Oy, it's also true. We want the budget, annual appropriations and appointment confirmations to be above that. They're the business of the government and shouldn't be impeded by politics."

"Good luck with that one, but I think that's a good idea."

"We also want it to be a CwC requirement that certain legislative business be completed on time, or pay and benefits stop, for the house that is remiss. My dad can get fired for not doing his job. Why shouldn't we hold Congress, the President or the Supreme Court responsible."

"You get my vote. Write it up and give it to Jane. Then keep on working. You're doing great work."

#

"The problem, Millie, is that the draft CwC only says that the citizen has an expectation of being taxed to pay for the government, a responsibility to pay his taxes and freedom from unfair or burdensome taxation, without good cause. In return, the government is responsible for fair taxation and has an expectation that taxes will be paid. But, the devil is in the details and the CwC doesn't include the details.

"What is a fair tax? When is taxation burdensome? What's best for the nation's economy, a flat tax, a value added tax, some renovated version of a sales tax? What do we do with capital gains taxes, inheritance taxes, excise taxes?

"And it's got to be tied to fiscal responsibility. No bill that spends money should be enacted unless the money is appropriated to pay the bill."

"Hey! Lighten up. I'm on your side, Beau, okay? I think we need to have an index or a data base or something that leaves behind the details that we know any section of the CwC is going to call out. It's just not our job to rebuild everything."

"I know. It's just frustrating. We can write in an idea, but some bureaucrat or 'sunsetter' legislator is going to try and make it work to his or her benefit. Just how do we keep that from happening?"

"Sitting here, now? Prayer seems to be all we have, I'm afraid."

August 4, 2017

"George, we need to have the DAs involved in some of what we're doing. Can we depend on them not obstructing or carrying information back to you or the Institute? We need their intelligence, insight and input, but we don't need or want interference."

George rubbed his eyes. "Millie, I wish I could accuse you of being unreasonable. I can't, though. The best I can say is that they are at your disposal. That's why they're here. They must report to me and I'll do what I can to keep anything in house. And before you ask, you can't pick and choose. You either work with all or none. Anything else is counterproductive and *will* haunt you later."

"That doesn't give me a warm and fuzzy, George. We're so close, but the details of transition, sunset, civil service, debt, international relationships, and a hundred other things are so far away from what we know. The individual working groups are starting to complain about being so buried in details, surprises and 'gotchas' that most are paralyzed."

George's attitude changed immediately. "We can't risk failure, Millie. I'll call them in and have a word with them. May I tell Dr. Elliot?"

Millie gave George a look that would have frozen a forest fire. "You may *not* tell *anyone* from the Institute, George, and you know very well why."

George winced, "Okay. But, you're going to need luck to keep the Institute from finding out what's going on. Some of the sponsors *want* a copy of the draft before it reports out. And, they'll do almost anything to get it."

#

Jay knocked on Jane's door. "Jane? Can you come to the day room, please? Some of us want to talk with you about a section of the CwC, that we don't think is right."

Jane saved her document and logged out. "Jay, you know that I'm supposed to have the freedom to write the draft. You will have your chance 'in convention' next week."

Jay was insistent. "I'm afraid the CwC will never get out of 'convention', if you don't listen to us now."

"I don't like the implied threat, Jay."

"We don't want it to be a threat, but no one will listen to us. And, if someone doesn't, we *will* disrupt the convention."

She sighed. "Alright, I'll come, but not alone. If there is some disruption planned, I want one of the EC there, too. If not Millie, then Al Lee."

"I'll talk to the group, but if one of you has to come, it should be Al, not Millie."

"Now, I'm intrigued. Why not Millie?"

"That's simple. She doesn't see things our way."

"And what makes you sure that I see things your way."

"Just come with me, Jane."

Jane made sure she was logged out. She consulted a contact list on her desk, picked up her cell phone and called Al Lee's number. "Al? Yes, it's Jane. I think we may have a problem brewing that lands in your lap." She paused and listened. "I told him, but his caucus, his word, is threatening to disrupt the convention. Can you meet us in the Day Room? Thanks." She stood. "Okay, let's go, Al will meet us there. And Jay? This better be worthwhile."

Al Lee was standing inside the door when Jay and Jane walked in. "Jane, can I talk with you?"

"Sure. I'll be right with you, Jay." She waited until he approached the group at the side of the room and began a conversation with them. "What's up?"

"I know this group. I'm surprised that they sent Jay to you. They're all evangelical or conservative Christians. They've been lobbying hard for protective clauses in the CwC and are just not willing to listen to either reality or reason."

"That would explain why Jay thought he could come directly to me. We're both LDS and, because my father is part of the church hierarchy, he thinks I should be as rabid as he is. He just doesn't quite understand what it means to be a good Mormon." Al started to say something. She held up a hand. "No, that's an internal thing, Al. I can deal with that. Let's go see what they have in mind." She walked to the front of the room and stood by Jay. Al moved to the side and sat in a folding chair. For the most part, the group didn't register that he was there.

"Good morning. Jay tells me that you have an issue, or issues, that you feel are not being addressed in the normal flow of our work. So, is there a spokesperson?"

"They want me to talk," offered Jay.

"I would prefer it from another member of this caucus, if you don't mind." Jay looked at her eyes. He didn't see the compassion that he expected from a sister.

"Okay," He turned toward the group. "Dinty? You're one of the more vocal in the caucus. Present your case." He turned back to Jane as an overweight young woman in tight pants and a long sleeved, high neck blouse walked toward the front. "Dinty is from Georgia."

"Hello, Dinty, did you say?"

The girl spoke for herself. "My name is Deanna, but my daddy said I looked like a Dinty, so Dinty is was."

Jane smiled. "Okay, Dinty. Jay's tossed the torch to you. What's bothering this group that can't wait until the open debate of the Convention?"

"Okay. We think you're writing God out of the CwC."

Jane cocked her head at the implication. "That's a very damning and very broad accusation, Dinty, and one with which I disagree, strongly. But, please continue."

"America is a Christian country. It always has been. You're taking Christ out of the country."

"Dinty, let's try and be a bit more concise. Where, exactly, have I written, your words, Christ out of the country? We may come back to that broad accusation, if we need to, but let's start small."

"Okay. I will." Her voice became insistent. "Your new paper doesn't address marriage as between a man and woman, or homosexuality as a sin or of abortion as murder." She crossed her arms and took a stance familiar to Jane, a righteous accusation daring Jane to refute what she had said.

"Dinty, let's first put the 'accusations' and the CwC into context. You contend that, for the sake of this argument, that the three items are the laws of God, right?"

"Don't you? Of course, they are." She turned and scowled at Jay. "Jay? I thought you said she was a good Christian."

Jay held out his hands. "I said, she is a member in very good standing of our Church, Dinty. I truly believe she is. Just listen, please."

Jane gave Jay a grateful glance and dipped her head in thanks. "Jay is right, Dinty, but my beliefs have no place in this conversation. I am acting as an agent of the Institute and this organization of 155 individuals. Now, would you agree that the CwC is a document meant to be the foundation of the government?"

"Sure, but ..."

"No 'buts' in this discussion, Dinty. Okay, we agree that there are two sides to this discussion, then; God's, if you will, and the government's. Okay?

"Well, I think they should be the same."

"You have that freedom of thought; even under the CwC, but you agree that there are two different items?"

"Uh, okay."

"Now, let's put a boundary around one of them. Do you know Mark 22:21?"

Dinty's eyes widened. "Uh, well, not off the top of my head, I guess. Can I get a Bible and look it up?"

"I don't think it will be necessary. I'm certain that Jay knows it. Jay?" Jay glanced at Jane and then a small smile lit up his face.

"They say unto him, Caesar's. Then saith he unto them, Render therefore unto Caesar the things which are Caesar's; and unto God the things that are God's."

"Do you know what they were referring to, Dinty?"

"Jesus was in the Temple."

"Well, actually, Matthew was referring to the statue of Caesar that was ordered placed in the temple. But, for the sake of the argument, let's just say that it means that some things are the provenance of God and others the provenance of governments, okay?"

"I guess."

"Good. Now, let's get to your three accusations.

"First, marriage. The Bible refers to marriage, but never defines it. Man, meaning throughout history, church hierarchies aplenty and governments galore, have all been the definers; not Jesus or the Almighty. In fact, the relationship of 'church', using that word in its most generic sense, and state with respect to marriage, dates to the Council of Trent. Marriage, in a legal sense, dates at least to ancient Rome and probably earlier in some context or another, at least in Jewish traditions. It is an establishment of property rights. Even the old testament establishes the wife as the property of her husband. So, we need to keep the sacraments of individual religious organizations separate from the legal implications of a union, as far as the CwC is concerned.

"Second, homosexuality. Again, the Bible makes peripheral reference to the act of sex between members of the same sex several times. Let's get it straight, though. The word 'homosexuality' was coined in the 19th century and has no Biblical or moral significance. And, the number of translations, over time, has significantly degraded the definition of 'unnatural acts' or 'sodomy' to a level of being indecipherable as to the intended meaning. Be that as it may, and as I hold in the explanation of marriage, does the government have the freedom to determine who sleeps with whom? Render unto Caesar, again.

"Third, abortion. I will grant you a much more emotional debate and one, in fact, with which I probably agree with you. It is a very tangled combination of women's reproductive rights and the right to life; of an infant, not a soul, but a life. Don't quote me, 'Thou shalt not kill.' When does life begin; at conception or when a fetus is a viable life-form outside a woman's womb? It's not my job to determine that, right now. Nor, does it have a place in the CwC; a road map for Caesar to follow.

"In all three of your arguments, it's my job to find common ground between morals and ethics, freedoms and responsibilities and to separate Caesar from God." She heard the crowd ready to pounce.

"Now wait. Before you respond with mob violence and 'storm the castle', let me continue. Let's deal with two of the specific topics from the standpoint of the CwC. First, you have the freedom to believe that marriage is a holy sacrament between one man and one woman. That's fine, so do I. But, someone from somewhere else, has the same freedom; that is, to believe that marriage is a legal contract between any two humans. As citizens, you both have the expectation that the law of the land will defend your freedom to believe that and that the government is responsible to ensure that your expectation is equitably fulfilled.

"You also have the freedom to hold the belief that a sexual relationship between consenting adults of the same sex is immoral and 'sinful'; 'wrong' in your religious sense. My example pair of gays has the same freedom, although they are free to believe that their relationship is as reasonable and 'moral' as yours; having no adverse effect on anyone else. Again, and in almost the same words, you both have the expectation that the law of the land will defend your freedom to believe that and that the government is responsible to ensure that your expectation is fulfilled on an equal basis to each. Remember that statue of Justice? She's blindfolded. My dad can remember when a black man could be sent to jail for marrying a white woman, and vice versa. Not today. With luck and the work we're doing, maybe someday our kids won't be able to remember a time when it mattered who married whom; so long as there was love and respect between them.

"What about my right to not recognize gay marriage?"

"Okay, let's deal with a pair of often misunderstood words. In fact, let's deal with an historical occurrence right along those lines. In Kentucky, in 2015, an elected official, a County Clerk to be exact, also an evangelical Christian, refused to issue marriage licenses that were legal under state law because the issuance of same offended her moral beliefs. Yet, by that action, she acted unethically. She broke the law in response to her moral outrage. The charge, misfeasance; or not doing her job.

"Let's explore 'moral' vs 'ethical' in this instance. A moral belief is a personal standard of 'right' and 'wrong'. Every one of us has moral standards; nearly all of them different in some way or another. No one set of standards is higher or lower, better or worse, 'more right' or 'more wrong'; except as they effect, in some way or another, fellow citizens. She was elected to be an official responsible for carrying out administrative details of the county under state law for *all* the citizens of her county. She was morally right, but ethically wrong. She could not separate Caesar from God. If she could not, in good moral conscience, carry out her duties, one of which was to issue marriage licenses to same-sex couples, then she had only one ethical choice, resignation.

"I apologize for the lecture. You each have the freedom to believe what you will. I have religious beliefs like Jay, here, yet largely foreign to Al Lee, in the back row. You have the freedom to not recognize gay marriage. You have the expectation that the government will defend your freedom. But you also have the responsibility to uphold the law of the land. The county clerk took two, but ignored the third. You have the freedom to refuse service to anyone you wish except as it violates the law, as in equality in housing; although, if you are in business, I can't see how it matters if your customers are gay, straight male or female, black or blue. On the other hand, anyone who disagrees with your freedom has the freedom to not patronize your business. Regrettably, both sides have had a tendency recently to believe that they can force the other to take their side by disrupting the business cycle through demonstration.

"Our nation, under the Constitution, is not perfect because man is not perfect. I am writing a document that I think best defends all Americans of all shapes, sizes, religions and belief systems, but the same human imperfections will exist. All I, or we can do, is try our best in our time; as the framers did in theirs. Who knows what the world will look like in another 230 years."

#

"Jane, I don't understand something."

Jane and Jay were walking back to her office. "I'm about talked out, Jay. What can I explain?"

"Don't be angry. I don't know how you did it, but you almost satisfied that group of religious conservatives. I know they don't like it, but you explained it in a way that made sense, in some way, to each one of them; including me. But, I don't understand how you can believe that God and Christ don't have a place in the CwC. For 230 years we've been a Christian country. Oh sure, we accept Jews and Chinese and Japanese and, now bunches of Muslims, but we're a Christian country. How can a Mormon, heck, a First Family who serves on the Quorum of Seventy, let the country change?"

Jane sighed and looked at her watch. She pointed at a bench. "Jay, I don't have time for this. Sit down."

"What?"

Sharply, she said, "Sit down!" Jay sat, and Jane sat at the other end of the bench, twisted toward him. "Look, If I don't write the CwC, if we don't approve it, as accepting all religious points of view, all of them, without exception, then no religious point of view is safe. One day it might be divorce outlawed, or, Saints preserve us, a belief that Jesus walked in America, as you and I believe He did. But, those points of view can have no impact on the processes of the Federal government. Remember, render unto Caesar?"

"But …"

"No 'buts' from you either, my friend. This has never been a Christian country. In no document, oath or law does the name of Jesus, or any of His associated names, appear. The closest you come is 'so help me God.' But, each of us defines 'God' in a way that suits our individual beliefs. The Founders used the word Providence to describe the actions of a Supreme Spirit. Even the Declaration simply said, 'our Creator'. Each of those words is generic enough to leave the question open to the heart of each citizen. We might as well remove Thanksgiving as a holiday, along with changing the name of Christmas. Valentine's Day celebrates a Catholic saint and Easter, for all its significance in Christianity, falls on a pagan holiday.

"Jay, religion simply has no place in a government for all the people. Even our beloved Utah has been forced, by necessity, to accept changes that seem un-Mormon. I've knelt beside you at services every Sunday as you or another priest conducted services. I pray every Sunday for a government that promises equality for all. If it doesn't, there is no promise of equality for any. It's as simple as that."

She stood and, without turning back, walked up the walkway to the Day Room.

The Good, the Bad and the Future

The Cabal

August 6, 2017 - Camp Donelson

"George, the sponsors are not happy."

George had been dreading this call. So far, he'd been fortunate. He sagged back in his chair. He'd already taken Marion Dixson's call. Now it was Harold Gilbert. "Harold, if by sponsors, you refer to the CEO, the Whip and their surrogates, I have tried every legal way to obtain a draft. Neither Sally nor Jane will release it, and they keep it on a Flash drive. The sponsors are just going to have to wait until tomorrow. Jane will send electronic copies to the extended Executive Committee at 9:00 tomorrow morning. I'm certain she knows that I will have a copy at 9:01, or as soon as I can convince the guys in IT to send it to me, as a Blind Copy. I've sent you every word I could get."

That wasn't quite true. George had kept very careful records of everything reported to him by the DAs. He felt that they had a pretty good idea of what the document said, at least in summary. He now knew that its name was the Contract with the Citizenry. He was absolutely astounded that a group of recent high school graduates could have conceived of a document with the depth of understanding and breadth of flexibility. And, he had sent none of that information to the Founders. He had kept his word to Millie. Or at least, he hoped he had.

"Well, you had better have a draft in my inbox before lunch, George. Marion called me and said that she wasn't sure where your loyalties were."

"Are *you* questioning them, Harold?"

"Not yet."

"My loyalties have always been with the charge given us. As I remember, it was 'to cause a new foundation document to be written, free of all interference and political pressure'."

He heard a chuckle at the other end. "You have a pretty good memory, George. It may well be better than that of some others. Keep up the good work."

"Thanks. I'll be in touch in the morning."

August 7. 2017

> From: George Hanover
>
> To: Harold Gilbert
>
> Marion Dixson
>
> Erick Leary
>
> Dean Elliot
>
> Subj: Draft Foundation Document
>
> Attach: Contract with the Citizenry of the United States (First Draft) - Not for Dissemination (Cwc-Draft-1.doc)
>
> Founders. Per your direction, I am attaching a copy of the draft Contract with the Citizenry of the United States (CwC), presented to the Executive Committee (extended), (ECe) at 9:00 this morning, August 7, 2017. This is an unauthorized copy. The plan is for the ECe to proof, modify and otherwise prepare the document and ancillary documentation, for presentation to the Committee of the Whole. They call it 'The Convention', at 9:00am, Thursday, August 10, 2017 for open debate. The enclosed document is, in almost its entirety, the creative work of Jane Manning Abrams -UT. This document is the product and analysis of 153 young Americans in an effort estimated at greater than 65,000 man-hours.
>
> George Hanover

From: Harold Gilbert

To: SponsorsList

Subj: Draft Foundation Document

Attach: Contract with the Citizenry of the United States (First Draft) - Not for Dissemination (Cwc-Draft-1.doc)

Attached is the document copy required by your correspondence dated 1 August 2017. It is provided over the objections of the Institute. The premature release of this document constitutes both a violation of the contract confidentiality clause and a breach of the security of the project. Unauthorized release or publication may seriously jeopardize the success of the project you are sponsoring and have grave negative impact on our nation. I urge you to be circumspect in discussion and comment and to keep all such commentary within the confines of the Sponsors, pending delivery of the document, hereinafter known as CwC, on Friday August 18, 2017.

Harold Gilbert

August 8, 2017 - Camp Donelson

"Mr. Gilbert?" His assistant leaned back from her desk to make eye contact with her boss.

"Yes, Mary?"

"The CEO is on line 2, sir."

Harold glanced at his watch. He shook his head and almost, but not quite, smiled. "Not bad, Mary. I sent the email at 5:13pm last night, so most of them would be gone for the day. Make a note. It's 8:03am."

He picked up the handset and pressed the line button blinking. "Good morning. This is Harold."

"Don't hand me that 'good morning' crap, Gilbert. Have you read this thing?"

"I have. I think it's remarkable."

"Well, I don't, and I'll bet a bunch of us won't. This destroys the structure that supports our country. The economy will go south if we let this get out! I can't even imagine what it would be like if it were ratified."

"And, I'm certain the sky is falling, too. However, this is exactly what you contracted for. I had it quoted to me just two days ago. Let's see, ah yes, 'to cause a new foundation document to be written free of all interference and political pressure.' I believe we've fulfilled that contract. I might add that it is filled in a manner that we could never have imagined."

"I don't care about that crap! This 'freedom, expectation, responsibility' BS gives the masses control. We can't have that. They've got no clue. They don't care like we do. Listen! I'm calling the other sponsors. We're going to kill this before it ever leaves Kentucky. You shut them down, Gilbert!" The line went dead.

Harold spoke into the dead handset. "You have a very fine day, too, sir." He sighed and placed the handset gently in the cradle. He looked at it for a moment and then spoke up.

"Mary?"

"Yes sir?"

"Would you see if Dr. Elliot is in, please?"

Gestation

"Millie? May I say something before we start?" The Executive Committee and their assistants were seated at tables formed in a rounded "U" shape, two to a table. The opening faced a large screen monitor with the CwC displayed. Sally sat at a table to the right, a keyboard on the table. She would make any edits voted by the EC.

Millie looked around the group and saw no objections. "Your nickel, Kathy."

Kathy stood and walked to stand in front of the screen. "Sally? Put the Preamble up, please." The screen faded and returned with a 64-word display. "Thanks. Friends, I read this and knew that what followed would be extraordinary. I was more than correct. Jane has taken our work, sometimes confused and always convoluted and created a document that, I believe, will stand as the view of what we want America to be. I move that Jane Manning Abrams be awarded John Hancock's honor of being first signatory of this document."

"Second!" Heads swiveled to see Al Lee grinning from his chair.

Millie laughed. "Sally, record that the first act of the Executive Committee reviewing the CwC, spell it out, please, was to vote on giving the honor of the first signature to Jane Manning Abrams of Utah. Now, all in favor? A show of hands." Seven hands were in the air. Only Jane's was in her lap; her head down. "Please show unanimous approval. Thank you, Kathy."

Jane raised her head, tears glistening in her eyes. "Thank you. You have no idea. But, you also know that we're not going to be the people signing this document, if, in fact, it is ever signed. We aren't the movers and shakers, the leaders and the politicians who will claim the honor of adding their names to a display in the National Archives. But, thanks anyway. Now, I suspect that we should get to work." She smiled broadly. "I'm flattered, but I know that you're just waiting to have at it. With your permission, Millie? Sally? Article 1 - Citizen Freedoms on the screen, please."

#

Beau flipped a page in his steno book. "I note that you've given the responsibility for any military action to the Congress, as it is in the Constitution. We know that the President has, since Vietnam, suborned that and that subsequent Chief Executives had the War Powers Act rammed through, to legitimize it. How do we prevent this from happening again?"

Al spoke up. "This is as ugly an issue as we will face, I think. It's not just an issue of separation of powers and potential executive abuse, but it has implications for budget. Remember that we required a balanced budget with specific provisos, one being a Congressionally-approved military action. It also has significant international implications. If the President promises an action to assist an ally, but Congress refuses, the view from across the pond is one of confusion and weakness. We cannot move the military from beneath the Executive. It belongs there. But, we can make controls stronger and more distinct than in the Constitution. Name the Executive Order as a tool in the Executive Section, yes. But, it carries a requirement to seek approve within a reasonable time limit. Disapproval means loss of funding; and that also disallows moving money around to bypass Congressional mandate. I think we need to put this one on the list to discuss with the DAs before the Convention, though. That is, unless, one of you has a truly creative way around this one."

Millie frowned. "We just seem to keep shuffling these decisions until later. Sally, put it on the list."

Tom McGinlay spoke for the first time. "Millie, the Framers didn't have anywhere near the complexities to deal with, that we face. They stood upon the shoulders of those who had gone before, Magna Carta and Rousseau, and wrote a document that defended them, as citizens, from what had happened to them in their recent past; illegal searches and billeting, taxation, repression etc.

We're not omniscient. And, we can't be expected to have workable solutions to every complex issue facing us today. It's taken 230 years to get us into this mess. We're not going to get out of it in eleven days and five pages single spaced. I expect that several libraries of clarifying and codifying documents will have to be written. The transition will take years and won't always be pretty. I imagine that the solution will, eventually, come from someone with a completely unique view of the problem; maybe even a high school sophomore, today." He smiled and sat back.

August 9, 2017

"I think you've captured the controls on the Executive in section II, but we need to strengthen the wording on the election, and elimination of the Electoral College, as an election method."

"What have you in mind, Oy?"

"Okay. Obviously, I'm looking at this from the standpoint of always being a citizen of a 'territory' and, to most of you, non-existent. Our votes have never counted, so we're victims of 'taxation without representation', if you will. If we have an 'every citizen has a vote' expectation, you bring us into the fold. That needs to be laid out; especially in view of the Geo-Economic entity Oceania.

"I also think we need to clarify the Vice-President. Both the Constitution and the 12th Amendment left the definition open to interpretation by the Electors. Since the Electors were, or are, political animals, the VP has historically been the running mate of the elected President. He, sorry, but they *have* all been men to date, didn't have to be. The running mate became vice-president for political reasons. It gave the Executive Branch an edge in the Senate. That could be viewed as a violation of the checks and balances as well as the separation of powers. Two centuries ago, with the VP largely ceremonial, that might have been acceptable. Today, it is not. He's become an assistant President. I suggest that the Vice President be the Presidential candidate who comes in second. "

Millie gasped in surprise. "Heck, the First Spouse has become a member of the administration with a paid staff. Abigail Adams would be beside herself at the audacity that she should be expected to represent the country, in any way. Imagine her lecturing a church group in Boston on the evils of the southern slave-based economy?" She paused for a giggle. "Anyway, you're proposing to undo the entire political power structure?" Oy simply smiled, his dark eyes twinkling.

"You know, there's merit there." Beau leaned forward and pointed at the monitor. "By breaking the hold of the Executive branch, it is possible to give more support to the Section I article that precludes unlimited blocking of legislation by minority caucus. Let's put in 'the candidate receiving the second highest number of popular votes shall be the Vice-President.'

"At the very least, I can see some input from the DAs on that one. Any objections?" Millie paused and swept her eyes around the table. Jane had her hand up enough to get Millie's attention. "Jane?"

"I'm not objecting; at least not on the principle that Beau is raising. I just think we need to think about the magnitude of change we're throwing at America all at once."

"I'm confused. You wrote the very document that you're criticizing?"

"No, not at all. I believe every word I wrote. And, I think all 153 of us believe it as well. But, if we're to be taken seriously, we need to ensure that we encourage the rest of America to understand and buy in. This isn't the 18th Century. The populace won't just accept what the leaders tell them is good for them. They're educated, involved and concerned. They're going to ask a lot, and I mean a lot, of questions. Someone had best have a good meaningful answer and not media spun double-talk."

"What are you driving at Jane?"

"If we're going to change the Executive branch as significantly as the proposal for Vice President, we need to have the political equivalent of a 'cost-benefit analysis' ready to go. 'Hem and Haw' with an answer and the proposal is dead. That means that our work, or someone's work, at any rate, isn't done when we ratify and hand off next week."

The Smell of Fear

August 9, 2017 - Alexandria, VA

"Elliot, I'm presuming that you've read this thing?"

Eight of the sponsors and Founders were standing in groups in the private bar/meeting room of the club on Fairfax Street. The sun, still high, was shining through the wavy period glass and dust motes sparkled with nearly as much intensity as the conversation.

Dr. Elliot tried not to appear upset by the condescension on the Whip's voice. "Of course."

"You can't believe that it's serious?"

"I believe the interns have written what they believe is a good foundation for the United States based upon their perceptions of the needs of today's population, yes."

"That's the most carefully shaped dodge and weave I've ever heard. This whole thing undermines the very structure that holds America together."

Dr. Elliot could play patronizing games, as well. "I think my Executive Committee might hold that they are protecting the real America from being used by a parasitic power structure."

The Whip's voice rose. "You're part of that power structure, you idiot! Are you a parasite? This thing takes our power away!" The room grew silent as heads turned toward the strident voice.

Elliot's voice was calm, and his face held a benign smile. "I believe they think that the 305 million Americans who are not millionaires ought to have more voice than the ten million who do." He turned to face, not just his adversary, but the entire audience of suit clad leaders. "All evening, we've heard fear of this document's effects, but less on America than on your personal and political power bases. Listen to yourselves. You sound like the British aristocracy of 1770 and Congress is behaving like Parliament. Use the colonists to increase our wealth. These kids know what you represent, and they've written a document that defines something that America needs to define; freedom, expectation and responsibility. Maybe we should listen? They're sending a message that," he smiled, "we parasites ought to read before we damn it."

"You're part of that ten percent, man. Are you going to let them take it away from you?"

"You've been reading your own P&L statements. Eight out of ten of that ten percent have investable assets between one and five million. If I remember my last issue of Forbes, eight of the ten major sponsors, including the legislators, are counted in the 45,000 of you with assets greater than $50 million; yourself included, sir. That is not lost on the Interns and won't be lost on the public when the 'great debate' begins."

"That doesn't matter. We'll spend them into silence. This is OUR America, not theirs!"

"Do you remember your Greek mythology, Don? Pandora's box? You opened it when you contracted with the Institute for a new foundation document. And now, 'they' as you so eloquently name them, are loose and looking around."

"You've got to stop this!" Every face was turned toward the voice of the retired bank CEO. "Dammit, you work for us. Stop it!"

"Put in a change request, Don. I'm busy right now with the primary deliverable of our contract. I'll look at the request on the 21st."

The Convention Convenes

August 10,2017 - Camp Donelson

The 200-seat theater was noisy and nearly full. The Institute Founders and the DAs were seated in the front row left. A representative group of five sponsors were seated front row right. Two tables, each with four chairs, were on the stage; one at each wing. The large movie screen was down and displaying a montage of scenic pictures of the United States. Between the screen and tables were two large HD TVs showing the audience from cameras that were at the extreme ends of the stage.

At precisely 10:00 am, the screen displayed a full-sized image of the United States flag. George walked onto the stage and stood at the center. Over the space of a minute, the crowd noise subsided, and the theater quieted. "Good morning. One administrative detail, if you will. Sally, please begin the recording devices. For everyone's information, there are two complete video and audio records being kept of these proceedings. One will be the working document of you, the interns. The second is a 'security' copy that will be under the protection of a private firm; the trendy blue sport coat you see seated at the back by the lighting panel." He paused for a moment. "Sally, is their camera on and recording?" He received a nod from Sally and a wave from the tech in the back.

"Right. Then, let the proceedings begin. Good morning. It is 10:00am, Eastern Daylight Time, August 10, 2017, at Camp Donelson, Kentucky. I now convene the Committee of the Whole, as authorized by contract with the Jefferson-Hamilton Institute for discussion that will, in the wording of the applicable contract clause, 'cause a new foundation document to be written free of all interference and political pressure'. I welcome the Founders,

Devil's Advocates and the Sponsors to this opening session. At the end of this session Sponsors, Founders, Devil's Advocates and I will, by agreement, leave the theater and the Committee of the Whole will meet in closed session for discussions, modifications and a final vote on acceptance, or ratification. The final vote will not be recorded. If the vote is three quarters in favor, the draft document will be certified by the voluntary signature of all 153 interns. The signed and certified document will then become deliverable no later than 10:00am Eastern Daylight Time, August 18, 2017, at the offices of the Institute on this compound. At that time, electronic copies will be delivered, as well. That delivery will constitute the end of this project and all interns will be released to return to your homes.

"The aforementioned having been presented, I now turn these proceedings over to Mildred Dickinson of Ohio, Chairman of the Executive Committee." George walked off the stage and took a seat with the Founders.

Millie turned on the portable microphone she was wearing, stood and walked to stage center. "Thank you, George. Good morning. On June 18th of this year, 155 recent high school graduates sat in this hall and received a charge. Today we meet to begin the final chapter that, we hope, will result in the successful execution of that charge. We have taken our governmental structure apart and analyzed it. We have taken the Constitution apart, section by section, and analyzed it. We have argued, discussed, negotiated, argued more, listened, heard and advised. In the end, we have caused to be written, to quote the contract, a new foundation document to be written free of all interference and political pressure. It is time to read that document in full for the first time.

"There can be but one author of any document. Thomas Jefferson wrote the Declaration of Independence and then sat through painful days of seeing it taken apart and reassembled. James Madison drafted the Constitution and then suffered through its gestation. The document that you have assisted in the creation of, has as its author, Jane Manning Abrams of Utah. I now ask her to rise and introduce you to the document she has created from all your hard work. Jane?"

Jane stood and, ringed binder in hand, approached the center. A security guard appeared from the wings with a portable stand and placed it center-stage. Jane placed her notebook on the stand, reached to her waist to turn on her wireless microphone and looked out over the audience. She took a deep breath.

"Sponsors, Founders, Devil's Advocates and, more importantly, members of the Committee of the Whole. I will now read, or cause to be read, the draft Contract with the Citizenry of the United States of America." She nodded at Sally and sixty-four words appeared on the screen.

"We are the People, who are the United States of America. We cherish our individual freedoms, wishing only to fulfill our expectations in life. In turn, we recognize our responsibilities to ourselves, our fellow citizens and, along with them, to the government with whom this Contract with the Citizenry is made, in order to seek a full, secure and fruitful life for ourselves, our families and the future of our nation."

She paused and looked at the Founders where she saw a mixture of rapt attention, the DAs, where she saw growing smiles and finally the Sponsors; the predominant expression there being more than a few frowns.

From the audience behind them came, at first, a few clapping hands, followed by a growing cacophony and finally a standing ovation of the full house. Jane turned to look at the Executive Committee. They, too, were standing and applauding. When she turned back, she saw that only the sponsors remained seated. She waited to see if it would end on its own. When she realized that it would not, she bowed her head for a moment, said a silent prayer, and raised her head with a broad smile. She raised her hands to quiet the applause. When it finally ended, she said, "Thank you all. It is my hope that it only gets better from here." She was rewarded with a few laughs and a smattering of applause.

"Please let the document be read in its entirety and without audience interruption. At the end, printed copies will be handed out and the entire document, in digital format, will be available on the network; but only to the interns. George tells me that the intern network is now separated from the rest of the camp network and the Internet for Computer Security, to protect our discussions. I'm asking George to read the document out loud. I want to watch reactions and make notes of my own, if you don't mind. George?"

George stood and mounted the stage. He gave Jane a hug and received the notebook from her. He reopened it and nodded at Sally. The screen went dark.

"Article I - The Citizenry. Section 1 - Citizen Freedoms ..."

A Winding Rocky Path

Details ... Details

August 12, 2017 - Camp Donelson

Beau pulled the microphone toward him and opened the morning session. "Good morning. It's Saturday and the EC decided, last night, that we would meet, as a whole, only until the lunch break. After that, we think it's time for individual thought and free discussion. By now, most of you have read the CwC enough times to have questions or thoughts that you might wish to discuss with those you've been working with, for the last two months. All the spaces, including the library and dining hall will be open for your use. The next scheduled session for all of us will begin at 8:00 am, Monday next, August 14.

"In case you don't have enough to assimilate, today is the date on which President Roosevelt signed Social Security into law. It's the date that Japan surrendered, officially ending combat in World War II. Oh, and it's the date on which the whiffle ball was invented. So, let's get to work."

"Madam Chairperson?" A male voice spoke up from the audience.

Millie squinted at the audience. "Turn the lights up high, please." After a brief delay, the remaining ceiling lights came on. "Okay. Thanks. I'm sorry, I don't recognize all 153 of us. Please give us your name, for the record, and the floor is yours."

"Jim Thornton, Millie, from Silver City, Nevada. I notice in Article 1, Section 2, the 'expectation of a healthy environment'. If that is an allusion to the broad area of health care, it's pretty nebulous."

Jane spoke up. "Absolutely correct, Jim. The problem with the citizenry expecting 'health care' is the definition of 'expectation of health care' itself. Are they expecting it to be free in all cases for everyone, regardless of need or diagnosis? If so, the cost is going to be astronomical and unfairly burdensome on some, including the healthy, the poor and even the well-to-do. I can toss all manner of buzzwords out like 'means testing' and 'preventative care' and 'end of life care'. If it's not free, then do the poor get less quality health care than the rich? Look at it in the bright light of reason. Someone with money can afford a Cadillac Escalade, while someone who lives paycheck to paycheck might not be able to afford a Ford Escort. Yet, they are both as likely to get cancer. Both are subject to the same genetic predispositions to obesity or diabetes. How far do we stretch government 'responsibility' and citizen 'expectation'?

"Now add nutrition oversight, safety of the food chain, drug purity and effectiveness and things like monitoring new sources of food, such as Genetically Modified Organisms, or GMOs. Congress will have to modify old laws or pass new laws that fit in the space between new citizen expectations and government responsibilities. Should government pay for medical research through tax dollars? That would reduce drug costs, maybe, but it has its own share of fairness issues with respect to taxation.

"Flip the coin, now. The government has a responsibility to provide solutions to the citizen expectation, but also an expectation that the citizenry must pay for anything they expect; that translates to either taxes or a medical bill for services rendered. That said, an expectation of 'free' means that it's paid for by someone else? We used to call that socialized medicine. I expect that it would be just as unacceptable under the CwC as it was under the Constitution. Am I making sense?"

"Some, but it sounds like you want to do away with Medicare and Medicaid."

"Jim, I, meaning me, Jane Abrams, or even us, meaning this convention, don't do away with anything. The whole issue is far larger and more convoluted than just Medicare and Medicaid.

What I'm saying is that all the framework of the CwC provides are expectations and responsibilities. The House and Senate will pass the laws and the President, through the Executive branch, will define how those laws are to be instituted. It is up to the citizens to elect legislators that understand this and will work toward sensible solutions, not pandering for the vote. The designed term limits make that less attractive.

"The best *we* can do is add a specific detailed item to the 'Intention of the Convention' document and Convention Transcripts."

"I guess I hadn't thought of all of that."

"Don't feel bad, Jim. At our age, and being healthy and dependent upon our families for nearly all financial support; at least up until now, it's unlikely that many of us have. This summer has, probably, been a crash course in the details and complexity of the health care issue. Add political conservatism or liberalism, private wealth or poverty and it becomes a life issue; perhaps the most important one. Certainly, it follows us from birth to death, individually and as a member of a family, a community or a nation.

"The few words in the CwC had to be carefully crafted to leave room for the legislature, through the citizenry, to make the critical decisions to guide both community and government."

#

"We have fifteen pages of 'Intentions' to your nine-page CwC, Jane, and it keeps growing."

"I'm not surprised, Sally. The word 'tax' is only alluded to in the Constitution and the Federal Tax Code is nearly 75,000 pages long. We're only laying a plan with boundaries and directions of flow. The real work will come after ratification and that will take so long that Al Lee will have both his B.A. and J.D. and be in the thick of it."

Sally giggled. "Why do I suspect that you and Millie will be right there with him?"

"You know, I always figured I would be a good Mormon wife, tending my family; very much as my mother and her mother. That may still happen, but I want to see this through. I can't wait until we can leave, and I can talk with mom, dad and grandpa about all of this. What are you going to do? You were on your way to school in Indiana, right?"

"Earlham, right. I still want to teach, but I think I might not do elementary school. I think I'll work on teaching Social Studies. I suspect that the next few years are going to be exciting, one way or the other, and I'd like to help kids grow up with open eyes and hearts."

"Sounds like you've got a worthy goal, girl. I wonder just how many of our 155 paths have changed; other than the two we know about, I mean. Even if you just sat and listened for two months, you couldn't have avoided hearing what was said and then thinking about it."

August 13, 2017 - Flagstaff, AZ

Bishop Benson peeked through his door and saw a pair of men, both in suits. He was as accustomed to suits, in his line of work, as he was to denim and boots. He opened the door.

"Nelson Benson?"

"Yes."

"I'm Martin Davies and this is Tom Klinitz. He handed the bishop a pair of business cards. We work for a large company who has an interest in a young man we understand that you may know, a Mr. Jay Brigham. Do you recognize that name?"

Benson was immediately on alert. "I know Jay, yes. He attends services at the church I serve. Is he okay?"

"We believe he's fine, sir. When did you last talk with him?"

"I believe I spoke with him in June; certainly not later."

"Did he discuss his job with you?"

"I'm afraid, gentlemen, that any dealings I have with a member of my church are of a bishop/member privileged relationship. I can't tell you what we spoke about. Even if I remembered, it would be inappropriate of me."

"Did he, perhaps, mention that he was working on rewriting some important government documents?"

"I'm sorry. As I've told you, even if I remembered, I couldn't tell you what we spoke about. Now, if you'll excuse me."

"A moment, please, Bishop. Yes, we know you're a bishop. We know that he called you at least twice this summer. We need to speak with him. Do you have any contact information for him, a cell number perhaps? It is very important."

Benson backed into his house and grasped the door. "I believe you told me that you work for a private company. I'm afraid you would have to talk with his employer and I do not know who that is. I do believe that he will be back by the beginning of the month to attend BYU. Now, if you will excuse me, I have evening services to prepare for." He closed the door. The two men heard the deadbolt set.

One spoke as the stood looking at the closed door. "I don't suppose they told you he was the pastor of the kid's church?"

"Nope, neglected that little detail. Back to square one?"

"At least back to Phoenix. Come on. You drive. I'll make the call."

#

Dr. Elliot was reading the first draft for the fourth or fifth time when his phone rang. He looked at the display and saw a familiar area code. He picked up the handset. "Dean Elliot."

"Mr. Elliot, this is Nelson Benson in Flagstaff, Arizona. I believe you visited me in June."

Dean remembered why he recognized the area code. "Yes, Bishop. How are you?"

"I'm fine thank you. You left a card and asked me to call you if I had any further contact with Jay."

"That's troubling. Has he called you again?"

"Oh, no. I assure you that I've not heard from him. However, two men were just here asking to contact him. Let's see, I've got those cards here. It was a Mr. Davies and a Mr. Klinitz from First Investigators. The address is Phoenix. Are they perhaps working for you? They said a big company has an interest in Jay."

Dean felt a cold chill and then rubbed his eyes as he thought. "No, sir. I don't think we've contracted with them, but I have an idea who might. If they or anyone else should contact you, please do not tell them anything; especially the subject that Jay raised with you. And, please get as much identification as you can from them and let me know. The project Jay is working on is nearing completion. To the best of my knowledge, he is working hard and well."

"I'm glad to hear it. I would hate for anything to imperil his college plans. He'll be the first of his family to attend college. Ranching is brutal, but infectious."

"The work he's doing is unbelievably important. He and his fellow workers are doing a magnificent job. Please call me, if you hear from them again."

"I will. Thank you. Good bye."

Dr. Elliot replaced the handset. Then, he picked it up again and pressed a speed dial. After a moment, he said, "George. Dean Elliot. Would you please come to my office?"

#

George set his glass of soda on the table where Jay and a pretty young intern were eating. "Jay, may I sit for a moment?"

"Uh, sure, George. Everything okay?"

"As far as I know, it is. Jean, isn't it?" The young woman nodded her head. "Would you be so kind as to refill Jay's glass? I need just a minute of his time."

Both young people showed some concern, but the young woman picked up the two glasses and walked away. She looked back over her shoulder. Jay nodded at her and smiled. "Whatever it is, I didn't do it." He tried to be light, but he was obviously concerned.

"We hope not. I'll cut to the chase before your friend returns. Have you had any contact with your Bishop Benson in Flagstaff?"

Jay looked up and his eyes got wide. "Oh, hell no! I might still be unsure about what we're doing, but I made you a promise. I haven't emailed, phoned or had any contact with him since June."

"We believe you, Jay. To be honest, we checked the phone records and they confirm what you're saying."

"Why are you asking?"

"We'd rather not say, but someone outside is asking questions in general, and trying to contact you, specifically. I need to ask you to let me know, immediately, if you are contacted by anyone outside the project with whom you are not personally acquainted ... and from before the project began. Can you do that?"

"Sure, but it sounds ominous."

"We hope it's far less so than it sounds, but it might just be important."

"Can I come back, now?" Jean had returned and was standing at the end of the table, glasses of soda in hand.

"Sure, Miss. Please sit down. We're through plotting and planning insurrection."

Jay looked surprised and then, realizing what George had done, smiled. He pushed her chair out and took one of the glasses."

"One final thing, Jay. Do you write your friends and folks routinely?"

"Only my parents, every weekend."

"Would you please ask them to have the same awareness of who is asking about you? If someone does, it would help if they got any information like names, phone numbers, companies they work for, etc. Will you do that?"

"I guess. I wrote them last night. Do you want me to write again?"

George thought for a moment. "No, that would be out of the ordinary. It can wait until next weekend. If you decide to write during the week, you can include it." He stood. "Enjoy the evening, you two." He picked up his glass and began table-hopping to appear that his visit with Jay was nothing more than that.

August 15, 2017

"I'm telling you that we need something in this thing to keep legacy entitlements, like Social Security, food stamps and farm subsidies, under control. If we don't, every funding/spending/taxing element throughout, is worthless. They grow without control and they become 'a right'."

"To Lin, we keep having this conversation. Social Security is not an entitlement!"

Millie jumped in. "Hold it! Both of you." She stood and walked to the table where the two antagonists sat. "Amy, we are aware of the definition of an entitlement. I don't want to have to restate it. But, let's not get into an argument over a single program. To Lin has a valid concern over the rising, and often unfunded, cost of many programs. These, like food stamps, unemployment, farm subsidies etc. have become less 'entitlements' than 'expectations'. First, I categorically state that the Social Security system, with which most of us have no real issue, is, by law, a program which would be self-supporting if Congress would stop raiding the fund."

To Lin held onto his argument, "Okay, but what about the other programs? Looking at it in the way we're writing the CwC, there is no specific additional freedom But, why, in the strongest terms, is there an expectation? That simply creates a 'nanny state'. That's what led to interference in our lives, like telling me what to teach my kids, what I can eat, etc. What's next? What I can read or say? My parents left a country where that was a way of life. I don't want to see it here."

Amy, her voice softer now. "To Lin, I might not understand what you're saying from the standpoint of experience, but I haven't seen much of the police state mentality here. I think they're separate arguments."

"Oh! Controlling school curriculum by funding and un-funding programs isn't a police state, in deed, if not in fact? George Orwell wrote about changing history, by changing the history taught in the schools."

Millie sounded exasperated. "Guys, let's stay on focus here. We are trying to deal with To Lin's query about entitlement programs, and only at the CwC level. Please. We just don't have that much time left.

"That does bring up a valid thought, though. Let's specify in the Article I section covering legislation, that preexisting programs must become fully funded within a certain period. Self-supporting programs, like Social Security may not be raided to fund them, nor can funding come from debt. Jane, what do you think?"

"Can't hurt. How do I word it?"

"Al, can you work up wording that you think will meet what you've heard here?"

Al Lee winced. "I can write it, but the bureaucrats are going to try and punch holes in it to protect rice bowls. This one is sure to bring the Conservatives and Liberals to fisticuffs."

"Let 'em eat cake!" To Lin added crossing his arms over his chest. Several rounds of applause from the assorted conservatives in the crowd erupted. The interns were heavily liberal, in bent, as most idealistic young people are. But, there was a solid core of conservatives in the room. They were also not the least bit reticent to voice their opinions. It made for spirited and productive debate ... most of the time.

Millie chuckled. "I think it was 'Let them eat brioche.' Anyway, Sally, add a one liner to identify all legacy entitlement programs and any funding associated with each. They're going to have to identify shortfalls if this is going to work."

Amy was trying to be conciliatory to a degree. "I would expect that taxes will have to account for the money IF we're not going to allow debt acquisition or funding reallocation."

"Cutting unfunded programs makes more sense. Taxes are already too high."

"Are you going to explain hunger to a child, To Lin? I can't. I'd rather cancel an aircraft carrier or sell a national park."

"Oh great!"

"Darn it! You guys won't let go." Millie walked between the two. "Sit down, both of you. You sound like Congress in an election year. We're not here for sound bites, photo ops or pity points. The job of funding, eliminating, identifying and all of that will belong to others. The wording and intentions state our case. That's all we can do." She shook her tight shoulders out, glared at both and returned to her seat. Speaking to no one in particular, "Now, let's move on."

#

"George, Marv Miller. Remember me?"

"I do. You're my resident digital trench coat." He heard a snort from the other end.

"I like that. The guys'll think it's a hoot."

"Glad I can give you some levity. What's up?

"You were right. We took the info on those suits in Arizona and tracked the company to a slick contract with a company related to the Minority Whip."

"Shit!"

"Not good, I take it."

"Not in the least. Are you certain?"

"Hey, am I a digital trench coat, or not? We're certain. We've got a trail of contracts and signatures. The only thing we don't have is his fingerprints on it. Can't be anyone else. Someone had knowledge enough to send them to Flagstaff. I presume you briefed them, on the initial incident?"

"Unfortunately, yes. We thought they deserved to know that we were protecting the project. That appears to have been a mistake."

"Buddy, never tell a politician something you don't want him to use for his personal gain. You might want to write that down."

"You're just a font of wisdom, my friend. Okay. Let me call the other Founders and see what we can do to plug this one."

"Right. See ya" The line went dead.

#

"Okay. I'm satisfied that, despite his best efforts, we've got this one plugged just in time. Any chance he knows about the kid you've got stashed in St. Elizabeth's?"

"Not unless he's got an 'in' to the NSA. Marv lent me a couple of his guys, not even agents, to pick her up and deliver her. Oh, don't get me wrong. The order to St. 'E's is a legal national security order, but it ends on Friday the 18th. She'll be brought back here, after the delivery, and sent home as if nothing happened."

Elliot thought for a moment. "I don't trust him not to have his own ears, even inside the NSA. He's lost his gambit to get to Jay. She's next. Move her today; now. Bring her back here today and squirrel her away in her room, guarded."

George looked at him. "Paranoid?"

"Just being overly careful. Bring her back."

"Okay. You're the boss. Can she attend the final meeting and vote?"

"Why not. One 'no' vote won't matter. Call now. I'll wait."

George shook his head and picked up his phone. He pressed a speed dial and waited. "Marv? George. The boss wants to bring Janice back today. Yeah, now. I know that. Thanks." He ended the call and set his phone down. "Done."

"Good, and the packets of printouts?"

"We've got those. She'll have nothing but memories and a paycheck, just like the rest of the kids."

"Seems a shame to use them like that."

"What do you mean?"

"Well, if this thing actually flies, their fingerprints are all over it, but their names will never be. Some politician will get the credit."

"Are you serious? You intend that the work they did be claimed by someone else?"

"It's not my intention, George. It's the way the contract was written. They contracted with us to write a new foundation document. We hired 155 high school grads to give us a fresh viewpoint. Nothing said we had to give them credit any more than the engineer who designed the engines on the Saturn V got credit for the moon landing."

George paused and said, in a quiet controlled voice. "That is unbelievably unfair."

"Life's a bitch, George. You hired on to do a job. Just do it. They hired on to do a job and they've done it."

August 17, 2017

"Hi, Marv. Thanks for coming on short notice."

"You did make it sound important, George."

"You won't know how important unless … well, let's just hope for the best outcome." George picked up his handset. "Would you please get hold of Millie Dickinson, Sally Jamison and Beau Williams. Ask them to meet me in the Day Room at 10:30. Thanks."

"Now, my digital trench coat, I need you to do your best NSA snoop imitation. Here's what I need."

August 18, 2017

"Good morning, guys. For the sake of the record, I am calling this final meeting of the Executive Committee - extended, to order at 8:00am, Friday August 18, 2017 at Camp Donelson, Kentucky. Present are all members of the ECe, and Sally Jamison, as recorder.

"Sally, turn off the recording systems for a moment. Wait, before you do that." She looked at the video camera. "I am stopping the recording to make some personal remarks, off the record, to my friends on the Executive Committee. Okay, turn it off.

"Before I turn that back on, I've a couple things to say. First, I cannot think of a better bunch of people to have worked with, on this project. Regardless of what happens, I hope we keep in touch. I really feel that, among the 155 of us, and that includes our two exiles, are the future leaders of this country of ours. Thank you all.

"Now, here's what's going to happen. We may be needed to help with the time line, although the DAs are mostly in charge. As soon as the CwC is ratified by the required majority, I will hand the voting records and the document to Dr. Elliot. He may or may not make some final remarks about the non-disclosure details. Following that, we will be asked to return to our rooms, gather our belongings and board a collection of buses headed to Nashville. Flights are arranged, as best they can be. Some of us will spend the night at motels in town, but by dinner all of us will be on our way home."

Beau asked, "We don't sign the CwC, like the Framers signed the Constitution?"

"Nope. I will sign the voting record as a true copy."

"But that's not attached, in any way to our work. We could be certifying a Spiderman comic, for all the good that does." Al didn't look happy.

"That's what they told me to do."

Beau spoke up again. "I've got an idea. We originally voted to let Jane sign it. Let's have her sign and date the last page, ceremoniously and in front of everyone, before you hand it over."

Jay stuck his hands in the air palms upward. "I remember a story of President Reagan saying 'Trust, but Verify' about something or other. Let's have her sign two copies and then scan one with a date stamp on it. That digital copy is to be included in the official record."

"Pretty cynical my friend."

Jay grinned. "Trust, but verify?"

"Who gets the second signed copy?"

"Jane, of course. Don't you think she earned it? Oh, and she gets a copy of the scan, too."

Millie looked at Jane. Tears were in her eyes. "Any objections?" She paused for only a second. "Done. Sally, turn it back on." Sally pressed a few keys, waited and then nodded at Millie.

"Okay, we've all had the night to review Jane's second draft of the CwC. I now ask for final comments." She looked from member to member, each of whom shook their heads in the negative. Then she looked at the three ex-officio members; receiving the same negative indication. "Hearing none, I will now call for a vote, by name; an 'aye' vote indicting acceptance of the document as written and revised by the Committee of the Whole.

"Alvin Lee?"

"Aye"

"Kathleen Greer?"

"Aye"

"Beau Williams?"

"Aye"

"Jane Manning Abrams?"

"Aye"

"And I, Mildred Dickinson, vote 'Aye'.

"The Executive Committee, having voted unanimously in favor of the Contract with the Citizenry of the United States of America, will now cause that document to be passed to the Committee of the Whole for a roll call vote; without comment. An affirmative vote of 120 or more of those present, will 'ratify' the document as accepted and deliverable to the staff of the Jefferson-Hamilton Institute in fulfillment of the contract specifications. The final page of the document will be signed, as a ceremonial gesture to the history of this nation, by its author, Jane Manning Abrams." Al Lee gave her a thumbs up.

"This meeting of the Executive Committee is adjourned. We will reassemble in the theater, at 10:00am, for the final vote."

Red Sky in Morning

The Vote

August 18, 2017 - Camp Donelson

Sally keyed the recording to start and looked at the two camera techs and her screen. Her monitor displayed four screens, two for the audience, the EC and an electronic voting board like that used by many state governments. She nodded at Millie.

"The chair will entertain a motion, from the floor, to vote on ratification of the Contract with the Citizenry of the United States of America, as modified by this assembly in Committee of the Whole." Millie sat at the table on center stage with the four members of the EC on either side of her.

"I so move." Millie strained to see who had offered the motion.

"Who was that?"

"Dinty, Millie."

Millie smiled, "Oh sure, sorry. Let the record show that a motion to vote is made by Deanna Mortenson of Georgia. Is there a second?"

Several 'seconds came from the audience. "I see and recognize Roy Tipton of Nebraska as having seconded the motion. Thank you all. A motion is made and seconded to call the question. By voice vote, all in favor?" A loud chorus of 'aye' sounded. "Opposed?" She heard a few expected representative 'nays'. "The 'aye's have it. The motion is approved to call the question. Sally will now call the roll. You may vote 'for', 'against' or 'abstain'. The vote will not return to you, if you abstain. I strongly recommend that you vote 'for' or 'against'. We believe we are making history today. I don't think any of us want to be remembered, or more likely forgotten, as not knowing what to do when it came down to the future of our nation. Sally?"

Sally stood and walked to the lectern, set her laptop on it and keyed the screen to display the tally board. "I will call the roll, alphabetically. Votes will be recorded as voiced. Please verify your vote on the board behind me.

"Jane Manning Abrams."

"For."

From the audience came the titter of laugher and one comment, "Ya think?" The tote board showed a 'yes' vote next to Jane's name.

"Jamal Barton"

"For"

"Jay Brigham" Millie held her breath. Jay had had enough reservations about the project early on, to have broken the NDA by contacting his pastor, in Arizona. He had been a willing and enthusiastic participant since then. How would he vote?

"I pray for the correct vote. For."

#

Al Lee was counting the votes as they were given. At the end of the Ks it was 50 'for' and 11 'against'. The vote could only manage 35 'against' votes. Al was comfortable, but not happy with the 'against' votes. Several were staunch liberals and conservatives; unwilling to yield on issues they felt were important. His head snapped up when he heard the next name.

"Janice Montesano"

"Against!" Her voice was loud and angry. The 'against' light next to her name was illuminated.

He wondered how she got there and why she was voting. Then, he did a quick calculation. He thought, '50 - 12', 80% for. He made a tick mark and listened for the next name.

"Terrance Nielson"

"For"

#

It was 125 'for' to 20 'against', when the long list of 'S' names was exhausted.

"Michael Taylor"

"Against" Michael had been removed from the process for passing information to the institute, early in the project. A vote against the document was no surprise.

Millie's cell phone vibrated. She glanced down and saw that it was a text message from George. She showed the screen to Alvin. He gave her a quizzical look and then pointed at Sally. Millie nodded, stood and, without interrupting the vote, walked to the lectern and placed her phone in front of Sally.

"William Walters" She looked at the screen and her head snapped up to look at Millie. Then she nodded in the affirmative and returned to the vote.

"For"

Sally reached into her pocket for a flash drive and plugged it into the USB port.

#

"Terrance Yancey"

"For"

"Madam Chairperson, the vote is concluded. It will take me a minute or two to tally and then recheck the figures for an accurate percentage of votes." She pressed several keys and glanced down at the USB drive.

"Well, boys and girls, that concludes the fun. In a moment or two, we will know the outcome of our two months of labor. Once tabulated, we will certify the total and pass the results to the Institute. It is 11:45. We are being paid for fifteen minutes we did not work. But, as we know, it *is* a government contract."

There were a few giggles at the allusion. "Regardless of the outcome, lunch will be our last meal here. At 2:00pm, all of us will board buses to Nashville. We will bid a fond adieu to beautiful Camp Donelson at that time. On behalf of the Executive Committee, thank you. I know that this experience changed my life and my perceptions of our government and nation. Please remember to leave your laptops and any notes in your rooms. The NDA that you signed, requires that nothing go with you, except memories. That NDA is in force until the CwC is publicly released or you receive correspondence otherwise." She glanced at Sally, who was typing furiously at her keyboard. Her last motion was to lift an index finger and point it at the keyboard. It descended. A moment later, she withdrew the Flash drive and placed it in her pocket. She nodded at Millie and Beau. Beau stood and walked into the wings.

"Ah! Sally has the results. Sally?"

Sally stood and walked to stand next to Millie. "Madam Chairperson. By a vote of 131 to 24, the Contract with the Citizenry of the United States is accepted by the Committee of the Whole. That is an 85% approval percentage."

"Ladies and Gentlemen, the measure is passed and will be so reported to the Institute. These proceedings are concluded." She gave Sally the sign to stop the recording. Sally pressed a few keys and then gave a 'cut' symbol to the cameramen. A moment later she nodded at Millie.

"Would you make two copies, please?"

"Already printing. They should be here in a moment." Beau walked in with two folders in his hands and presented them to Millie.

"Thank you." She held up the two folders and faced the audience. "Here it is. I wonder how the Framers felt when they were handed the first copy of the Constitution after the vote. We are not required to sign this. After all, we are merely handing a draft to those who paid us to write it." There were a few moans. "Now, the Executive Committee has decided on a ceremonial acceptance, anyway. The honor of signing the document is awarded to Jane Manning Abrams, author and, as the luck of the alphabet goes, caster of the first vote for acceptance."

Applause broke out for a few moments. "Madame Chairperson?"

Millie heard the unmistakable southern drawl of JR Robbins and looked out to find him. "Just Millie, now, JR? What's up?"

"Millie, I move that all of us sign the document, required or not. We are, after all, the 'Framers' of the twenty-first Century and, regardless of what happens how, deserve to feel that we completed something."

Millie wasn't quite sure what to say. Al Lee stood, grinning. "Millie, this is still a convened meeting and a motion is proposed. I suggest that you call for a 'second'."

"Second" was heard at least four times from the audience.

Millie shrugged her shoulders. "A motion is made and seconded, for all 155 members of this assemblage to sign the CwC. All in favor?"

A thunderous approval was heard. "Okay. Al, would you let the dining room know that we'll be half an hour late? Guys, help me move this table." She looked at one of the cameramen. "Jim, would you disconnect from the network and record the signing for us?" She received a thumbs up as he pushed the tripod into position.

A moment later, Jay put his phone down. "They'll hold everything for us."

Millie looked out at the audience. "Okay, remember that you and your bags have to be in front of the residence at 2pm. Sally, read the roll."

"Jane Manning Abrams." Sally stepped to the table and signed both copies in a bold hand. She bowed her head for a moment and stepped away.

"Jamal Barton"

#

Sally place one signed copy in a folder and handed it to Millie. The other she handed to Jane Abrams. Then, she removed the Flash drive from her pocket and gave it to Jane, as well. "Take care of this, Jane. It's history. Now, let's go to lunch."

"I'll meet you guys there. I've got to deliver this, and we're late." Millie took her folder, gave Jane and Sally a hug and then walked out of the theater. She hurried down the walk to the Institute offices. She glanced at her cell phone, 1:04. No lunch for her, she still had final packing to do. She mounted the steps and the doors opened, George holding them.

"We wondered where you were. The Founders are in the conference room." He closed the door behind her, and led the way to the conference room. She walked in and saw the four Founders and the Devil's Advocates, all standing.

She walked to the end of the table where Dr. Elliot stood. She held out the folder and a Flash drive. "Dr. Elliot, the Committee of the Whole has accepted and endorsed the draft version of the Contract with the Citizenry of the United States by a vote of 85% 'yes' votes. I believe this concludes the contract with the interns."

Elliot took the folder and glanced at the document. Then he set it on the table in front of him. "Millie, you and your compatriots surprised us at every turn of this project from packing the softball team to the design of the document. We will now pass it to the Sponsors for action. I note that you all signed it. That was unnecessary, you know. This isn't the official copy, should there ever be one. It's just a draft."

"It was a nearly unanimous desire to make a ceremonial gesture of our involvement. You never know what history might do. Do you know when it might be published for public discussion?"

"Unfortunately, no. I know that the sponsors are very interested in seeing it. They've been calling for days trying to get an advance copy of it. Other than the original draft that we saw on the 10th, we've been unable to get any information. Your people are incredibly loyal."

"Less loyal, I think, than dedicated to the idea that we've created a document that supports the America we want to live in, and for a few of us, someday help govern. Now, if you'll excuse me, I have to get my bags out of my room. I've got a bus to catch."

"Millie. Thank you very much." Dr. Elliot put his hands out and took hers in them. "Safe travels and, whatever happens, you've done good work." She looked at him trying to figure out that last statement as he dropped her hand. George stepped in and gave her a hug.

As he did, he whispered in her ear. "I'll be in touch. Did you get my text?"

"Mmm hmm", Millie hummed. "Good bye." She gave George's arm a squeeze, turned and left.

#

The interns dribbled out of the residence, many towing roll-on bags behind them. As they stepped outside, they were met, one last time, by the DAs at a table. Their IDs were collected, as were their room keys. The ID was scanned and then shredded. The program that they were scanning, changed the password for network access; effectively isolating them from any information stored on the servers or on their laptop. Each intern was then handed a folder that held an itinerary, tickets or boarding passes, a final paycheck and, if necessary, a reservation slip at an airport hotel. The folder was marked with a bus number.

At exactly 2:00 pm, four large tour buses made their way to the curb near the residence. Millie was the last one out of the residence. She turned in her ID and key and received her folder. She was assigned to bus 4 and would be spending the night at the Airport Hampton Inn. She glanced at her itinerary. The flight to Dayton didn't leave until 8:30am the next morning. She sighed. At least she could call home and talk with her mom and dad.

Luggage was loaded and then the young people boarded. There were no staff members present to even wave to them. The interns had done their job and they were going home. Few looked out to see the windows of the conference room. Dr Elliot, George and Harold Gilbert were watching. As the last bus pulled away in a cloud of diesel exhaust, Harold turned to the other two. "I hated to give them hope that what they've written will ever be seen".

George gave him a quizzical look. "Why should it not? The sponsors went to a great deal of trouble and expense to get this document written. Why would they want to bury it? Did you really read it? It's visionary and extraordinary."

Dr. Elliot shook his head slowly. His eyes looked as old as he felt just then. "Pure politics George. I overheard several them after the presentation on the 10th. They had expected it to be a rewrite of the Constitution; one that repeated much of the structure that gave them power and, with luck, put some boundaries around some of today's problems. In their arrogance, they completely underestimated the desire of these teenagers to define their own future. In short, they forgot the spirit that they had at that age. Instead, they heard a document that completely gutted that power structure. They will be running scared to think of what the rest of the country would do if they began to think in terms of 'freedom', 'expectation' and 'responsibility'. These kids gave the power back to the citizens and that, my friends, has them spooked.

August 18, 2017 - Nashville International Airport

Jane was sitting in the boarding area for her flight to St. Louis and reading a novel on her tablet, when Al Lee sat down next to her. "Hey. How long until your flight?"

Jane, glanced at the time on her tablet and closed it. "I've got an hour or so before boarding. You?"

"My flight to DC was delayed by weather, so I'll be here an hour or two longer. With luck and no traffic on 66 and 81, I'll be home by dinner. Mom's making her lasagna."

They sat for a few minutes, watching people go about their travels. Finally, Jane spoke quietly, not looking at Al. "Do you suppose that any of them will ever know who we are or what we did?"

Al smiled and responded softly. "You can answer that question yourself, Jane. Name me five signers of the Constitution."

Jane closed her eyes and thought. "George Washington, Ben Franklin, James Madison, Alexander Hamilton and," she paused as she thought, "oh, John Dickinson. Thanks Millie."

"Good for you. That puts you ahead of most of the people in this concourse. Now, name me another."

Jane thought hard for nearly a minute. "I can't."

Lee smiled. "I believe your question was something like, 'Will any of these people ever know who we are or what we did?' I think you've answered your own question."

Jane sighed. "I suppose you're right. I guess our legacy is more the document than the names of a bunch of kids headed to college, who got together one summer in Kentucky. Can you imagine that 'back to school' assignment? 'What I did on my summer vacation'."

Al's head tipped back as he laughed out loud. "Well, you've got the only souvenir for 'show and tell'." He stood up and held out his hand. "Keep in touch, Jane. I expect that we'll see each other across an aisle someday."

Jane had to think and then remembered the folder in her carry on. She touched her pocket and was reassured when she felt the bulge of the Flash drive.

August 18, 2017 - Hampton Inn, Nashville International Airport

Millie sat with Sally in the coffee shop. Both were catching the same flight to Dayton in the morning. Sally would be met by her boyfriend and they would drive to Richmond, Indiana where she would register at Earlham early in the week. Millie would be met by her parents. They were planning a trip to Pennsylvania and Delaware. Millie had asked to see some of the family historical places. Her parents, although curious, were just pleased that she wanted to spend time with them before she left for Penn State.

Surprisingly, the varied subjects of their dinner conversation had been those expected of eighteen-year-old girls going off to college and not the events of the summer. Those seemed to be fading behind the excitement of the next few weeks. Neither expected to see or hear anything about the CwC until fall. It would take the sponsors time to prepare any program for release and begin the path to acknowledgment.

"Why isn't your boyfriend insisting that you go to Indiana with him?"

Sally thought for a moment. "I think because we both applied to Notre Dame. I was accepted, but didn't get any scholarship. He didn't get in." She grinned. "You don't suppose he felt intimidated?"

Millie snorted. "Intimidated by mild little ole Sally? Perish the thought." At that moment, her phone text notification sounded as the phone skittered on the table to the vibration. She didn't recognize the number, so she ignored it.

"Aren't you going to check it?"

"One of the nice things about the summer was that I didn't get much SPAM. It looks like it's starting again." She opened the message.

'Millie, Use this email for contact. Don't lose it and don't tell anyone you have it. George.'

"That's strange." She showed the text to Sally.

"Between the text during the voting and this, I wonder what's going on."

"I don't know, but I'm going to send Jane a quick message."

August 18, 2017 - Camp Donelson

George had just sent the text to Millie from his personal cell phone when his office phone rang. "This is George."

"George, Marv."

"Hey, what's up?"

"This is strange, man. I thought we were all working for the same people. What's going on?"

"I have no idea what you're talking about Marv. We do work for the same people, The Institute."

"Well, there's the rub, old buddy. NSA works for the government, and I just got a strange directive from a 'cutout' in Congress."

"Huh?"

He heard a chuckle. "You just don't read enough spy novels. Some office that does nothing but pass along messages, assignments and stuff that keeps the originators 'invisible'. Anyway, this one says to copy and then wipe your network. What's weird is that it says to do it right now. Do you have any idea what's going on?"

"Not in the least. Dr. E told me to have IT collect the laptops today and then back up the network and scrub the laptops on Monday."

"Well, when I push the button, and I don't have much time before I need to push the button, like minutes, you're not going to have anything to back up. I'm supposed to do this without leaving a digital fingerprint, too."

Without thinking, George put a Flash drive in his laptop and copied the 'Documents' folder to it. "That's bothersome. Can you give me a few minutes to talk with Dr. Elliot and the others here; if they're still here? How long can you hold off?"

"Not gonna help. I have to report completion within an hour. Someone up there doesn't want extra copies of your work hanging around."

"I think I know where it came from. Give me fifteen minutes, Marv. Call it a favor. I'm going to call IT really quick."

"Fifteen is all I can give you, George. And, I never called." The line went dead. George speed dialed IT.

"Dan? George. How quickly can you back up the server to a removable?"

"If I've got one, it'll take about 30 minutes. Why? We're supposed to do that Monday. I've just let nearly everyone go."

"Crap! Find a drive, Dan and start backing up ... right now! We've got fifteen minutes before it all goes away."

"What?"

George shouted into the phone. "Don't talk! Just do it!" He hung up and speed dialed Dr. Elliot.

August 18, 2017 - Alexandria, Virginia

"You know that you've just broken any number of laws under the 'cyber intrusion' statutes."

"Prove it." The minority Whip walked to the table and poured himself another scotch. "My NSA people are loyal to me. In an hour, nothing will remain of the 'We the People' project that isn't in our possession. 'We the People', what a ridiculous name for a bunch of wet-behind-the-ears kids." He took a long sip and returned to his wing chair.

The industrialist sat back. "If there are any notes, you could be in big trouble."

"Phah! Some kid with a notebook of scribbles? I've got the files; judiciously edited, of course. And, I've got the spin-doctors and friendly press. Who's gonna believe a college freshman? That thing they put together is pie-in-the-sky utopianism at its worst. I should never have bought off on that project."

"I suspect that the White House interest might have had something to do with it?"

"Yeah, well, if he makes any noise about it, I'll bury him in mid-terms. You don't realize just how much money I have backing us in keeping the structure just like it is."

"What about the Institute people? They're not kids. Will they be a problem?"

"Not if they ever want another contract from us."

The door opened, and a liveried servant stepped in. "Mr. Eldridge is on the phone, sir."

The minority Whip stepped to the phone. "Eldridge? What's the status?"

"Sir, the remote location is scrubbed back to the c: prompt and any laptops, too. We've backed up the files here. Marv wasn't happy with doing that without an Executive Directive. I had to tell him that the order came from the Congressional leadership, to get him to do it, without a signed order. Where do you want these files stored?"

"If he makes any more noise, I want him listening to cell conversations in Platte, Nebraska. Put everything on removables and have them delivered here. Then, scrub your servers, too. Those files never existed." He hung up, turned and smiled. "Poof!"

"Did all ten of us agree to this? I know the VP and two or three others really liked what they heard on the 10th."

The Whip turned to the window. "Poof!"

Up From the Ashes

Down in Flames

October 30, 2017 - Trenton, New Jersey

From: Mildred Dickinson

To: George Hanover

Subject: We the People

George, It's been more than two months since the project closed. I keep getting emails from the guys, more than twenty so far, asking what's going on. What can you tell me?

Millie

#

From: George Hanover

To: Mildred Dickinson

Subject: We the People

Millie, I'll check with Dr. E, but my office has received no news. The draft and notes were turned over to the sponsors, the Monday after you left. We're just as concerned as you, that we've heard nothing. But, from the professional standpoint, remember that you had a job to do and you all did remarkably well, regardless of what happened to your product.

George

#

"You know, I felt like I was lying to Millie, Harold. I've told the same story to Jay and half a dozen others. You know damned well that the sponsors are bottling up the CwC. Why can't we tell the kids the truth?"

"George, I'm as sorry as you are at this turn of events. Obviously, they don't intend to let the CwC go public and as long as they don't release it for discussion, the NDA stays in force. Unfortunately, that means the same NDA rules apply to us."

"How about talking with the Vice President? I didn't get the impression that he was among those who don't like the CwC."

"I could, but what's he going to do. We don't know the President's position, George. If we guessed wrong, it would be the last contract the Institute ever saw. I do have the partners to consider."

"So, you're taking the position of doing nothing and hoping for the best? I don't suppose I could trot out that old saying, 'evil men succeed when good men do nothing.' We can't just sit here."

Harold sighed. "George, as long as you work for me, you will take no action that may imperil the Institute. All of our good work would be lost, if we go up against a power position."

George stood and started for the door. "It worked for David against Goliath."

November 5, 2017 - Salt Lake City, Utah

"Dad? Got a minute?"

Jane's dad closed his Bible and sat back. "Sure, Janey. Something troubling you? I suspected such when you drove down from Ogden for the weekend. I'm certain you wouldn't lose study time unless it were something important."

Jane hugged her father and then pushed his feet aside and sat on the hassock. "Maybe I just missed my family."

Her dad smiled knowingly. "Among your good traits, and they are legion, I've never found you a good liar. Your eyes betray you. And, you were preoccupied in church today. You hardly paid attention, at all. Now, tell me what's troubling you. Mother will be putting dinner on soon."

"I remember telling you a bit about what we did this summer in Kentucky, right?"

"Yes, you told me you were doing research on some esoteric government legal issues that required many man-hours of research. Was that not true? I rather doubt that you were cavorting in Cancun." He grinned. "You left your passport at home."

"Funny, daddy. Funny. I can't imagine a good Mormon girl cavorting in Cancun, where half the entertainment is forbidden by the Doctrine and Covenants. No, I told you the truth, but very generically. I signed a non-disclosure agreement that forbade me from telling you what we were doing."

"And you are no longer bound by that promise?"

"That's the problem that's bothering me. The work we did was supposed to be released by now. Or at least, we thought it was. Once it was released, we could talk about it. I've asked the Institute folks, but I think they're dancing around the issue. What we did was important, daddy. I mean really important to the country. And, in some ways, it will be important to the church, as well."

"I'm not sure I see your problem, yet."

She took a deep breath. "Before we left, the Executive Committee and, I think, the Institute, entrusted me with a copy of the document we wrote as well as a Flash drive with most of the major notes and analysis on it. I want, so much, to print a million copies and send them to everyone."

"What do your friends have to say about it?

"Millie, she was the chair person, and Al Lee, he's related to Robert E. Lee, both tell me to keep it safe until the right time. But, I think someone, or some group of people doesn't want to release it. Daddy, it would be such a shame. Not releasing it would mean the country would continue down a track that you and I know already know is wrong for everyone."

He reached out and held her cheek. "Honey, Brigham Young gave us a quote, that I can see would work either way in this instance. You must decide which of the two ways, holding your voice or speaking out, is the road to follow. He said, 'True independence and freedom can only exist in doing what's right.' You, and only you, can decide what's right. I have faith in you and faith that God will show you the correct path." He stood and held out his hand to his daughter. "Now, I believe that mother has dinner on the table."

November 13, 2017 - New York City

The two men shook hands. The industrialist showed him to a small table in a dark corner. Security details for both made overhearing the conversation impossible. "Mr. Minority Whip, welcome. You don't often set foot outside the beltway. What brings you to Gotham?"

"I'm getting some serious queries from other sponsors about that damned piece of paper. I've been dancing around the issue so much that I feel like I'm on 'Dancing with the Stars - Politician Edition'. We've got to do something. Apparently, doing nothing isn't going to work. It's not going to go away."

"Just ignore it. You've got the document and the only copies of the files. What can they do, put a headline in the tabloids?" He laughed out loud. "I can see it. 'Mr. Speaker, What's the Whip hiding?' Priceless, worthless and just as unlikely. You're losing your grip."

"You're not listening to me. I don't give a rat's ass about the public. I'll be reelected because I own the machine in my state. The problem is that I'm getting questions from people just as powerful as you or me. I don't need that."

"Then do something about it to defuse it before it has a chance to blossom. Can't you leak something to discredit the project, or the kids; like they were partying and doing drugs or something like that?"

"Damn it. Take this seriously. There were far too many people to invent something. If any document comes out, it's going to have to be the real one and 85% of those stupid kids think it's the best thing since James Madison, along with all the Institute folks and more than half the sponsors; fools that they be."

"You'll think of something." The industrialist clipped a cigar and lit it. "I suppose you don't have much choice. Just make sure that cursed piece of paper never gets published."

The Whip rubbed his eyes, "For Christ's sake you don't need to tell me that. I figured that one out for myself."

November 14, 2017 - Washington, DC

"Print this file for me, Jane. It's highly confidential. I advise you not to read it. Just print it and put it in a folder and hand it to me."

"Yes, sir. I'll have it for you in a moment." The Whip turned and walked back into his office. The aide held up the Flash drive to the other aide in the office.

His office mate simply shook his head. "He couldn't just print it from his laptop?"

"That would have been a loss of face. Honest work? Really?" He plugged the Flash drive into his laptop to print the sole document on it cwc_draft1.doc.

#

The draft was finished. He sat back and looked at the pages of notes and analysis that he had gleaned from the files he had removed from Kentucky. It looked perfect enough to fool the press. "Fool the press and you've fooled the public", he said to himself. He'd been fooling the press for years. His own machine was expert at it. It would work. The day after Thanksgiving was perfect, too. He smiled at his genius.

November 24, 2017 - Washington Post

Unnamed sources within the beltway confirm that a three-million-dollar project funded by an ultra-liberal think tank employed recent high school graduates to produce a mock 'updated' Constitution. The document, so flawed and 'Utopian' that it failed an acceptance vote by even its own authoring mob of children. A congressional financial oversight agency report alleged that it was 'another example of unfettered government spending abuse'. Despite threats of publication, the minority Whip was quoted, off the record at his home for the holiday. 'The We the People Contract with the Citizenry, is an unrealistic insult to the magnificent Constitution written by none other than James Madison. To actually believe that high school teens could possess the wisdom and foresight to supplant that marvelous document is delusional.'

Up From the Ashes

November 24, 2017 - Trenton, New Jersey

"Dr. E, have you seen the snow job the Minority Whip has dumped in the Post?"

"I saw it, George. The Times sent me a copy of the 'confidential release' his puppets sent out. He even included the last page of the CwC; a supposed proof that it failed. It had twenty-four bogus signatures."

"Can he get away with that?"

"He's got the only files and the original copy. The guy is a career politician with an ego that requires a semi to move it around. Do you have a magic wand?"

"You seem all too willing to roll over, Dean. This is a blatant power grab. We can't let it go."

"George. You are a great research lead with good instincts and are one of our hidden assets, but you lack political savvy. The Institute, for all its fancy name, remains a government funded 'independent research agency'; a 'think tank' in other words. Our futures and fortunes are invested in this, along with the livelihoods of, on any one day, a hundred employees; yourself included. We live and die by Federal contract. We can't afford to take on his machine. He'd bury us in bad, if false, press."

"It still sucks. The kids are going to see that and be really hurt. Some are going to be deeply hurt."

"Life's a bitch, George. Call it a learning experience for them."

December 4, 2017 - Trenton, New Jersey

George sat at his desk. He was staring out the window; looking at nothing, his fingers drumming on his desk. In fact, he was pondering the follow-up opEd in today's Post, about the Institute's contract for the CwC. It was slanted toward decrying waste and the liberal agenda of the Institute. He shook his head. The article was obviously planted by the Whip's machine to further undermine the' We the People' initiative. Beneath the paper, in the stack, was a printout of the CwC and several pages of the research and analysis done; saved before the original files had been deleted at the direction of higher authority.

The whole affair gnawed at him. He thought back to the Fourth of July briefing and the enthusiasm of most of the Sponsors for the project. Only three or four, led by the Minority

Whip, showed disdain for the effort, yet that minority had seized and squelched, what George and the Institute considered, a superior effort to salvage the lumbering governmental process.

Suddenly, he decided. Saying to the window, "It's a blatant power grab by a few. Hell, in a third world country, our intelligence guys would call it a 'coup d'état'. Not going to happen on my watch." He pushed the newspaper aside and pulled a folder from the middle of the stack.

December 5, 2017 - Charlottesville, Virginia

From: Al Lee

To: Mildred Dickinson

Subject: WTP

Millie, I'm presuming you have seen that smelly pile dumped in the Post just before Thanksgiving. If not, look up bullshit in the dictionary. I expect a picture of the Minority Whip will be right next to it. At any rate, we can't just stand by and let this A-hole do that. Can we get together during the break, somewhere in the middle?"

Al

December 6, 2017 - Richmond, Indiana

From: Mildred Dickinson

To: Al Lee

Cc: Jane Abrams, Beau Williams, Sally Jamison

Bc: George Hanover

Subject: WTP

Al, you get my vote. I've copied the EC to see where and when we can meet. My dad knows enough to understand why I'll miss a day or so of vacation. Keep in touch.

Millie

Trenton, New Jersey

From: George Hanover

To: Mildred Dickinson

Subject: Holiday Greetings

Attach: Holiday_2105.pdf

Millie, lest you believe your work is forgotten, we, at the Institute wish you a happy holiday season and the best of luck in your college career.

George

#

Millie looked at the very strange email. She and George had been exchanging emails intermittently since she had left for Earlham. This one was entirely out in left field. She clicked the attachment to open it. Her eyes grew wide when she saw that it was a scan of a typed note.

Millie,
My friends at NSA tell me that they've been ordered to scan for emails, sent between the former Executive Committee members. He couldn't tell me who sent down the order, but said they've trapped several that mention the project. Do not use email to discuss anything you did last summer. I can't tell you what to do. I can just tell you to be very careful. Whoever is doing this is powerful and has the money and friends to do you and your friends

great harm, if you try to dispute their story. The Institute can't help, and you have no proof.

Just be careful. Find a way to communicate that will take them a while to find. Give Jane my best wishes for the success and great dividends from her savings plan.

George

Millie looked at the message and was confused by the last sentence. Then, a smile began to spread across her face.

December 7, 2017 - Trenton, New Jersey

"Marv? George."

"Hey, George. I'm surprised to hear from you. I figured you'd be running for cover, just like your bosses."

"Not gonna go there. How much do you love your job?"

"I'm not sure I want to hear the rest of this conversation."

"Something stinks, Marv. I've made my choice. I'm asking where your loyalties lie, your country and the law or your paycheck?"

"That bad?"

"I think so, but I can't prove it … yet. I need your skills. Off the record and unattributable."

"Do you have any idea how deep the pile is that would hit the fan?"

"That same pile is nearing the fringe on the flag, buddy. Trust me on this one."

"I say again, that bad?"

"Well, historically, I can say that only Secretary Stanton's actions after Lincoln's assassination compare."

"Aw, come on."

"By the time you finish doing me this favor, I think you'll agree. Tell you what. If I haven't made my case based on what you find, burn it and tell me to go away. No harm, no foul."

"I guess I can live with that. What's the favor?"

"I want you to scan some area codes for some keywords and only during a certain period. That keeps it out of the realm of illegal tapping, right? If you get hits, I'll see if I can get warrants. I'll bet I can."

"You sure about this? I might get fired, but you'll be weeding beans in Pennsylvania."

"Don't make me beg, buddy."

"Okay. Now, I'm intrigued. Give me the area codes and the rest. God help you if you're wrong. I won't ever have heard of you."

December 8, 2017 - Trenton, New Jersey

"George? Marv."

"I'm really glad you called back. Did you get anything?"

"I've just emailed you a file as a Blind Copy."

"Why the BCC, Marv?" The phone went silent for a few seconds. "Marv?"

George heard a long sigh. "The original intercepts and transcripts were sent to the Attorney General, George, with a copy to the Speaker."

"Worse than I thought?"

"I had no choice. Wear your raincoat when it hits the fan, old buddy."

George maximized his email program and opened the message from Marv. He read through the intercepts and rubbed his eyes. He took one deep breath and hit 'Forward' on the message.

From: George Hanover

To: Mildred Dickinson

Subj: FW: and he overtyped the subject with a new subject line, Merry Christmas, Millie

Dear Millie,

December 8, 2017 - Dayton, Ohio

From: Mildred Dickinson

To: Alvin Lee, Beau Williams, Kathryn Greer, Jane Abrams

Subj: Holiday Greetings

Hey all, I thought we might get together for some holiday cheer. I know it's short notice, but, darn it, we had so much in common in Kentucky, that we should get together and swap tales. So, anticipating that we all think it's a good idea to discuss what's happened since we left, I've gotten a block of rooms at the Hampton Inn in Lexington, Kentucky for two nights, 12/15-16. RSVP to me, but call 502-555-7211 and confirm a room in your name.

I look forward to seeing you all there. If we have fun, I'll bet we can plan a real party for early Spring and invite everyone.

Happy holidays. Millie

December 11, 2017 - Chicago, Illinois

"Yeah, I read the report from the NSA taps. I told you those kids were no problem. They're planning a Christmas party, for God's sake. I told you there was nothing they could do about it."

"Listen, Congressman. Except for being in Kentucky last summer, these kids have absolutely nothing in common. You've got blue blood, blue collar, black, white, Mormon, Protestant and Catholic. Hell, they don't even celebrate Christmas the same. I'm telling you, there's something weird about this little soiree."

"You're paranoid. What do you want me to do? Send in SpecOps or the CIA to run a honey pot on the Lee kid? They're fucking college freshmen! They can't find their beanies without a study guide. You actually think they can try to cause us problems that my machine can't make go away? You're an idiot, if you do. I can manage the Chinese, the French and the President. I'm not worried about five kids away from home that want to party."

"Look, at least keep the taps on their phones and emails."

"I should send you a bill for wasting taxpayer money. Okay. If it'll keep you from soiling your panties, I'll keep the taps on till the first of the year, but not a day longer. Good bye."

December 15, 2017 - Lexington, Kentucky

Kathy, shoulder bag over her shoulder, walked up to the reception desk. "I'm Kathryn Greer. I believe you have a reservation for me?"

The clerk keyed in her name. "Yes, Miss Greer. The room is paid for already. May I see a photo ID please?"

Kathy pushed her driver's license across the counter. "Who paid for the room?"

The clerk looked at the ID, checked it against the information on the screen and looked at Kathy. He smiled and passed it back to her. "Thank you. I've no idea, Miss. It just says it was paid with a credit card. Oh," he pushed an envelope across the counter, along with a room key card. "The envelope was waiting for you. You're in room 224. Just take the elevator up to the second floor and turn right. The continental breakfast is from 7 to 10 am on weekends. Ice and vending machines are on each floor and the coffee pot is right there." He pointed to his left. "Welcome to the Hampton Inn."

#

Kathy threw her shoulder bag on one of the two double beds and flopped onto the other. She slid her thumb under the flap of the envelope and tore it open. It held a short hand-written note.

Kathy, Thanks for coming. We'll meet for dinner at 7 pm in the Denny's next door. Al's plane doesn't arrive until 5:30 and I want us all there. See you. Millie.

#

Jane stood and gave Kathy a hug when she walked in. "You go, girl-friend. Looking good. Welcome to the grand conspiracy. How's Brown?"

Kathy looked at her for a moment, wondering about the 'conspiracy' comment. "Probably the same as BYU, confusing and full of freshman stress. I'll bet the food's better in Utah, though." She glanced at the table. Millie was reviewing a document with Al and Beau was thumbing his phone screen. "Hey guys!" She sat between Beau and Jane. "Okay, my 'spidey sense' tells me that this is no Christmas party. What's up?"

Millie took the reins. "You would be absolutely right. This is about an attempt to bury the CwC before it has a chance to be seen by anyone but the sponsors. Apparently, some of them think they have the right and power to throw our work away. I, for one, am proud that we wrote something that represents the way we want *our* country to run. I'm not going to let some political animal or some industrialist or anyone else decide for me. *We* are going to do something about it."

"Uh huh. Us and what army? If it's who the papers are saying, he's got an awful lot of powerful friends and more money than any of us; more money than most third world countries in fact."

"Kathy. I know Connecticut isn't out in the sticks, but you're late to the party." She slid a piece of paper across the table; the same one she had been going over with Al. "Read, but don't read it out loud."

Kathy skimmed the sheet. Then, she looked at Al. He had an enigmatic smile on his face. She reread the sheet in detail and as if she were reading the answers to a test on a study guide. "You've got to be kidding. Even if you tried this, you couldn't possibly keep it a secret long enough to pull it off. Besides, where's your evidence? Innuendo is the same crap they used to smear the CwC to start with. And, what about that damned non-disclosure agreement?"

"Actually, we have the proof, Kathy." Al slid a folder to her.

She opened it and looked at the phone records and transcripts of taps. Her voice dropped a half octave. "How did you get this?"

"You didn't hear it from me, but George has gone under cover to feed us information. He drove down to see me a week ago with this. The Institute won't do anything because they don't want to lose work, but he knows that Dr. Elliot would like to see something done and he thinks the other Founders would come around if it weren't perceived that they had released this. As for the NDA, the minute that 'they' leaked the name and published that bogus back page, it was abrogated. Al checked with one of his law professors at Virginia."

A smirk crossed her face. Al reached for the file. She said, "I'm listening."

"Then, welcome, fellow un-indicted co-conspirator. Jane is providing the special gifts for the Grinch and his friends. After dinner, we're going to my room and address Christmas cards to 150 of our closest friends."

December 16, 2017

"Okay. Here's the rest of the plan. Al will drop these at a post office in West Virginia on his way home. They'll go out Monday and everyone, except the guys in the territories and maybe Alaska and Hawaii, will have it by Thursday. That means that RSVP cards will start arriving by Monday next. Each of us has twenty-five RSVPs addressed to us. Wednesday the 27th, send me an email with the numbers of supporters and which ones will 'actively' participate; based on the requests in their Christmas cards. Absolutely no phone calls from now on and no inference in the emails except for totals and the ID number of the intern from the list I just gave you. The website will be up on Tuesday of next week. The URL is in the letter and on the documents you have. The only real risk is that one of us actually supports the cover up conspiracy and will leak this."

Beau shook his head. "I'm thinking that won't happen. We had interns that didn't like the document, but I never heard, all summer, anyone ever supporting underhanded political crap. They all hated the way the government manipulated the truth; whether they liked what was being manipulated or not. No, if someone doesn't want to get involved, they'll just say 'no' and sit back. Incidentally, those quotes at the top and the bottom are worth more than the text in the middle. Great thinking."

"Thank Jane for those."

"My dad gave it to me. He said it would take me a while to figure out what 'the right thing' is. When you called me, I knew."

Millie stood. "Join me in holding hands." They all stood and stacked hands. "Folks, I say ye, 'The United States of America, one nation belonging to all the people'."

Ten hands went up and down, clasped together. "Hear, Hear!"

January 3, 2018 - Chicago, Illinois

The Minority Whip was annoyed at the doorbell ringing at 8:15 in the morning. "I'll get it, Ellen." He set his cup and paper down and looked through the peep hole. His heart caught as he opened the door. "Mr. Speaker? Majority Leader? What are you doing here? Please come in."

The Speaker and the Majority Leader stepped in, followed by two uniformed officers. The Whip checked, one was Chicago PD, the other Washington DC. "Mr. Minority Whip, you are under arrest for tampering with federal documents under the cyber-security acts. In addition, I am bringing charges against you, in the House, for malfeasance, tampering and conspiracy to defraud. In both instances, the charges require that all access to classified material be suspended. As such, you are relieved as Minority Whip, pending trial in the Senate and in the court of law. These gentlemen will escort you to the local precinct, where you will be served with the extradition paperwork required for your return to the Capitol.

The Whip blustered, "Just a cotton-picking minute ..."

"Jim, you have the right to remain silent. I strongly recommend you just shut up!"

#

"Hello?"

"Clark? Have you seen the paper?"

"No, what's up?"

"Remember those high school kids that you said the Whip wasn't worried about?"

"Uh, yeah." A cold chill ran through him.

"Well, apparently, they're as capable of 'dirty tricks' as the Whip. Open the paper. If my research is right, the headline is in 64 papers this morning, including the Post, the Times, the Chronicle and the Tribune." The phone went silent. The industrialist set the handset on the cradle and picked up the paper sitting on the side table by a carafe of coffee.

"Oh my God!" The paper fell to the floor as he dropped into the chair

#

Government Cover-up!!

New Constitution Secretly Quashed!

Minority Whip indicted for intimidation, bribes and corruption.

About the Author

Karl Bogott is, truly, a 'Baby Boomer'; a child of the fifties and sixties. Born in Modesto, California he, his mother and brother followed his dad, a WWII veteran back and forth across the country in pursuit of the good life. He's lived in Ohio, New Mexico and Colorado, where he went on active duty as a U.S. Navy enlisted sailor. He served in the USS Tawakoni (ATF114), an ocean-going tug, and on Midway Island. He reentered the Navy, as a commissioned officer, serving in three ships and at three shore stations before retiring in 1995, as a Commander in the U.S. Navy Supply Corps. Married 45 years with two children and three grandchildren, he and his wife now reside in Virginia Beach, VA.

He's never been shy about traveling to 'far away places' and has been to the bottom of the Grand Canyon and the top of St. Peters in Rome, along with Macchu Picchu in Peru and sailing the Cape of Good Hope, the Suez Canal and the Panama Canal. He's never too shy to ask 'why' and to seek unique solutions to lingering problems.

We the People is his first novel. He hopes it will generate controversy, conversation and maybe, just maybe, unique solutions to the problems facing the country we all love.

His second novel, The Old Lady of Elm Street, is available from Amazon and on Kindle. It is a story of the renovation of a 1905 Victorian home. In discovering what holds the old home together, the couple doing the work also discovers what held the family that lived in that home together and what tore them apart. It's a romance of discovery and renewal.

Thank You. Now, please don't stop here.

I'm pleased that you've read <u>We the People</u>. I hope you enjoyed it
and that it might make you think critically about our government,
our country and our future. Getting the word out about a self-
published book takes work and I'm asking for your help. Help me get
the story out. Here are some ideas.
1. Write a review, e.g. for Amazon or your local newspaper
2. Talk about the book on Facebook, LinkedIn or Twitter
3. Recommend it to friends and bloggers
4. Promote it in the newsletter of your church, school, civic club
   or business
5. Lend your copy to a high school teacher or local government
   leader and ask for them to comment on it.
6. Suggest it as the selection for your reading club
7. Give a copy to someone who cares as deeply about our
   country as I do.

Thank you for the time you've spent reading my book and for
helping others discover the story of the young people who wanted to
make their country … *theirs*.

– Karl Bogott

www.ingramcontent.com/pod-product-compliance
Lightning Source LLC
Chambersburg PA
CBHW062129280526
45788CB00001B/109